P

56

D1130245

The Collected Works of Paul Valéry

Edited by Jackson Mathews

VOLUME 8

PAUL VALÉRY

LEONARDO POE MALLARMÉ

Translated by
Malcolm Cowley
and
James R. Lawler

ROUTLEDGE & KEGAN PAUL

LONDON

First published in England 1972
by Routledge & Kegan Paul Ltd.
Broadway House, 68–74 Carter Lane
London, E.C.4
Copyright © *1972 by Princeton University Press, Princeton, N.J.*

THIS IS VOLUME EIGHT OF THE
COLLECTED WORKS OF PAUL VALÉRY.
IT IS THE THIRTEENTH VOLUME OF THE
COLLECTED WORKS TO APPEAR

ISBN 0–7100–7148–5
Printed in Great Britain
at the University Printing House, Cambridge
(Brooke Crutchley, University Printer)

CONTENTS

CONTENTS

Preface

IT IS ACCURATE—and more than merely accurate—to say that Leonardo, and Poe, and Mallarmé each had a deep influence upon me at the age when we usually fix upon the object, the field, and the conditions of our will to inner activity. The works of these men enchanted, dominated me, and—as was only fitting—tormented me as well; the beautiful is that which fills us with despair. But their sway was not so much that of the works themselves as of the idea of their authors which those works impressed on me. I would imagine their minds, and from that it was an easy step to forming an image of the mind, a pursuit to which I have devoted the best of my time—the free time that was always measured out to me and which I still yearn for, at my age! In truth, the work that interests me deeply is the work that incites me to picture the living and thinking system that produced it—an illusion, no doubt, but one that develops energies not to be found in the attitude of a purely passive reader.

But if I was changed by those three creators of forms and ideas, the change had to be in accordance with my own nature. I cannot enter into the detail of my reactions in the spiritual presence of these three masters of the art of abstraction. All three were very diversely committed to the difficulties and enchantments of the same problem, which, in brief, is that of calculating the combinations to be made between the products of the sensibility and the operative powers of the intellect.

PAUL VALÉRY

LEONARDO

Introduction to the Method of
Leonardo da Vinci

[1894]

To Marcel Schwob

WHAT A MAN leaves after him are the dreams that his name inspires and the works that make his name a symbol of admiration, hate, or indifference. We think of how he thought, and we are able to find within his works a kind of thinking derived from ourselves that we attribute to him; we can refashion this thought in the image of our own. It is easy to picture to ourselves an ordinary man; his motives and elementary reactions can be supplied quite simply from our own memories. The commonplace acts that form the surface of his life and those that form the surface of ours are linked in the same fashion. We too can serve as the bond that holds the acts together, and the circle of activity suggested by his name is no wider than our own. If we choose an individual who excelled in some respect, we shall find it harder to picture the workings and the ways of

In the embarrassment of having to write on a great subject, I felt impelled to consider and state the problem before trying to solve it. That is not what usually happens with the literary mind, whose instinct is to leap across the crevasse, not to measure the depth of it.

3

Today I should write this first paragraph in a very different fashion, while preserving its essence and function.
For its purpose is to make us think about the possibility of any project of the sort—that is, about the situation of and the means available to a mind that sets out to imagine a mind.

his mind. In order to go beyond an indiscriminate admiration, we shall be forced to stretch in some particular way our conception of his dominating quality, which we doubtless possess only in the germ. But if all the faculties of the chosen mind were widely developed at the same time, or if considerable traces of its activity are to be found in all fields of endeavor, then the figure of our hero grows more and more difficult to conceive in its unity and tends to escape our strivings. From one boundary to another of this mental territory there are immense distances that we have never traveled. Our understanding fails to grasp the continuity of this whole—just as it fails to perceive those formless rags of space that separate known objects and fill in the random intervals between; just as it loses myriads of facts at every moment, beyond the small number of those evoked by speech. Nevertheless, we must linger over the task, become inured to it, and learn to surmount the difficulties imposed on our imagination by this combination of elements heterogeneous to it. In this process all our intelligence is applied to conceiving a unique order and a single motive force. We wish to place a being in our like-

4

ness at the heart of the system we impose on ourselves. We struggle to form a decisive image. And our mind, with a degree of violence depending on its lucidity and breadth, ends by winning back its own unity. As if produced by mechanism, a hypothesis takes shape and proves to be the individual who achieved all these things, the central vision where all this must have taken place, the monstrous brain or strange animal that wove a pure web connecting so many forms. These enigmatic and diverse constructions were the labors of this brain, its instinct making a home for itself. The production of such a hypothesis is a phenomenon that admits of variations but not of chance. It has the same value as the logical analysis of which it should be the object. It is the basis of the method that we will take up to serve our purpose.

I propose to imagine a man whose activities are so diverse that if I postulate a ruling idea behind them all, there could be none more universal. And I want this man to possess an infinitely keen perception of the difference of things, the adventures of which perception might well be called analysis. I see him as aiming at all things: he is

In reality man *and* Leonardo *were the names I gave to what then impressed me as being the power of the* mind.

Universe—*a better word would have been "universality." What I wished to designate was not so much the* fabulous totality *that the word "universe" generally tries to evoke, as the feeling that every object belongs to a system containing (by hypothesis) that which is necessary to define every object.*

always thinking in terms of the universe, and of rigor.* He is so formed as to overlook nothing that enters into the confusion of things; not the least shrub. He descends into the depths of that which exists for all men, but there he draws apart and studies himself. He penetrates to the habits and structures of nature, he works on them from every angle, and finally it is he alone who constructs, enumerates, sets in motion. He leaves behind him churches and fortresses; he fashions ornaments instinct with gentleness and grandeur, besides a thousand mechanical devices and the rigorous calculations of many a research. He leaves the abandoned relics and remnants of unimaginable games and fancies. In the midst of these pastimes, which are mingled with his science, which in turn cannot be distinguished from a passion, he has the charm of always seeming to think of something else. . . . I shall follow him as he moves through the density and raw unity of the world, where he will become so familiar with nature that he will imitate it in order to use it, and will end by finding it difficult to

* *Hostinato rigore,* obstinate rigor—Leonardo's motto. [P.V., as all footnotes in this section.]

conceive of an object that nature does not contain.

This creation of our thoughts requires a name that will serve as a limit to the expansion of terms usually so far removed as to escape each other. I can find none more suitable than that of *Leonardo da Vinci*. Whoever pictures a tree must also picture a sky or background from which the tree stands forth; in this there is a sort of logic that is almost tangible and yet almost unknown. The figure I am presenting can be reduced to an inference from this type. Very little that I shall have to say of him should be applied to the man who made this name illustrious: I will not pursue a coincidence that I think would be impossible to define incorrectly. I am trying to give one view of the details of an intellectual life, one suggestion of the methods implied by every discovery, *one*, chosen among the multitude of imaginable things—a crude model, if you will, but preferable in every way to a collection of dubious anecdotes, or a commentary upon museum catalogues, or a list of dates. That kind of erudition would merely falsify the purely hypothetical intention of this essay. I am not ignorant of such

An author who composes a biography can try to live his subject or else to construct him, and there is a decided opposition between these two courses. To live him *is to transform oneself into what is necessarily incomplete, since life in this sense is composed of anecdotes, details, moments.* Construction, *on the other hand, implies the* a priori *conditions of an existence that could be* completely different.
This sort of logic is what leads by way of sensory impressions to the construction of what I have just called a universe. *Here it leads to a personage.*
In short, the problem is to use the full potential of one's thinking, under the control of the highest

7

possible degree of consciousness.

matters, but my task above all is to omit them, so that a conjecture based on very general terms may in no way be confused with the visible fragments of a personality completely vanished, leaving us equally convinced both of his thinking existence and of the impossibility of ever knowing it better.

I should express all this quite differently today, but I can recognize myself in the double effort I was making: to imagine the labor, and at the same time to picture the accidental circumstances that may have engendered the works.

The effects of a work are never a simple consequence of the circumstances in which it was generated. On the contrary, we might say that the secret aim of a work is to make us imagine that it created itself, by a process as remote as possible from the real one.

Many an error that distorts our judgment of human achievements is due to a strange disregard of their genesis. We seldom remember that they did not always exist. This has led to a sort of reciprocal coquetry which leads authors to suppress, to conceal all too well, the origins of a work. We fear the latter may be humble; we even suspect them of being natural. And although there are very few authors with the courage to say how their work took shape, I believe there are not many more who venture even to understand the process. Such an understanding can only begin with one's painfully relinquishing all laudatory epithets and notions of glory; it will not allow for any idea of personal superiority or delusion of grandeur. It leads to the discovery of the relativity that underlies the apparent perfection. And this research into origins is neces-

8

sary if we are not to believe that minds are as radically different as their productions would make it seem. Certain scientific works, for example—and particularly those of the mathematicians—are so limpid in their structure that it is hard to believe they have an author. There is something *inhuman* about them, and this quality has not been without its effect. It has led to the belief that there is such a great distance between certain disciplines, notably the sciences and the arts, that the minds devoted to each have been set as widely apart, in the common view, as the results of their labors seem to be. And yet these labors differ only in their variations from a common basis: by the part of the basis that each preserves, and the part that each neglects, in forming their languages and symbols. We must therefore be a little suspicious of books and expositions that seem too pure. Whatever is fixed deceives us, and whatever is made to be looked at is likely to change its appearance, to seem nobler. The operations of the mind can best serve our purpose of analysis while they are moving, unresolved, still at the mercy of a moment—before they have been given the name of enter-

Is it possible to make anything except under the illusion that one is making something else?—The objective of the artist is not so much the work itself as what people will think about it, which never depends simply on what it is.

An outstanding difference between the sciences and the arts is that the former must aim at results that are either certain or immensely probable, whereas the latter can only hope for results of an unknown probability.

Between the mode of generation and the

9

fruit, *there is an enormous difference.*

Pascal's famous Pensées are not so much straightforward private thoughts as arguments, or weapons or stultifying poisons, for others. *Their form is sometimes so finely wrought and deeply studied that it reveals the will to falsify the true "thought" by making it more imposing and terrifying than any thought could be.*

tainment or law, theorem or work of art, and, being perfected, have lost their mutual resemblance.

Within the mind a drama takes place. Drama, adventure, agitation, any words of the sort can be used provided that several of them are used together, so that one is corrected by another. Most of those dramas are lost, like the plays of Menander, but we do have Leonardo's manuscripts and Pascal's dazzling notes. These fragments insist that we examine them. They help us to realize by what starts and snatches of thought, by what strange suggestions from human events or the flow of sensations, and after what immense moments of lassitude, men are able to see the shadows of their future works, the ghosts that come before. But without having recourse to such great examples that they might be dismissed as exceptional cases, we need merely observe someone who thinks he is alone and left to himself: he *recoils* from an idea, *grasps* it, denies or smiles or stiffens, and mimes the strange predicament of his own diversity. Madmen often act like this in public.

By such examples, physical movements that can be measured and defined are shown to be closely related to the personal drama of which I was speaking. The actors in the drama are mental images, and it is easy to understand that, if we eliminate the particular features of the images and consider only their succession, frequency, periodicity, varying capacity for association, and finally their duration, we are soon tempted to find analogies in the so-called material world, to compare them with scientific analyses, to postulate an environment, to endow them first with continuity, velocities, properties of displacement, then with mass and energy. Thereupon we may realize that many such systems are possible, that any one in particular is worth no more than another, and that our use of them—which is rewarding, since it always casts light on something —must be continually watched over and restored to its purely verbal function. For, in precise terms, analogy is only our faculty of changing images, of combining them, of making part of one coexist with part of another, and of perceiving, voluntarily or involuntarily, the connections in their structure. And this makes it impossible to describe the mind, where images exist. In the mind words lose their force.

I should be inclined to say that what is most real in our thinking is not the part of it that consists in forming a simple image of perceptible reality. Rather it is the process of observation—precarious and often untrustworthy as it may be —of what takes place within us and induces us to believe that the variations in the two worlds are comparable. This process enables us, at least in a rough way, to express what is properly the psychic world in terms of metaphors taken from the perceptible world, and particularly from acts and operations that we can effectuate. Thus, note the relation of "thinking"

*and "weighing"
(penser and peser),
of "grasping" and
"comprehending,"
of "hypothesis"
and "synthesis,"
etc.
"Duration" comes
from the same root
as dur, "hard." All
this amounts to giving
certain visual, tactile,
and motor images—
or their combinations
—a double value.*

They are formed, there they leap forth, under its *eyes*; it is the mind that describes words to us.

And so man carries away *visions*, whose power becomes his power. He connects it with his history, of which his visions are the geometrical site. From this process arise those decisive acts that astound us; those perspectives, miraculous divinations, exact judgments; those illuminations, those incomprehensible anxieties, and stupid blunders as well. In certain extraordinary cases, invoking abstract gods —genius, inspiration, a thousand others —we ask with stupefaction how these marvels came to be. Once again we believe that something must have created itself, for we worship mystery and the marvelous as much as we love to ignore what goes on behind the scenes; we ascribe logic to miracle, although the inspired author had been preparing for a year. He was ripe. He had always thought of this work, perhaps unconsciously; and while others were still not ready to see, he had looked, combined, and now was merely reading what was written in his mind. The secret—whether of Leonardo, or of Bonaparte, or that of the highest intelligence at a given time—lies and can only lie in the relations they found—and were compelled to find—*among things of which we cannot grasp the law of continuity*. It is certain that, at the decisive moment, they had only to complete definite acts. Their supreme achievement, the one that the world admires, had become a simple matter—almost like comparing two lengths.

From this point of view we can perceive the unity of the method with which we are concerned. It is native and elemental to this environment, of which it is the very life and definition. And when thinkers as powerful as the man whom I am contemplating through these lines discover the implicit resources of the method, in a clearer and more conscious moment they have the right to exclaim: "*Facil cosa è farsi universale!*—It is easy to become universal!" They can, for the moment, admire the prodigious instrument they are—at the price of instantly denying the element of prodigy.

But this final clarity is attained only after long wanderings and inevitable idolatries. A consciousness of the operations of thought, which is the unrecognized logic I mentioned before, exists but rarely, even in the

The word "continuity" was not at all the right choice. I remember having written it in place of another word that could not be found. I meant to say: among things that we cannot transpose or translate into a system of the totality of our acts—that is, into the system of our powers.

13

keenest minds. The number of conceptions, the ability to prolong them, and the abundance of discoveries are something different, and are produced without respect to one's judgment of their nature. Yet the importance of that judgment is easy to appreciate. A flower, a proposition, and a sound can be imagined almost simultaneously; the intervals between them can be made as short as we choose; and each of these objects of thought can also change, be deformed, lose its initial qualities one after another at the will of the mind that conceived it, but it is in one's consciousness of this power that all its value resides. That consciousness alone permits us to criticize these *formations*, to interpret them, to find in them nothing more than they contain, and not to confuse their states with those of reality. With it begins the analysis of all intellectual phases, of all the states that consciousness will have the power to define as fallacy, madness, discovery—which at first were only nuances impossible to distinguish. Equivalent variations of a common substance, they were comparable one to another, existed at indefinite and almost irresponsible levels, could sometimes be named, and all

14

according to the same system. To be conscious of one's thoughts, as thoughts, is to recognize this sort of equality or homogeneity; to feel that all combinations of the sort are legitimate, natural, and that the method consists in arousing them, in seeing them precisely, in seeking for what they imply.

At some time in this process of observation, this double life of the mind that reduces ordinary thinking to something like the dream of a wakened sleeper, it appears that the sequence of the dream—with its mass of combinations, contrasts, and perceptions, either grouped around some project or moving forward indeterminately, at one's pleasure—is developing with *perceptible* regularity, with the obvious continuity of a machine. The idea then arises (or the wish) that this movement might be accelerated, that the terms of the sequence might be carried to their *limit*, to that of their imaginable expressions, *after which everything will be changed.* And if this mode of being conscious becomes habitual, it will enable us, for example, to consider beforehand all the possible results of an imagined act and all the relationships of a conceived object, and

This observation (about carrying psychic processes to their limit) is one over which the author might well have lingered. It would suggest a further investigation of time, of the mental process I have sometimes described as subjecting ideas to the pressure of time,

15

of the part played by external circumstances, and of the willed establishment of certain thresholds. Here we should be entering an area of extremely delicate psychic mechanics, in which particular durations play an important part, are included one in another, etc.

then to proceed further to the faculty of putting them aside, of divining something ever more intense or exact than the given object, to the ability to rouse oneself from any thought that was lasting too long. Whatever its nature, a thought that becomes fixed assumes the characteristics of a hypnosis and is called, in the language of logic, an idol; in the domain of art and poetic construction, it becomes a sterile monotony. The faculty of which I speak—one that leads the mind to foresee itself and to picture as a whole whatever was going to be pictured in detail, together with the effect of the sequence thus presented in brief—is the basis of all generalization. In certain individuals it manifests itself with remarkable energy, becoming a veritable passion; in the arts it is the cause of each separate advance and explains the continually more frequent use of contraction, suggestion, and violent contrast; while the same faculty exists implicitly, in its rational form, at the base of all mathematical concepts. It is very similar to the operation which, under the name of reasoning by recurrence,★ extends the application of

My opinion is that the secret of this reasoning process or mathematical induction resides in a sort

★ The philosophical importance of this form of reasoning was demonstrated for the

these analyses—and which, from the type of simple addition to infinitesimal summation, does more than save us from making an infinite number of useless experiments; it produces more complex structures, since the conscious imitation of my act is a new act that envelops all the possible adaptations of the first.

of consciousness that the act in itself is independent of its subject matter.

This tableau of drama, agitation, lucidity stands in opposition to other scenes and movements that we call "Nature" or "the World." But we can do nothing with this natural world except to distinguish ourselves from it, and then immediately replace ourselves within its frame.

Philosophers have generally concluded by implying our existence in the notion we hold of nature, and nature in the notion we hold of ourselves; but they seldom go beyond this point, for we know they are more inclined to dispute the ideas of their predecessors than to look into the problem for themselves. Scientists and artists have exploited nature in

Here we have the essential vice of philosophy. Philosophy is something personal, but does not wish to be personal.
It hopes to accumulate a steadily increasing capital of transmissible values, as science has done.

first time by M. Poincaré in a recent article. When consulted by the author, the eminent scientist confirmed our statement of his priority.

Hence all the philosophical systems that pretend to have no author.

their different fashions: in the end the former measured, and then constructed; the latter came to construct as though they had measured. Everything they have made finds a place of its own accord in the natural world, where it also plays a part, helping to extend it by giving new forms to its constituent materials. But before generalizing and building we observe. From among the mass of qualities that present themselves, our senses— each in its own fashion, with its own degree of docility—distinguish and choose the qualities that will be retained and developed by the individual. At first the process is undergone passively, almost unconsciously, as a vessel lets itself be filled: there is a feeling of slow and pleasurable circulation. Later, one's interest being awakened, one assigns new values to things that had seemed closed and irreducible; one adds to them, takes more pleasure in particular features, finds expression for these; and what happens is like the restitution of an energy that our senses had received. Soon the energy will alter the environment in its turn, employing to this end the conscious thought of a person.

The universal man also begins with

simple observation, and continually renews this self-fertilization from what he sees. He returns to the intoxication of ordinary instinct and to the emotion aroused by the least of real things, when one considers both thing and instinct, so self-contained in all their qualities, and concentrating in every way so many effects.

Most people see with their intellects much more often than with their eyes. Instead of colored spaces, they become aware of concepts. Something whitish, cubical, erect, its planes broken by the sparkle of glass, is immediately a house for them—the House!—a complex idea, a combination of abstract qualities. If they change position, the movement of the rows of windows, the translation of surfaces which continuously alters their sensuous perceptions, all this escapes them, for their concept remains the same. They perceive with a dictionary rather than with the retina; and they approach objects so blindly, they have such a vague notion of the difficulties and pleasures of vision, that they have invented *beautiful views*. Of the rest they are unaware. In this one instance, however, they feast on a concept that

Why artists are useful: they preserve the subtlety and instability of sensory impressions.
A modern artist has to exhaust two-thirds of his time trying to see what is visible—and above all, trying not to see what is invisible. Philosophers often pay a high price for striving to do the opposite.

19

swarms with words. (A general rule that applies to the weakness existing in all branches of knowledge is precisely our choice of *obvious* standpoints, our being content with definite systems that facilitate, that make it easy to grasp. In this sense one can say that the work of art is always more or less didactic.) Even these beautiful views are more or less concealed from ordinary observers; and all the modulations so delicately contrived by little movements, changing light, and tiring eyes are lost to them, neither adding to nor subtracting from their sensations. Since they know that the level of still water is horizontal, they fail to observe that the sea is *upright* at the horizon. Should the tip of a nose, the whiteness of a shoulder, or two fingers happen to dig into a pool of light that isolates them, our observers never think of regarding them as new jewels enriching their vision. Those jewels are fragments of a person, and the person alone exists, is known to them. Moreover, since they utterly reject anything that lacks a name, the number of their impressions is strictly limited in advance!*

A work of art should always teach us that we had not seen what we see.

The deeper education consists in unlearning one's first education.

* See proposition CCLXXI of Leonardo's treatise *On Painting:* "*Impossibile che una memoria possa riserbare tutti gli aspetti o muta-*

The exercise of the opposite gift leads to analyses in the true sense. One cannot say that the gift is exercised in *nature*. This word, although it seems general and apparently contains every possibility of experience, is altogether personal. It evokes particular images, determining the memory or history of one man. In most cases it calls forth the vision of a green, vague, and continuous eruption; of some great elemental work as opposed to everything human; of a monotonous quantity that will some day cover us; of

That is, the gift for seeing *more than one* knows.
These remarks are the naïve expression of a doubt long held by the author, as to the true value or function of words. *The words of ordinary speech are not* made for *logic. The permanence and universality of their meanings are never assured.*

zioni d'alcun membro di qualunque animal si sia. . . . È perchè ogni quantità continua è divisibile in infinito—It is impossible for any memory to retain all the aspects of any limb of any animal whatever. This is because any continuous quantity is infinitely divisible."

What I have said of sight also applies to the other senses, but I have chosen sight because it seems to me the most *intellectual* of them all. In the mind, visual images predominate. It is between these images that the analogical faculty is most often exercised. When we make analogies between any two objects, the inferior term of the comparison may even originate in an error of judgment caused by an indistinct sensation. The form and colors of an object are so evidently uppermost in our minds that they enter into our concepts of qualities relating to another sense. If we speak of the hardness of iron, for example, the visual image of iron will almost always be produced, and seldom an auditive image.

In short, errors and analogies result from the fact that an impression can be completed in two or three different fashions. Land, a cloud, or a ship are three different ways of completing a certain appearance on the horizon, at sea. Desire or expectation puts one of these words in our minds.

something stronger than we are, entangled in itself and tearing itself apart while sleeping on and working on; of something to which, personified, the poets accorded cruelty, kindness, and several other motives. Hence, our ideal observer must be placed not in nature, but in any corner whatever of that which exists.

An early attempt of mine to represent an individual universe. An " I " and its Universe—if we admit that these myths are useful— should have, in any system, the same relation that exists between a retina and a source of light.

The observer is confined in a sphere that is never broken. It has variations that will reveal themselves as movements or objects, but its surface remains closed, although every portion of the sphere is renewed and changes position. At first the observer is only the condition of this finite space; at every moment he *is* this finite space. He is troubled by none of his memories or powers so long as he equates himself with what he sees. And if I were able to conceive of his remaining in this state, I should conceive that his impressions differed hardly at all from those received in a dream. He is vaguely conscious of pain, pleasure, and a sense of tranquility,* all imparted

* Without touching on physiological questions, I might mention the case of a man suffering from a form of depressive psychosis. This patient, whom I once saw in a clinic, was in a state of retarded life; he

to him by these indefinite forms, among which is numbered his own body. And now, slowly, some of the forms begin to be forgotten, almost disappearing from sight, while others make themselves visible for the first time—in the place where they had always been. It must also be noted that changes in vision resulting from the mere duration of one's attention, and from tired eyes, are likely to be indistinguishably confused with those due to ordinary movements. Certain areas in one's field of vision become exaggerated, in the same way as an ailing limb seems larger and, because of the importance it acquires from pain, distorts our notion of the body. These exaggerated areas will be more amenable to observation and easier to remember. At this point the spectator begins rising from simple perception to reverie; henceforth he will be able to extend the particular characteristics derived from the first and most familiar objects to other objects in greater and greater number. Remembering a precedent, he perfects the

Inequalities are certain to appear. Consciousness is by essence unstable.

recognized objects only after an extraordinary delay. Sensations took a very long time to reach his mind. He felt no needs. This form of insanity is exceedingly rare.

There is a sort of liberty with regard to groupings, corres-pondences, and neutralizations that is exercised in the entire field of per-ception. If several persons are speaking at the same time, we can, if we choose, listen to only one of them.

These are intuitions *in the narrow and etymological sense of the word.*
An image can serve as the anticipation of another image.

given space. Then, at his pleasure, he can arrange or undo his successive impressions. He can appreciate the value of strange combinations: a group of flowers, or of men, a hand or a cheek seen by itself, a spot of sunlight on a wall, a gathering of animals brought together by chance—all these he regards as complete and solid beings. He feels a desire to picture the invisible wholes of which he has been given some visible parts. Thus, he infers the planes designed by a bird in its flight, the trajectory of a missile, the surfaces delimited by our gestures, and the extraordinary fissures, the fluid ara-besques, the formless chambers created in an all-penetrating medium by the grating and quivering of a swarm of insects, by trees that roll like ships, by wheels, the human smile, the tide. Traces of what he imagined can some-times be seen on water or on rippled sand; and sometimes his own retina, as the moments pass, can compare some object with the form of its movement.

The persistence of impressions has an essential role.
There is a sort of symmetry in these mutually inverse transformations.
Corresponding to the

From such forms, born of move-ment, there is a transition to the move-ments into which forms may be dissolved by means of a simple change in duration. If a drop of rain appears to be a line, a thousand vibrations to be a continuous sound, and the irregularities of this paper to be a polished plane, and if duration is taken to be the sole cause of these impressions, then a stable form may be replaced by a sufficient rapidity in the periodic registration of a thing (or element) chosen for the purpose. Geometricians will be able to introduce time and velocity into the study of forms, just as they can eliminate both from the study of movements. In common speech, by a similar process, a road will *climb*, a jetty will *stretch*, a statue *rise*. And the intoxication of analogy, as well as the logic of continuity, will carry these actions to the limit of their tendency, to the impossibility of their ever being halted. Everything moves by gradations, imaginarily. Here in this room, and because I concentrate on this one thought, the objects about me are as *active* as the flame of the lamp. The armchair decays in its place, the table asserts itself so fast that it is motionless, and the curtains flow endlessly away. The result is an infinite complexity. To regain control of ourselves in the midst of the moving bodies, the circulation of their contours, the jumble of knots, the paths, the falls, the whirlpools, the confusion of velocities, we

spatialization of linear movements is something I once described as the chronolysis of space.

Something like this might be seen from a certain level of observation, if light and the retina were continuous—but then we should no longer see the objects themselves. Hence the function of the "mind" here is to combine two incompatible orders of size or quality, two levels of vision that are mutually exclusive.

It is thanks to the hierarchy of the senses and the varying duration of our perceptions that we can oppose to this chaos of palpitations and substitutions a world of solid masses and identifiable objects. There are only two things we perceive directly: persistence *and* averages.

must have recourse to our grand capacity for deliberately forgetting—and without destroying the acquired idea, we introduce a generalized concept, that of the orders of magnitude.

And so, by the extension of the "given quantity," we lose our intoxication with these particular objects, of which there can be no science. When we look at them fixedly, they change if we think of them; and if we do not think of them, we fall into a lasting torpor, of somewhat the same nature as a tranquil dream; we stare as if hypnotized at the corner of a table or the shadow of a leaf, only to waken the moment they are *seen*. There are men who feel with special delicacy the pleasure that is derived from the *individuality* of objects. What they prefer and are delighted to find in a thing is the quality of being unique—which all things possess. Their form of curiosity finds its ultimate expression in fiction and the arts of the theater and is called, at this extreme, the *faculty of identification*.★ Nothing seems more deliberately absurd when described than the temerity of a person who declares that he *is* a certain object and feels its

Always the motive force of inequality.

★ Edgar Allan Poe, "On Shakespeare" (*Marginalia*).

26

impressions—especially if the object is inanimate.* Yet there is nothing more powerful in the imaginative life. The chosen object becomes as it were the center of that life, a center of ever multiplying associations, depending on whether the object is more or less complicated. Essentially this faculty must be a means of exciting the imaginative vitality, of setting potential energy to work. Carried too far it becomes a pathological symptom and gains a frightening ascendancy over the increasing feebleness of a decaying mind.

From a pure observation of things to these complex states, the mind has merely extended its functions, forming concepts in response to the problems offered by all sensation and solving the problems more or less easily, depending on whether a larger or smaller production of such concepts is demanded. It is evident that we are touching, at this point, on the very *springs* of thought. Thinking consists, during almost all the time we devote to it, in wandering among themes

Inequality again. The transition from the less to the more is spontaneous. The transition from the more to the less is deliberate and rare,

* Whoever explains why identification with a material object *seems* more absurd than that with a living object will have taken a step toward explaining the problem.

27

since it has to go against the customary practice and appearance of comprehension.

about which we know, first of all, that we know them *more or less well.* Hence, things can be classified according to the ease or difficulty they afford to our comprehension, according to our degree of familiarity with them, and according to the various resistances offered by their parts or conditions when we try to imagine them together. The history of this graduated complexity remains to be conjectured.

If everything were irregular, or if everything were regular, there would be no thinking—for thinking is only an effort to pass from disorder to order. It requires the former as an occasion for being exercised, and the latter for models to imitate.

The isolated, the exceptional, the singular are inexplicable—that is, they have no expression but themselves.
The insurmountable difficulties presented by prime numbers.

The world is irregularly strewn with regular arrangements. Crystals are of this nature; so are flowers and leaves, many striped or spotted ornaments on the fur, wings, or shells of animals, the patterns made by the wind on water or sand, etc. Sometimes these effects depend on a sort of perspective and on temporary juxtapositions. Distance produces or disfigures them. Time reveals or hides them. Thus, the number of births, deaths, crimes, and accidents presents a regularity in its fluctuations, one that becomes more and more evident as we follow the record through the years. The most surprising events, and the most *asymmetrical* in relation to neighboring moments, return to a semblance of order when considered in relation to

28

longer periods. One might mention other examples in the realm of instincts, habits, and customs, as well as the semblances of periodicity that have given rise to so many philosophies of history.

The knowledge of regular combinations is divided among the different sciences; or, where none can be established, it comes under the calculation of probabilities. For our purpose *—which has overrun* we need only the observation made *almost all of Physics* on introducing this topic: that regular *since 1894.* combinations, whether of time or space, are irregularly distributed in the field of investigation. Mentally they seem to be opposed to a vast number of formless things.

I think they might be described as "first guides of the human mind," except that such a proposition is immediately reversible. In any case they represent continuity.* Any thought permits of a change or transfer (of attention, for example) among ele-

* Here the word is not employed in its mathematical sense. It is not a question of inserting a numerable infinity and an innumerable infinity of values into an interval; it is only a question of simple intuition, of objects that suggest laws, of laws that are evident to the eyes. The existence or possibility of such things is the first—and not the least surprising—fact of this order.

ments apparently fixed in their relation to the thought, which it selects from memory or immediate perception. If the elements are perfectly similar, or if their difference can be reduced to mere distance, to the elementary fact of their existing separately, then the *labor* to be performed is in turn reduced to this purely differential notion. Thus, a straight line will be the easiest of all lines to conceive, because there is no smaller effort for the mind than that exerted in passing from one point of a straight line to another, each of the points being similarly placed in relation to all the rest. In other words, all portions of the line are so homogeneous, however short we may conceive them to be, that they can all be reduced to one, always the same; and that is the reason why the dimensions of shapes are always expressed in terms of straight lines. At a higher degree of complexity, periodicity is employed to represent continuous properties; for this periodicity, whether it exists in space or time, is nothing else than the division of an object of thought into fragments, such that they can be replaced one by the other under certain conditions—or else it is the multiplication of an object under those same conditions.

The easiest to conceive, but extremely difficult to define. This whole passage is a youthful and not very successful attempt to describe the simplest *intuitions—by means of which the world of sensory images and the system of* concepts *can sometimes be brought together.*

Why is it that only a part of all that exists can be so reduced? There is a moment when the figure becomes so complicated, or the event seems so new, that we must abandon the attempt to consider them as a whole, or to proceed with their translation into continuous values. At what point did our Euclids halt in their apprehension of forms? What was the particular degree of interruption that set a limit to their notion of continuity? They had reached what appeared to be the furthest point of a research at which one cannot fail to be tempted by the doctrines of evolution. One is loath to admit to oneself that this limit could be final.

It is certain, in any case, that the basis and aim of every speculation is the extension of continuity with the help of metaphors, abstractions, and special languages. These are employed by the arts in a fashion to be discussed in a moment.

We have arrived at the conception that parts of the world let themselves be reduced, here and there, to intelligible elements. Sometimes our senses suffice for the task; sometimes the most ingenious methods must be employed; but always there are voids. The

We are now—1930 —at a stage in which those difficulties have become pressing. What I awkwardly tried to express in 1894 is the state we are in today. We have come to despair of finding any figurative—or even any intelligible— explanation.

Langevin is hopeful on this point; I, not at all. Discussed at the Société de Philosophie, 1929.

What takes place, in other words, is a sort of adaptation to the diversity, multiplicity, and instability of facts.

attempts remain lacunary. It is here that we find the kingdom of our hero.

By now—after thirty-six years—this hypothesis has been curiously confirmed. Theoretical physics of the boldest and most difficult sort has been forced to abandon images *and the whole notion of visual and motor representation. In its effort to subjugate its vast domain—to unify its laws and make them independent of the place, time, and movement of the observer—it has no other guide than the* symmetry *of its formulas.*

He has an extraordinary sense of symmetry that makes him regard everything as a problem. Wherever the understanding breaks off he introduces the productions of his mind. It is evident how extremely convenient he can be. He is like a scientific hypothesis. We should have to invent him, but he exists; the universal man can now be imagined. A Leonardo da Vinci can exist in our minds, without too much dazzling them, in the form of a concept; our dream of his power need not be quickly lost in a fog of big words and ponderous epithets conducive to inconsistent thinking. Could one believe that Leonardo himself would be satisfied with such mirages?

This *symbolic* mind held an immense collection of forms, an ever lucid treasury of the dispositions of nature, a potentiality always ready to be translated into action and growing with the extension of its domain. A host of concepts, a throng of possible memories, the power to recognize an extraordinary number of distinct things in the world at large and arrange them in a thousand fashions: this constituted

Leonardo. He was the master of faces, anatomies, machines. He knew how a smile was made; he could put it on the façade of a house or into the mazes of a garden. He disordered and curled the filaments of water and the tongues of flames. If his hand traces the vicissitudes of the attacks which he has planned, he depicts in fearful bouquets the trajectories of balls from thousands of cannon; they raze the bastions of cities and strongholds which he has just constructed in all their details, and fortified. As though he found the metamorphoses of things too gradual when observed in a calm, he adores battles, tempests, the deluge. Regarding them from a height, he can see them as mechanical processes; and he can feel them in the apparent independence or life of their fragments; in a handful of sand driven by the wind; in the stray idea of any fighter distorted by passion and inner torment.* He is there in the "shy and blunt" little bodies of children, in the constricted gestures of old men and women, in the simplicity of

* See the description of a battle, of the deluge, etc., in his treatise *On Painting* and in the manuscripts at the Institut de France (ed. Ravaisson-Mollien). Drawings of tempests, bombardments, etc., can be seen in the Windsor manuscripts.

the corpse. He has the secret of composing fantastic beings and of making their existence seem probable; the logic that harmonizes their discordant parts is so rigorous that it suggests the life and the naturalness of the whole. He makes a Christ, an angel, a monster, by taking what is known, what exists everywhere, and arranging it in a new order. Here he profits by the illusion and abstraction of painting, an art that depicts only a single quality of things, but thereby evokes them all.

He passes from the headlong or seemingly retarded movement of the avalanche and landslide, from massive curves to multitudinous draperies; from smoke sprouting on roofs to distant tree-forms, to the vaporous beeches of the horizon; from fish to birds; from the sea glittering in the sun to birch leaves in their thousand slender mirrors; from scales and shells to the gleams that sail over gulfs; from ears and ringlets to the frozen whorls of the nautilus. From the shell he proceeds to the spiral tumescence of the

Sketches of this type are often to be found in Leonardo's manuscripts. His precise imagination

waves; from the skin on the water of shallow pools to the veins that would warm it, and thence to the elemental movements of crawling, to the fluid serpent. He vivifies. He molds the

34

water round a swimmer* into clinging scarves, draperies that show the effort of the muscles in relief. As for the air, he transfixes it in the wake of soaring larks as ravelings of shadow; it is pictured in the frothy flights of bubbles which these aerial journeys and delicate breaths must disturb and leave trailing across the blue-tinted pages of space, the dense, vague crystal of space.

He reconstructs all buildings, tempted by every mode of combining the most diverse materials. He enjoys things distributed in the dimensions of space; vaults and beams and soaring domes; rows of galleries and loggias; masses held aloft by the weight in their arches; bridges flung from pier to pier; the depth of green in trees rising into the air from which it drinks; and the structures formed by migratory birds, those acute triangles pointing to the south, revealing a rational combination of living beings.

He makes sport of difficulties, and, growing bolder, he translates all his feelings with clarity into this universal language. The abundance of his metaphorical resources makes this possible.

* Sketch in the manuscripts of the Institut de France.

creates the sort of effects that photography has since revealed as fact.

From this point of view his intellectual labors are part of the slow transformation by which the notion of space—at first that of a complete vacuum or an isotropic volume—has little by little developed into the notion of a system inseparable from the matter it contains, and from time.

His desire to probe utterly the slightest fragment, the merest shard, of the world renews the force and cohesion of his being. His joy finds an outlet in his decorations for fêtes and in other charming inventions; when he dreams of constructing a *flying man*, he sees him soaring to the mountaintops for snow and coming back to scatter it over the streets of cities pulsing with the heat of summer. His emotion delights in pure faces touched by a frown of shadow and in the gesture of a silent god. His hate knows all weapons: all the artifices of the engineer, all the stratagems of the general. He establishes terrible engines of war and protects them with bastions, caponiers, salients, and moats which he provides with water-gates, so as suddenly to transform the aspects of a siege; and I recall—while savoring the fine Italian wariness of the *cinquecento*—that he built strongholds in which four flights of steps, independent round the same axis, separate the mercenaries from their leaders and the troops of hired soldiers one from the other.

He worships the human body, male and female, which measures and is measured by all things. He can feel its height; how a rose can grow up to its

lips while a great plane tree leaps
twenty times higher, in a jet whence
the leaves hang down to its head. He
knows that a radiant body will fill a
possible room, or the concavity of a
vault that is deduced from the human
form, or a natural background that is
measured by its steps. He studies the
lightest footfall; spies on the skeleton
silent in the flesh, the concurrent
motions of the human walk, and all
the superficial play of heat and cool-
ness over naked flesh, perceiving these
as a diffused whiteness or bronze
welded over a mechanism. And the
face, that enlightening and enlightened
thing—of all visible things the most
particular, the most magnetic, the
most difficult to regard without studying it—the face haunts him. In each
man's memory there remain in-
distinctly a few hundred faces with
their variations. In his, they were classified and proceeded consecutively from
one physiognomy to another, from
one irony to another, from one wisdom
to a lesser wisdom, from benignity to
the divine—by way of symmetry.
About the eyes—fixed points of variable brilliance—he adjusts the mask
that hides a complex structure of bones
and distinct muscles under a uniform

37

skin; then drawing the mask tight, he makes it reveal all.

Among the multitude of minds, this mind impresses us as being one of the *regular combinations* already mentioned. In order to understand it, one does not feel that, like most of the others, it has to be attached to a nation, a tradition, or a group practicing the same art. Its acts, by virtue of their number and intercommunication, together form a symmetrical object, a sort of *system complete in itself,* or completing itself continually.

Perhaps this highest degree of self-possession deprives an individual of all particularities— except the very one of being master and center of himself? . . . In the "Note and Digression" this notion is developed at some length.

Leonardo is bound to be the despair of modern man who, from adolescence, is directed into a speciality, where it is hoped he may excel simply because he is confined to it. The variety of methods is offered as an excuse, and the quantity of details, and the constant accumulation of facts and theories, with the result that the patient observer, the meticulous accountant of existence, the individual who reduces himself—not without earning our gratitude, if the phrase has any meaning here—to the minute aptitudes of an instrument, is confounded with the man for whom this work is done, the poet of hypothesis, the architect of analytical materials. The first needs patience, monotonous direction, specialization, and time. The absence of thought is his virtue. But the other must circulate through barriers and partitions. His function is to disregard them. At this point I might suggest an analogy between specialization and the state of stupor due to a prolonged sensation that was mentioned above. But the best argument is that, nine times out of ten, every great improvement in a field of endeavor is obtained by the intrusion of methods and notions that were not foreseen within it. Having just attributed those advances to the formation of images, then of idioms, we cannot evade this consequence, that the number of such idioms possessed by any man has a singular bearing on his chance of finding new ones. It would be easy to demonstrate that all the minds that have served as substance to generations of seekers and quibblers, all those whose remains have nourished, for centuries on end, human opinion and the human mania for echoing, have been more or less universal. The names of Aristotle, Descartes, Leibniz, Kant, Diderot are sufficient confirmation.

Here we are verging on another topic, the joys of *construction*. I shall

What I should write today is that the number of ways an individual can employ a single word is more important than the number of words at his disposal. Cf. Racine and Victor Hugo.

Diderot is unexpected here. His one truly philosophic quality

was the lightness of touch that all philosophers should have—and so many of them lack.

try to justify the preceding remarks with a few examples and to show, in its application, the possibility and almost the necessity of a general interplay of thought. I should like to point out that the particular results I shall mention in passing would be difficult to obtain without our employing a number of apparently unrelated concepts.

The arbitrary creating the necessary. . . .

He who has never been seized—were it in a dream!—by a project he is free to abandon, by the adventure of a construction already completed when others see it only beginning; who has never experienced either the fire of enthusiasm that utterly consumes a moment of himself, the poison of conception, the scruples, the chill of interior objections, as well as that struggle between alternative ideas in which the stronger and more universal must triumph, even over habit, even over novelty; the man who never, in the whiteness of his paper, has seen an image troubled by the possible and by regret for all the symbols that will not be chosen, any more than he has seen, in the limpid air, a building that does not exist; the man who has not been haunted by the intoxication of a distant aim, by anxiety as to means, by the foreknowledge of delays and despair, by the calculation of successive phases, or by the reasoning that is projected into the future to designate the very things that must not be reasoned about *even then*: that man, however great his knowledge, will never know the riches or the broad intellectual domains that are illuminated by the conscious act of *constructing*. And it was from the human mind that even the gods received their gift of *creation*, because that mind, being periodic and abstract, can expand any of its conceptions to the point at which they are no longer conceivable.

Constructing takes place between a project or a particular vision and the materials that one has chosen. For one order of things, which is initial, we substitute another order, whatever may be the objects rearranged: stones, colors, words, concepts, men, etc. Their specific nature does not change the general conditions of that sort of music in which, at this point, the chosen material serves only as the timbre, if we pursue the metaphor. The wonder is that we sometimes receive an impression of accuracy and consistency from human constructions made of an agglomeration of seeming-

This independence is essential to the pursuit of form. *But the artist*, in another phase, *tries to restore the particularity, even the singularity, that he had begun by eliminating from his attention.*

41

ly incompatible elements, as though the mind that arranged them had recognized their secret affinities. But the wonder passes all bounds when we perceive that the author, in the vast majority of cases, is himself unable to give an account of the paths he followed, and that he wields a power whose motive forces he does not know. He can never lay claim in advance to a success. By what process are the parts of an edifice, the elements of a drama, the factors in a victory, reconciled one with another? By what series of obscure analyses is anyone led to the production of a work?

In such cases it is customary to explain everything by instinct, but that leaves instinct itself to be explained.

Instinct is a mental force of which the cause and the purpose are both immeasurable—*if we admit that* cause *and* purpose *have any meaning in this connection.*

In the present case, moreover, we should be making our appeal to strictly personal and exceptional instincts, that is, to the contradictory notion of "hereditary habit," something that would be no more habitual than it was hereditary.

The act of constructing, as soon as it leads to some comprehensible result, would lead us to think that some common measure of terms has been applied, an element or principle already presupposed by the simple fact

42

of our becoming conscious, and which can have only an abstract or imaginary existence. We cannot conceive of a whole composed of changes—a picture or an edifice of multiple qualities—except as the locus of the modalities of a single *matter* or *law*, of which we affirm the hidden continuity in the very same instant that we recognize the edifice as a unified whole, as the limited field of our investigation. Here again we encounter that psychological postulate of continuity which, in our faculty of knowing, resembles the principle of inertia in mechanics. Only such purely abstract, purely differential combinations as those of numbers can be constructed with the aid of fixed units; and it is to be noted that the relation of these to other possible constructions is the same as that of the regular portions of the world to the irregular portions.

The word differential *is not used here in its technical sense. What I meant was that the combinations would consist of identical elements.*

In art there is a word that can be applied to all its modes and fantasies, while suppressing, at a stroke, all the supposed difficulties involved in the opposition or resemblance between art and the nature that is never defined, and for good reason: that word is *ornament*. Let us only recall in succes-

Ornament, that answer to emptiness,

43

that compensation of the possible, in a sense completes and is also the annulment of a liberty.

sion the groups of curved lines and balancing sections that cover the oldest known objects, the profiles of vases or temples; then the lozenges, volutes, ova, and striae of the ancients; the crystallized forms and voluptuous wall-surfaces of the Arabs; the skeletal Gothic symmetries; the waves, the flames, the flowers on Japanese lacquer or bronze; and in each of these eras the introduction of the likenesses of plants, animals, and men, the perfecting of those resemblances: painting, sculpture. Or think of speech and its primitive melody, the separation of words from music and the branching development of each; on the one hand, the invention of verbs, of writing, the *figurative* complexity of language that becomes possible, and the occurrence —so peculiar—of abstract words; on the other hand, the system of tones rendered more flexible, extending from the voice to the resonance of materials, enriched by harmony, then varied by the use of different timbres. And finally let us observe a similar progression in the structures of thought, first through a sort of primitive psychic onomatopoeia, then through elementary symmetries and contrasts, till it reaches the ideas of substances, metaphors, a faltering sort of logic, formalism, entities, metaphysical concepts. . . .

All this multiform vitality can be regarded from the standpoint of ornament. The manifestations we have listed can be considered as finished portions of space or time containing different variations. Some of these are known and characterized objects, but their meaning and ordinary use are ignored so that only their order and mutual reactions may subsist. On this order depends the effect. The effect is the aim of ornament, and thus the work of art takes on the character of a machine to impress a public; to arouse emotions and their corresponding images.

From this point of view the conception bears the same relation to the particular arts that mathematics bears to the other sciences. Just as the physical notions of time, length, density, mass, etc., exist in mathematical calculations merely as homogeneous quantities and do not recover their individuality until the results are interpreted, so the objects chosen and arranged to obtain an effect are, as it were, detached from most of their attributes, which they only reassume

Here is another word —homogeneous— that is not being used in its technical sense. I simply wished to say that quantitative symbols are assigned to widely different

45

qualities, and that the qualities do not exist for and during a mathematical calculation except as numbers.
Likewise a painter, when planning a picture, regards objects as colors and colors as the elements with which he operates.

in the effect—that is, in the open mind of the spectator. Hence it is by a process of abstraction that works of art are constructed; and the process is more or less powerful, more or less easy to define, depending on whether the elements taken from reality are more or less complex. Inversely, it is by a sort of induction, by the production of mental images, that works of art are appreciated; and this process likewise demands more or less energy, causes more or less *fatigue*, depending on whether it is set in motion by a simple pattern on a vase or by one of Pascal's broken phrases.

The painter disposes pigments on a plane surface and expresses himself by means of their lines of separation, their varying thicknesses, their fusions and clashes. What the spectator sees is only a more or less faithful representation of bodies, gestures, and landscapes, as though he were looking out through a window of the museum. The picture is judged in the same spirit as reality. Some complain that the face is ugly, others fall in love with it, still others are psychological and verbose; a few look only at the hands, which they always say are unfinished. The fact is that the picture, in accordance with unconscious demands, is supposed to represent the physical and natural conditions of our own environment. Light radiates and weight makes itself felt, just as they do here; and anatomy and perspective gradually assumed a foremost rank among pictorial studies. I believe, on the contrary, that the surest method of judging a picture is to identify nothing at first, but, step by step, to make the series of inductions demanded by the simultaneous presence of colored masses in a definite area; then one can rise from metaphor to metaphor, from supposition to supposition, and so attain, in the end, to knowledge of the subject— or sometimes to sheer consciousness of pleasure, which we did not always feel in the beginning.

I have made a similar suggestion for poetry: that one should approach it as pure sonority, reading and rereading it as a sort of music, and should not introduce meanings or intentions into the diction before clearly grasping the system of sounds that every poem must offer on pain of nonexistence.

No example I could give of the general attitude toward painting would be more amusing than the celebrated "smile of Mona Lisa," to which the epithet "mysterious" seems irrevocably fixed. That dimpled face has evoked the sort of phraseology justified in all literatures, under the title of "Sensations" or "Impressions" of art. It is buried beneath a mass of words and disappears among the many paragraphs that start by calling it *disturbing* and end with a generally vague description of a state of *soul*. It might deserve less intoxicating studies. Leonardo had no use for inexact observations or arbitrary symbols, or Mona Lisa would never have been painted. He was guided by a perpetual sagacity.

In the background of *The Last Supper* there are three windows. The one in the middle, which opens behind Jesus, is distinguished from the others by a cornice that forms the arc of a circle. If we prolong the arc, we obtain a circumference with Christ as its center. All the great lines of the fresco converge at this point; the symmetry of the whole is relative to this center and to the long line of the table of the agape. The mystery, if one exists, is to know how we come to regard such combinations as mysterious, and that, I fear, can be explained.

It is not from painting, however, that we shall choose the striking example we need of the communication between the different activities of thought. The host of suggestions rising from the painter's need to diversify and people a surface; the resemblance between the first attempts of this

48

order and certain dispositions in the natural world; the evolution of visual sensibility—all these will be disregarded at this point, for fear of conducting the reader into all too arid speculations. A vaster art that is the ancestor, as it were, of painting will serve our purpose better.

The word *construction*—which I purposely employed so as to indicate more forcibly the problem of human intervention in natural things and so as to direct the mind of the reader toward the logic of the subject by a material suggestion—now resumes its more limited meaning. Architecture becomes our example.

The monument (which composes the City, which in turn is almost the whole of civilization) is such a complex entity that our understanding of it passes through several successive phases. First we grasp a changeable background that merges with the sky, then a rich texture of motifs in height, breadth, and depth, infinitely varied by perspective, then something solid, bold, resistant, with certain animal characteristics—organs, members—then finally a machine having gravity for its motive force, one that carries us

49

What physics discovers in matter today is no longer an edifice of any sort, but rather the indescribable in essence —and the unforeseen! 1930.

in thought from geometry to dynamics and thence to the most tenuous speculations of molecular physics, suggesting as it does not only the theories of that science but the models used to represent molecular structures. It is through the monument or, one might rather say, among such imaginary scaffoldings as might be conceived to harmonize its conditions one with another—its purpose with its stability, its proportions with its site, its form with its matter, and harmonizing each of these conditions with itself, its millions of aspects among themselves, its types of balance among themselves, its three dimensions with one another —that we are best able to reconstitute the clear intelligence of a Leonardo. Such a mind can play at imagining the future sensations of the man who will make a circuit of the edifice, draw near, appear at a window, and by picturing what the man will see; or by following the weight of the roof as it is carried down walls and buttresses to the foundations; or by feeling the balanced stress of the beams and the vibration of the wind that will torment them; or by foreseeing the forms of light playing freely over tiles and cornices, then diffused, encaged in rooms where the sun touches the floors. It will test and judge the pressure of the lintel on its supports, the expediency of the arch, the difficulties of the vaulting, the cascades of steps gushing from their landings, and all the power of invention that terminates in a durable mass, embellished, defended, and made liquid with windows, built for our lives, to contain our words, and out of it our smoke will rise.

Architecture is commonly misunderstood. Our notion of it varies from stage setting to that of an investment in housing. I suggest we refer to the idea of the City in order to appreciate its universality, and that we should come to know its complex charm by recalling the multiplicity of its aspects. For a building to be motionless is the exception; our pleasure comes from moving about it so as to make the building move in turn, while we enjoy all the combinations of its parts, as they vary: the column turns, depths recede, galleries glide; a thousand visions escape from the monument, a thousand harmonies.

(Many a project for a church, never realized, is to be found among Leonardo's manuscripts. Generally we may guess it to be a St. Peter's in

The most difficult problem for architecture as an art is to provide in advance for these endlessly varied aspects. It is the test of a monument—and a fatal test for any building designed as if it were a stage setting.

Rome; the St. Peter's of Michelangelo makes us wish it had been. At the end of the Gothic period, during a time when ancient temples were being unearthed, Leonardo found, between these two styles, the great design of the Byzantines: a cupola rising above cupolas; domes topped with swelling domes that cluster round the highest dome of all. His plans, however, show a boldness and pure ornamentation that Justinian's architects never mastered.)

The monument, that creature of stone, exists in space. What we call space is relative to the existence of whatever structures we may choose to conceive. The architectural structure interprets space, and leads to hypotheses on the nature of space, in a quite special manner; for it is an equilibrium of materials with respect to gravity, a visible static whole, and at the same time, within each of its materials, another equilibrium—molecular, in this case, and imperfectly understood. He who designs a monument speculates on the nature of gravity and then immediately penetrates into the obscure atomic realm. He is faced with the problem of structure, that is, to know what combinations must be imagined in order to satisfy the conditions of resistance, resilience, etc., obtaining in a given space. We can see the logical extension of the problem and how one passes from the architectural domain, usually handed over to the specialists, into the most abstruse theories of general physics and mechanics.

Thanks to the docility of the imagination, the properties of an edifice and those inherent in a given substance help to explain each other. Space, as soon as we try to represent it in our minds, at once ceases to be a void and is filled with a host of arbitrary constructions; and in all cases it can be replaced by a juxta-position of forms, which we know can be rendered as required. However complicated we may suppose an edifice to be, it will represent, when multiplied and proportionally dimin-ished in size, the basic unit of a forma-tion of space, and the qualities of the formation will depend on those of the unit. Thus, we can find ourselves sur-rounded by and moving among a multitude of structures. Let us note, for example, in how many different fashions the space around us is occu-pied—in other words, is formed, is conceivable—and let us try to grasp

This might be the place for a few remarks on space, a word that changes its meaning with one's angle of vision or manner of speaking. The space of ordinary

practice is not quite the same as that of the physicists, which is not quite the same as that of geometricians—since none of these is defined by all the same experiences and operations. It follows that the cardinal properties of identity do not apply equally in the different fields. In chemistry, for example, there is no infinitely small. *Today, in physics, one is privileged to doubt whether a* length *is infinitely divisible. This means that the idea of division and the idea of the thing to be divided are no longer independent. The operation itself is no longer conceivable beyond a certain point.*

the conditions implied in our being able to perceive the variety of things with their particular qualities: a fabric, a mineral, a liquid, a cloud of smoke. We can form a clear idea of any of these textures only by enlarging a single particle and by inserting into it a structure so organized that, by simple multiplication, it will form a substance having the same qualities as the substance under consideration. . . . With the aid of concepts like these we can move continuously through the apparently quite separate domains of the artist and the scientist, proceeding from the most poetic, even the most fantastic, construction to one that is tangible and ponderable. The problems of composition and those of analysis are reciprocal; and when our age abandoned oversimplified concepts with regard to the constitution of matter, it gained a triumph no less *psychological* than that of abandoning similar concepts with regard to the formation of ideas. Dogmatic explanations of matter and substantialist reveries are disappearing at the same time; and the science of forming hypotheses, names, models, is being liberated from preconceived theories and the idol of simplicity.

I have just indicated, with a brevity for which the reader who differs will either thank or excuse me, an evolution I believe to be important. I could give no better example of it than to quote, from the writings of Leonardo himself, a sentence of which one might say that each of its terms has been so purified and elaborated as to become a concept fundamental to our modern understanding of the world. "The air," he says, "is full of infinite lines, straight and radiating, intercrossing and interweaving without ever coinciding one with another; and they *represent* for every object the true FORM of their reason (or their explanation)." *L'aria e piena d'infinite linie rette e radiose insieme intersegate e intessute sanza ochupatione luna dellaltra rapresantano aqualunche obieto lauera forma della lor chagione.* (Manuscript A, folio 2.) The sentence seems to contain the first germ of the theory of light waves, especially when it is compared with other remarks that Leonardo made on the same subject.* It

* See Manuscript A, *Siccome la pietra gittata nell'acqua...*, *etc.*; also the curious and lively *Histoire des sciences mathématiques*, by G. Libri, and the *Essai sur les ouvrages mathématiques de Léonard*, by J.-B. Venturi, Paris, An. v (1797).

gives the skeleton, as it were, of a system of waves all the lines of which are directions of propagation. But I do not set much store by scientific prophecies of this sort, which are always suspect; too many people think that the ancients discovered everything. Besides, a theory acquires value only through its logical and experimental developments. In this instance all we have is a few *assertions* based intuitively on the observation of rays, as found in waves of sound or water. The interest of the quotation resides in its form, which gives authentic light on a method, the very one I have been discussing throughout this essay. Leonardo's explanation does not *as yet* assume the character of a measurement. It consists merely in the emission of an image, a concrete mental relation between phenomena— or, let us say to be exact, between the images of phenomena. He seems to have engaged consciously in this form of psychic experimentation, and I believe that nobody else clearly recognized the method during the three centuries after his death, although everyone made use of it—necessarily. I also believe—though perhaps it is going too far—that the famous and

As I said above, the phenomena of mental imagery have received far too little attention. I remain firmly convinced of their importance. I hold that certain laws proper to the field are essential and have an extra-ordinary range of application. If we investigated such phenomena as the variations of images, the restrictions

age-old question of whether there is such a thing as empty space can be related to one's awareness or unawareness of this *imaginative logic*. An action at a distance is something that cannot be imagined. We can explain it only by using an abstraction. In our minds only an abstraction can make a leap, *potest facere saltus*. Even Newton, who gave their analytic form to "actions at a distance," realized that his explanations were inadequate. It was Faraday who rediscovered Leonardo's method as applied to the physical sciences. After the glorious mathematical researches of Lagrange, d'Alembert, Laplace, Ampère, and many others, he came forward with admirably bold concepts that were literally only the projection, in his imagination, of observed phenomena; and his imagination was so remarkably lucid "that his ideas were capable of being expressed in the ordinary mathematical forms, and thus compared with those of the professed mathematicians."* The *regular combinations* formed by iron filings round the poles of a magnet were, in his mind, models of the transmission of the former "actions at a distance."

imposed on those variations, and the spontaneous production of reflex images or their complements, we would be able to reunite worlds as distinct from one another as the worlds of dream, of the mystical state, and of deduction by analogy.

* Preface to the treatise on *Electricity and Magnetism*, by J. Clerk Maxwell.

Today there are still lines of force traversing all space, but one can no longer see them.
Might they perhaps be heard? It is only the mental flights suggested by melodies that can give us some idea or intuition of trajectories in space-time. A sustained note represents a point.

Like Leonardo he *saw* systems of lines uniting all bodies, filling the whole of space, and in this way *explained* electrical phenomena and even gravity; such lines of force can be regarded, for the purpose of this essay, as those of least resistance to the understanding. Faraday was not a mathematician, but he differed from mathematicians only in the expression of his thoughts and by the absence of analytical symbols. "Faraday, in his mind's eye, saw lines of force traversing all space, where mathematicians saw centers of force attracting at a distance; Faraday saw a medium where they saw nothing but distance."* Beginning with Faraday a new era opened for physical science; and when J. Clerk Maxwell translated his master's ideas into the language of mathematics, scientific imaginations were filled with dominating visions of much the same type. The study of the medium that he discovered, a scene of electrical activity and intermolecular reactions, remains the principal occupation of modern physics. Inspired partly by the demand for more and more precision in representing the modes of energy, partly by the will to *see*, and partly by something that

* J. Clerk Maxwell.

58

might be called the kinetic mania, hypothetical constructions have appeared that are of the greatest logical and psychological interest. Lord Kelvin, for example, feels such a pressing need to express even the subtlest of natural processes by mental images, and to carry these to a point at which they can be reproduced in tangible form, that he believes every explanation should lead to a mechanical model. Such a mind rejects the inert atom, the mere point imagined by Boscovich and the physicists of the early nineteenth century, and replaces it with an already extremely complex mechanism caught in a web of ether, which itself becomes a rather elaborate construction as a result of the many different conditions it is asked to fulfill. It is no effort for a mind like his to pass from the architecture of crystals to that of stone and iron; in our viaducts, in the symmetries of beams and girders, he finds the symmetries of resistance that quartz and gypsum offer to compression and cleavage—or, in a different fashion, to the passage of light waves.

We no longer think of the atom as a mechanism. Today it is another world.

Such men seem to have had an intuitive grasp of the methods discussed in this essay. We might even permit ourselves to extend those methods beyond the physical sciences; and we believe that it would be neither absurd nor entirely impossible to create a model of the continuity of the intellectual operations of a Leonardo da Vinci, or of any other mind, determined by the analysis of the conditions to be fulfilled. . . .

The artists and art-lovers who have turned these pages in the hope of renewing some of the impressions to be obtained at the Louvre, or in Florence and Milan, must excuse me for disappointing them. Nevertheless, I doubt if I have strayed too far from their favorite occupation, in spite of appearances. I believe, on the contrary, that I have touched on their central problem, that of composition. Some of them will doubtless be astonished to hear me saying that questions concerning the effect of a work of art are usually discussed and answered with the help of words and notions that not only are obscure but involve a thousand difficulties. More than one critic has spent a lifetime changing his definition of *the beautiful*, or *life*, or *mystery*. Ten minutes of simply considering one's own mind should suffice to destroy those idols of the cave and make one realize the inconsistency of attaching an abstract noun, always empty, to an always personal and strictly personal vision. In the same way, most of the disappointments that artists suffer are based on the difficulty or impossibility of *rendering*, through the medium of their art, an image that seems to lose its color and wither as soon as they try to capture it in words, on a canvas, or in a certain key. A few additional moments of *consciousness* might be spent in ascertaining that we merely delude ourselves when we wish to reproduce the fantasies of our own minds in those of others. It might even be said that the attempt is nearly incomprehensible. What is called in art a *realization*, is in fact a problem of rendering—one in which the private meaning, the key attributed by every author to his materials, plays no part, and in which the principal factors are the nature of those materials and the mentality of the public. Edgar Poe, who in this century of literary perturbation was the very lightning of the confusion, of the poetic storm, and whose analysis sometimes ends, like Leonardo's, in mysterious smiles, has clearly established his reader's approach

Nothing seems harder for the public—and even for critics—to admit than this incompetence of the author with regard to his own work, once he has completed it.

on the basis of psychology and probable effects. From that point of view, every combination of elements made to be perceived and judged depends on a few general laws and on a particular adaptation, defined in advance for a foreseen category of minds to which the whole is specially addressed; and the work of art becomes a machine designed to arouse and assemble the individual formations of those minds. This suggestion is quite opposite to the ordinary notion of the sublime, and I can guess the indignation it might arouse; but that very indignation would help to confirm what I am saying—without this essay's being in any respect a work of art.

I can see Leonardo da Vinci exploring the depths of this mechanism, which he called the paradise of the sciences, with the same natural power with which he dedicated himself to the invention of pure and misty faces. And that same luminous territory, with its docile throng of possible beings, was the field of those activities which slowed down and solidified into distinct works of art. Leonardo himself did not feel that these expressed different passions. On the last page of that slender notebook, deeply scored with his secret script and those risky calculations in which he gropes toward his favorite research, aviation, he exclaims—in a flash that strikes at his imperfect labors, and illuminates his patience and its obstacles with the vision of a supreme spiritual aim, an obstinate certainty: "The great bird will take his first flight mounted on the back of his great swan, and filling the universe with stupor, filling all writings with his renown, and eternal glory to the nest where he was born! —*Piglierà il primo volo il grande uccello sopra del dosso del suo magno cecero e empiendo l'universo di stupore, empiendo di sua fama tutte le scritture e gloria eterna al nido dove nacque.*"

Here is an astonishing prophecy, though one that would be easy to dismiss if it were merely a view of the possible. All its sublimity is due to its being proffered by the first man who really studied the problem of flight, and the first to imagine its technical solution— at the beginning of the sixteenth century!

Note and Digression

[1919]

And why, one might ask, did the author make his hero go to Hungary? Because he wanted to include a piece of orchestral music with a Hungarian theme. This he freely confesses. He would have sent the hero anywhere else if he had found the slightest musical reason for so doing.

HECTOR BERLIOZ, *The Damnation of Faust,* Foreword

In fact the word "method" was more than a bit strong. "Method" suggests some fairly definite order of operations, whereas I was merely thinking of the curious habit I had of transforming all the questions in my mind.

I MUST APOLOGIZE for having chosen such an ambitious and truly misleading title as *Introduction to the Method of Leonardo da Vinci*. When I attached it to this brief study, I had no idea of imposing on the reader. But twenty-five years have passed since I put it there, and now, looked at with a colder eye, it seems a bit strong. So the pretentious title could be toned down. As for the text... but I shouldn't even dream of writing it today. *Impossible!* common sense would exclaim. When the game of chess played between knowledge and being has reached its *n*th move, a man flatters himself that he has learned from his opponent; he

64

assumes the opponent's air, turns pitiless toward the young man he is forced
to acknowledge as his ancestor, discovers inexplicable faults, which were
the audacities of the younger man, and
reconstructs his unsophisticated past.
All of which amounts to making him
more stupid than he really was—but
stupid by necessity, stupid for strategic
reasons! No temptation is keener or
closer to the heart, and none, perhaps,
is more productive than that of denying oneself. Each day is jealous of the
other days, and rightly so; the mind
struggles desperately to deny that it
was ever more powerful; the insight
of any given moment refuses to illumi-
nate past moments that were brighter
than itself; and, at the touch of the sun,
the first phrase stammered by the
awakening brain, the first to go echoing through this Memnon, is: "To
reckon nothing accomplished, *nihil
reputare actum.*"

*Today feels that
yesterday was weaker
than itself, or
stronger, and is
offended by either
sensation.*

To reread, then; to reread after having
forgotten—to reread *oneself*, without
a hint of tenderness, or fatherly feeling;
coldly and with critical acumen, and
in a mood terribly conducive to ridicule and contempt, with an alien gaze,
and a destructive eye—is to recast one's

work, or feel that it should be recast, into a very different mold.

Such an aim would be worth the effort, but has always been beyond my power. Consequently, I never dreamed of attempting it: this little essay owes its existence to Mme Juliette Adam, who, toward the end of the year 1894, on the gracious advice of M. Léon Daudet, asked me to write it for her journal, *La Nouvelle Revue*.

It was my first commission.

Twenty-three though I was, my problem was immense. I was only too well aware that I knew Leonardo a great deal less than I admired him. I regarded him as the principal character of that Intellectual Comedy which has still to find its poet and would, in my judgment, be far more valuable than *La Comédie Humaine*; more so, even, than *The Divine Comedy*. I felt that this ruler of his own resources, this master of draftsmanship, of images, and of calculation, had found the central attitude from which the enterprises of knowledge and the operations of art are equally possible; successful cooperation between analysis and action is more than probable—a marvelously stimulating thought.

I always make

But also a thought too immediate,

a thought without value, infinitely diffuse, a thought to be spoken, not written.

I was charmed to the height of my senses by this Apollo. What could be more seductive than a god who rejects mystery; who does not base his power on the agitation of our senses, or address his power to the darkest, most tender, most sinister part of our natures; who forces our minds to agree, not to submit; whose miracle is to clarify, and whose profundity is a carefully deduced perspective? Is there any surer sign of a real and legitimate power than its not being exercised under a veil?—Never had Dionysus a more deliberate enemy, or one more pure and armed with insight, than this hero who aimed less at bending and breaking monsters than at examining their structure; who disdained to pierce them with arrows because his questions went deeper; not so much their conqueror as their superior, he demonstrates that the most effective triumph is to understand one's foes— almost to the point of reproducing them; and once having grasped their principle, he can shrug them aside, derisively reduced to the humble con-

a distinction between these two ways of thought.
If I did only what tempted me, I should never write except to seek or to preserve. The unwritten word finds before *seeking.*

dition of very ordinary cases and explainable paradoxes.

His drawings and manuscripts, little as I had studied them, filled me with a sort of awe. From his thousands of notes and sketches I gained the extraordinary impression that an hallucinating shower of sparks was being struck by all sorts of hammer blows involved in some fantastic work of production. Formulas, maxims, advice to himself, trials of a reasoning that checks itself, now and then a finished description; now and then a word to himself as an intimate. . . .

But I had no desire to repeat that he was this and that, not only a painter but a mathematician and. . . .

And, in a word, the artist of the world itself. This is known to all.

I was too little versed in the subject to dream of explaining his researches in detail—of trying, for example, to determine the exact nature of the *impeto* that plays such a great part in his dynamics, or of discussing the *sfumato* he pursued in his painting— and I was not scholarly enough (still less inclined enough toward scholarship) to give me hope of contributing

To tell the truth, I could not see what interest was to be found in the mass of details that scholars hunt for in libraries. What is the importance, I said to myself, of something

68

any addition whatever to the known facts. For true learning I felt less enthusiasm than is its due. The astonishing conversation of Marcel Schwob impressed me more by its peculiar charm than by its subject matter. I drank in every word he said and had the pleasure of erudition without its effort. But then I would come back to myself; my idleness would rise in revolt against the notion of the disheartening studies, the endless collations, and the scrupulous methods that preserve us from certainty. I would tell my friend that scholars run more risks than the rest of us, because they make bets and we stay out of the game, and because they have two ways of being wrong—our way, which is easy, and theirs, which is laborious. That even if they are lucky enough to rediscover certain events for our benefit, the very number of material facts established in this way is a threat to the reality we are seeking. Fact in the raw is more false than falsehood. Documents give us a haphazard view of rules and exceptions. Even a diarist likes to set down the peculiarities of his time rather than its generally accepted customs.

But everything that is true of an age or a person does not always add

that happens only once?

History is a stimulant for me, not a nutriment. What we learn from history is not changed into types of action or into functions and operations of the mind. When the mind is wide awake, it needs only the present and itself. I am not given to the quest for the past, which I would rather reject. My mind only enjoys action.

The truest, the most essential part of an individual, is his potential self, which might or might not be revealed by his life. What happens to him may not draw from him powers unknown to himself. If a bell is never struck, it never gives forth what would be its funda-mental tone.

That was why my endeavor was to conceive and describe in my own way a potential *Leonardo, rather than the Leonardo of history.*

to our real knowledge of one or the other. Nobody is equal to the exact sum of his appearances; and is there any man who has never said, or has never done, something that was not *him*? Sometimes imitation, sometimes a lapse—or chance—or merely the accumulated boredom of being exactly what one is, of being oneself, distorts that self for a moment. We are sketched during a dinner; the drawing is handed down to a posterity of scholars, and so there we are—a pretty sight for the whole of literary eternity. A scowling face, if photographed at the moment, is an irrefutable docu-ment. But show it to the friends of the victim and they cannot guess who it is.

Dislike of prolonged labors being so ingenious, my reluctance had many other sophistries to choose from. Nevertheless I might have faced these tedious tasks if I had believed they would lead me to my desired aim. In my outer darkness I loved the inner law of the great Leonardo. I was not interested in his biography, nor even in the productions of his mind. Of that brow loaded with laurels, I dreamed only of the *kernel*.

Having refuted so much, what was I to do—rich in desires, if in nothing else, and drunk with intellectual greediness and pride?

Should I let myself go—contrive to contract some literary fever? Cultivate its delirium?

I was yearning for a splendid theme. How little that amounts to, on the page!

Doubtless a great thirst illumines itself with streaming visions; it acts upon who knows what secret substances as does invisible light on Bohemian glass impregnated with uranium; it reveals what it is looking for; it sets pitchers with diamonds and an opalescent shimmer upon carafes....But the beverages it cools for itself are mere illusions; and I believed, and still believe, that it is ignoble to write from enthusiasm alone. Enthusiasm is not a state of mind for a writer.

However great the energy of fire, it becomes useful and a motive force only by virtue of the engines in which it is confined by human skill. There must be well-placed restraints to keep it from being wasted. Some obstacle must be opposed to the inevitable return of equilibrium; otherwise noth-

Some found this aphorism a scandal, because they took it as a reflection on themselves instead of for what it was, a simple statement of fact.
An eternal confusion of ideas leads to a demand that the emotions of the reader

71

should directly *depend on or result from the emotions of the writer, as if* the work did not exist. *" To move me to tears," it is said, " you must weep." You will make me weep, or perhaps laugh, with the literary product of your tears. Even Pascal and Stendhal have their* crossed out *passages. Despair and passion keep searching nevertheless for the word that will tell most powerfully on* persons unknown. *The inspired writer corrects himself. Such has to be the case. Otherwise these great authors would not have been* writers. *And besides, with greater resistance, there is all the more self-criticism.*

ing is gained from the futile dissipation of heat.

In the case of writing, however, the author feels himself to be at once the *source* of energy, the *engineer*, and the *restraints*. One part of him is impulsion; another foresees, organizes, moderates, suppresses; a third part (logic and memory) maintains the conditions, preserves the connections, and assures some fixity to the *calculated* design. *To write* should mean to construct, as precisely and solidly as possible, a machine of language in which the released energy of the mind is used in overcoming *real* obstacles; hence the writer must be divided against himself. That is the only respect in which, strictly speaking, the whole man acts as *author*. Everything else is not *his*, but belongs to a part of him that has escaped. Between the emotion or initial intention and its natural ending, which is disorder, vagueness, and forgetting—the destiny of all thinking—it is his task to introduce obstacles created by himself, so that, being interposed, they may struggle with the purely transitory nature of psychic phenomena to win a measure of renewable action, a share of independent existence.

Perhaps in those days I exaggerated the evident defect of all literature, which is never to satisfy the whole of the mind. I did not like the notion of leaving some faculties idle while the others were being employed. I might also say (and it amounts to the same thing) that I valued nothing above *consciousness*; I would have given many masterpieces that I believed to be un-premeditated for one page visibly directed by the mind.

There are authors, and not the least famous ones, whose works are only an elimination of their emotions.
Such works are capable of touching but not of teaching their authors; by producing them they do not learn how to do what they could not do or be different from what they were.

These illusions would be easy to defend, and I am still not so firmly convinced of their barrenness that I do not return to them on occasion. But they poisoned my efforts at the time. Not only were my precepts too insistent and too definite; they were also too universal to serve me in any given circumstance. So many years must pass before the truths we have fashioned for ourselves become our very flesh!

Thus, instead of finding in myself these requirements, these obstacles equivalent to exterior forces, which enable one to drive against one's first impulses, I would be checked by ill-assorted quibbles and I would deliber-ately make things even harder than they should have seemed to such young eyes. As an alternative to this, I could see nothing but whims, opportunism, and nauseating facility: an effortless fluency, idle as that of dreams, stirring and mixing together the infinite world of hackneyed properties.

If I let chance direct my pen, I found myself writing words that bear witness to the weakness of one's thinking: *genius, mystery, profound, ...* attributes that properly belong to chaos and tell less about their subject than about the writer. I tried to deceive myself, but that mental strategy had a short issue: I was so quick to counter my budding ideas that the result of these transactions, at any given moment, was zero.

As a crowning misfortune I worshiped precision, confusedly but passionately; I laid indefinite claim to the right of directing my thoughts.

The will cannot operate in or on the mind *except indirectly—through the* body. *It can* repeat so as to obtain, *but can do little more.*

I realized, to be sure, that the mind is forced to depend on its own happy accidents; it is made for, gives forth, and receives the unforeseen; its definite expectations are without direct results; and its willed or regular operations are useful only as hindsight as though in a second life which it granted to the most lucid part of itself. I did not believe,

74

however, in the innate power of delirium, in the necessity of ignorance, in revelations from the absurd, or in creative incoherence. What is engendered in us by accident always bears some resemblance to its parent!

Our revelations, I reflected, are only events of a certain order; and we still have to interpret—we must always interpret—these *conscious events*. Even our happiest intuitions are in some sort inexact *by excess*, as compared with our ordinary thinking; *by deficiency*, as compared with the infinite complexity of the minute objects and real situations they pretend to bring under our control. Our personal merit—after which we yearn—consists not so much in undergoing the inspirations as in seizing them; not so much in seizing as in revising them.... Our riposte to the daemon is sometimes better than his thrust.

And besides, we know to our cost that the laws of probability are against the daemon. Shamelessly the spirit whispers a million absurdities for every fine idea it concedes to us; and the value of that lucky chance depends, even so, on our ability to shape it to our ends. It is so with ores, which have no value in their hidden veins

Our thinking can never be either too complicated or too simple.
For it hopes to attain the real, which cannot be of an infinite—inexhaustible—complexity; and, on the other hand, it cannot grasp anything, or make use of what it has grasped, except by reducing it to a simple form.

75

and beds; they become useful only in the light, as a result of work performed above ground.

Far from its being the intuitive elements that lend importance to works of art, take away the works and your inspirations will be nothing but intellectual accidents, lost in the statistics of the local life of the brain. Their true value is not derived from the obscurity of their origins, or from the supposed depths from which we naïvely like to think they emerged, or from their giving us a feeling of amazed delight; it depends rather on their meeting our needs, and, in the last analysis, on the conscious use we make of them—in other words, on the collaboration of the whole man.

A statistical hypothesis.

Once it is agreed that our greatest insights are closely intermingled with our greatest chances of error, and that our average thoughts are of no great significance, then it is the part of us that chooses, the part that organizes, which must be exercised at every moment. The rest depends on no one, and we invoke it as vainly as we pray for rain. We may give it a name, torment it, make a god of it, but the only result will be a greater amount of pretense and fraud—things so naturally allied with intellectual ambition that one hardly knows whether they are its cause or its effect. The practice of taking a hypallage for a discovery, a simile for a demonstration, a vomit of words for a torrent of capital information, and oneself for an oracle— that is our infirmity from birth.

Leonardo da Vinci has no connection with such disorders. Among the multitude of idols from which we have to choose, since at least one of them must be worshiped, he fixed his eyes on that Obstinate Rigor which proclaims itself the most exacting of all. (But it must be the least vulgar of idols, since all the others concur in hating it.)

Once rigor has been instituted, a positive liberty is possible. Apparent liberty, on the other hand, is only the privilege of obeying every chance impulse; the more of it we enjoy, the more we are chained to the same spot; we are like a cork on the waves, which is attached to nothing, disturbed by everything, and on which all the forces of the universe contend and are canceled out.

All the productions of the great Vinci can be deduced solely from his great purpose; and his thinking, as if it belonged to no particular person, seems to be more universal, more detailed, more consecutive, and more isolated than that of any individual mind. The very superior man is never an *eccentric*. His personality is as insignificant as you please. Few disproportions; no intellectual superstitions; no vain fears. He is not afraid of analysis; he guides it—or perhaps is guided by it—to remote consequences; he returns to the real without effort. He imitates, he innovates; he rejects neither the old because it is old or the new for being new; but he consults something in himself that is eternally of the present.

The career of this antithesis has been extraordinary. I fear it has done little but harm in the realm of the intellect.

Leonardo was totally unaware of the crudely defined opposition between the spirit of finesse and the spirit of geometry that would be proclaimed, three half-centuries later, by a man who was completely insensitive to the arts and could not conceive of any such delicate but natural union of distinct talents; who thought that painting was vanity and that true eloquence laughed eloquence to scorn;

People were shocked by this statement. But where would mankind be if all the

who launches us into a wager in which he engulfs all finesse and all geometry; and who in the end, having changed his new lamp for an old one, wasted

78

hours sewing papers into his pockets, at a time when he might have honored France by discovering the infinitesimal calculus. . . .

others of equal talent had followed his example?

No revelations for Leonardo. No abyss opening on his right. An abyss would make him think of a bridge. An abyss might serve for his trial flights of some great mechanical bird. . . .

And he must have seen himself as the model thinking animal, supple and responsive, gifted with several types of movement, and, without resistance or delay, capable of passing from one gait to another at the rider's slightest whim. Spirit of finesse or spirit of geometry, he adopted them both, then abandoned both, as if they were the successive paces of a well-trained horse. . . . The supremely coordinated being need only prescribe to himself certain secret modifications, very simple as concerns the will, and at once he passes from the category of purely formal transformations and symbolic acts to that of imperfect knowledge and spontaneous realities. To possess this freedom to change oneself profoundly, to employ such a wide register of adaptations, is merely to be a man in all his integrity, such a

The ancients had too little knowledge not to be free in their mental attitudes.

man as we imagine to have existed among the ancients.

A superior elegance is disconcerting. This freedom from fuss, from attitudes of prophecy or pathos; these exact ideals; this even division between curiosity and capability, always restored by a master of equilibrium; this disdain for artifices and illusion; and, in the most versatile of men, this ignorance of self-display—such qualities, in our eyes, are so many scandals. For creatures like ourselves, who make a sort of profession of being sensitive, who assume to possess everything in a few elementary effects of contrast and nervous resonance; to apprehend everything when we give ourselves the illusion of being melted into the shifting and iridescent substance of our lives on earth—what could be more difficult to conceive?

But Leonardo, passing from research to research, quite simply becomes the ever more admirable riding master of his own nature. He trains his thoughts with endless care, exercises his vision, teaches obedience to his acts; he guides one hand or the other through admirably precise drawings; he relaxes or concentrates, tightens the relation between his ambitions and his abilities, drives his reasoning further and further in the realm of art, and still preserves his grace.

An intelligence that is so detached will sometimes assume strange attitudes—as a ballet dancer amazes us by the poses she can strike and hold for a time, although they are born of pure instability. The independence of Leonardo shocks our instincts and makes sport of our desires. There is nothing more free, which is to say nothing less humane, than his judgments on love and death. He lets them be inferred from a few fragments in his notebooks.

"Love in its fury"—he says in almost these words—"is so ugly a thing that the human race would die out (*la natura si perderebbe*) if those who practice it could see themselves." Many of his sketches are evidence of that scorn, since for certain things the height of scorn is finally to examine them at one's leisure. Here and there he has drawn anatomical unions, horrible cross sections of love itself. He is fascinated by the erotic machine, the mechanics of living bodies being his favorite domain; but sweat against

This cool look at the mechanics of love is, I think, unique in our intellectual history. When love is coldly analyzed, many curious ideas come to mind. What roundabout ways, what a complexity of methods, to bring about fecundation! Emotions, ideals, beauty, all intervening as the means of stimulating a given muscle.

The essential feature of the function becoming an incidental, its accomplishment something to be feared, eluded....
It would be hard to find better evidence of the degree to which nature *is* devious.

sweat, the panting of the *opranti*, a monster formed of clashing muscular structures, and the final transfiguration into beasts, all seem to excite only his repugnance and disdain....

His judgment of death must be reconstructed from a very short text, truly classical in its richness and simplicity. Perhaps it was meant to be placed in the introduction to a never-completed treatise on the human body.

This man who dissected ten cadavers to follow the course of a few veins thinks to himself: "The organization of our body is such a marvelous thing that the soul, although *something divine*, is deeply grieved at being separated from the body that was its home. *And I can well believe*, says Leonardo, *that its tears and its suffering are not unjustified....*

Let us not go into the kind of doubt, heavy with meaning, implied by these words. It is enough to consider the enormous shadow projected here by an idea in process of formation: death interpreted as a *disaster for the soul*! Death of the body as a diminution of the *divine thing*! Death moving the soul to tears and destroying its dearest work, by the ruin of the structure that the soul had designed for its dwelling!

I do not care to deduce a Vincian metaphysic from these reticent words; but I will allow myself a fairly obvious comparison, since it occurs to me of itself. For such a student of organisms, the body is not something contemptible, a mere rag; it has too many properties and resolves too many problems; *it possesses too many functions and resources not to answer some transcendent need, which is powerful enough to construct the body and not powerful enough to dispense with its complexity.* The body is the creation and the instrument of someone who has need of it, does not willingly cast it aside, and laments its loss as one might weep for vanished power. . . . Such is the feeling of Vinci His philosophy is wholly *naturalistic*, outraged by *spiritualism*, firmly attached to the letter of the physico-mechanical explanation; and yet, on the subject of the soul, he is very close to the philosophy of the Church. The Church, at least in so far as it is Thomist, does not grant a very enviable existence to the departed soul. There is nothing more destitute than a soul that has lost its body. It has scarcely more than being; it is a logical

As a matter of fact, we are interested only in the sensibility. If we also worry about the intelligence (a scholastic distinction, I grant), basically that is only because of the many varied effects it has on our sensibility.
Now, the latter can be abolished for an extended period while we are still living. In

83

theological terms, the soul has not left the body, but the I has disappeared during this lapse of time. What we regard as ourselves has been reduced to a cipher, and the possibility of its being restored in integrum *left at the mercy of the slightest accident. All we know for certain is:* we are capable of—not being.

minimum, a sort of latent life in which the soul is inconceivable to us, and doubtless to itself. Power, desire, and perhaps knowledge have been taken away. I am not even sure the soul can remember that somewhere, at some time, it was the *form* and *act* of its body, all that's left is the honor of its autonomy.... Fortunately this vain and colorless condition is only temporary—if the word has any meaning outside the bounds of time. Reason demands, and dogma imposes, the restitution of the flesh. The qualities of this supreme flesh will doubtless be very different from those of the former body. Here we are obliged, I suppose, to conceive of something quite other than a mere realization of the *improbable*. But it is idle to venture beyond the limits of physics, and to dream of a glorious body whose mass would be in another relation than ours to universal gravity, while the relation between this variable mass and the speed of light would be such that the promised *agility* could be achieved. In any case the naked soul must, according to theology, recover a certain functional life in a certain body, and, by means of this new body, a sort of matter that will allow it to function and to replenish its empty intellectual categories with incorruptible marvels.

A dogma that concedes to the bodily organism this more than secondary importance, which strikingly diminishes the function of the soul; that forbids and spares us the folly of trying to imagine what the soul must be; that even insists on its assuming a new body before participating in the full splendor of eternal life—such a dogma, so much the opposite of pure spiritualism, distinguishes the Church in a most striking manner from most of the other Christian confessions. But it seems to me that the religious literature of the last two or three centuries has passed over no article more lightly. Apologists and preachers hardly mention it. I fail to see the reason for this half-silence.

I have wandered so far into Leonardo that for the moment I do not know how to come back to myself. . . . Well! Any road will lead me there; that is the definition of the self. It simply cannot be lost; we can only lose our time.

So let us continue to follow, at least for a little while, the bent and inclination of the mind. We can follow

Nothing could more clearly illustrate the superficial character

85

*of our thinking than
the type of observa-
tions and reflections
it is capable of
making about the*
body.
*It belongs to the
body, sets it in
motion, ignores it, is
dependent on it,
forgets it, is surprised
by it. . . .*

them without fear, unfortunately, for they lead to no real depth. Even our most "profound" thinking is limited by the insuperable conditions that make all thinking "superficial." We can merely enter a forest of transpositions; or else it is a palace walled with mirrors, peopled by a solitary lamp which they multiply to infinity.

But even so, let us see whether our unaided curiosity can bring to light the hidden system of an individual of the first magnitude; and let us try to imagine how he must appear to himself, when he sometimes pauses in the course of his labors to consider himself as a whole.

First he views himself as subjected to common necessities and realities; then he withdraws into the privacy of separate knowledge. He has our way of seeing and his own. He has a reasoned opinion of his nature, and a sense of its artifice. He is absent and present. He maintains the sort of duality that a priest has to maintain. He knows that he cannot define himself completely in his own eyes in terms of ordinary circumstances and motives. *To live*, and even to live well, is only a means for him. When he eats, he also nourishes another marvel than his life, and half his bread is consecrated. *To act* is still only an exercise. *To love* —but I doubt whether he finds it possible. As for glory, no. To shine in others' eyes is to get from them the glitter of false jewelry.

He must, however, find who knows what points of reference, so placed as to reveal an orderly relation between his particular life and the *applied life* he has worked out for himself. His imperturbable clear-sightedness, which seems to represent—though without altogether convincing him—the whole of his being, would like to escape from the relativity that it cannot fail to recognize in everything else. But even though it transforms itself, and reproduces itself day after day as pure as the sun, still this apparent identity of his carries with it a feeling of being deceptive. It knows, in its fixity, that it is subjected to mysterious propulsions, to unseen modifications; and hence it knows that always, even in its clearest state of lucidity, it includes a hidden possibility of failure and total ruin—just as a dream however precise is likely to include an inexplicable germ of nonreality.

It is a sort of luminous torture to

That is how we came to invent Time, which represents to us the common fate of all that is not the " I." But this " I " no longer contains anything, since it is the fixed limit of the fundamental and continuous operation of the intelligence— which consists of an endless rejection of everything.

87

feel that one sees all things without ceasing to feel that one is still *visible* and conceivably the object of an alien attention, and without ever finding the place and the look that would leave nothing behind them.

Durus est hic sermo, the reader would be justified in saying. But in matters like these, what is not vague is difficult, and what is not difficult is nil. Let us press on a little farther.

For a presence of mind so utterly conscious of itself, one that closes on itself after making a circuit of the "universe," all events and all categories of events—life, death, ideas— are only subordinate *symbols*. Since every *visible thing* is at the same time alien, indispensable, and inferior to the *thing that sees*, it follows that the importance of these symbols, however great it may seem at any moment, will diminish on reflection, giving way before the sheer persistence of the attention in itself. Everything yields before this pure universality, this in-surmountable general law which consciousness feels itself to be.

If any given events have the power of suppressing the consciousness, they are, by the same token, deprived of all meaning; if they preserve the consciousness, they become part of its system. The intelligence does not know that it was born or that it will perish. It is aware, no doubt, of its fluctuations and final disappearance, but only by means of a notion that is essentially no different from the others. It might believe, quite easily, that it was exempt from loss or change, had it not been led by its experiences, at some time or other, to recognize the range of ominous possibilities and the existence of a certain downward trend that leads beyond the lowest depths. One can sense that this trend may become irresistible; it announces the beginning of a permanent separation from the spiritual sun, from the ideal maximum of clearness, solidity, and the power of distinguishing and choosing. One can visualize that downward path hidden from sight by a thousand psychological impurities, beset with boomings and dizziness, winding on through the confusion of times and the disturbance of functions, then losing itself amid the inexpressible confusion of the very dimensions of knowledge till it arrives at the instantaneous and undivided state that dissolves this chaos into nothing.

Hence the idea of immortality and its continuing vigor. We cannot conceive of a suppression of consciousness that is not accidental, or could be definitive. Consciousness is able to conceive only of what it can do, and it can do nothing but re-exist.

89

Nevertheless, a complete system of psychological substitutions, opposed to death as it is to life, becomes more conscious and self-sufficient the more it becomes detached from any origin and, in some sort, less exposed to any chance of rupture. Like a smoke ring this system, composed though it be of interior energies, lays miraculous claim to perfect independence and perfect indivisibility. In a very clear consciousness, memory and phenomena are so interrelated, so expected, so responded to; the past is so well utilized, the new so promptly balanced, and the relationship of the whole so definitely established, that apparently nothing can begin and nothing can end inside this almost pure state of activity. The perpetual interchange of *things*, of which it consists, would seem to assure it of indefinite continuity, for it is attached to none of these. It contains no *ultimate*—no particular object of thought or perception so much more real than all the rest that no other object can come after it. There is no idea that so completely fulfills the unknown conditions of one's consciousness that it leads to the disappearance of consciousness. No thought is such that it destroys, and

There is no such thing as a last thought, *a thought that comes last by virtue of some in-*

90

concludes, the power of thinking; there is no position of the bolt that closes the lock forever; and there is no particular thought whose relation to thought in general is that of a conclusion inherent in its development—resolving, like a final harmony, this permanent dissonance.

Since the mind has set no limit for itself, and since no idea completes the task of consciousness, it must perish in some incomprehensible disaster, one which was predicted and for which it was prepared by the anguish and the curious sensation of which I was speaking. These give a glimpse of unstable worlds, incompatible with the fullness of life; inhuman, infirm worlds, comparable with those suggested by the geometrician when he plays with axioms, and by the physicist when he postulates other than the admitted *constants*. Dreams, anxieties, and ecstasies; all those half-possible states that might be described as introducing into the equation of knowledge approximate values, or transcendental solutions, exist between the clarity of life and the simplicity of death, forming strange degrees, varieties, and ineffable phases—for there are no names for

herent quality.
For the male insect of certain species, there is a last act, the act of love, after which they die. But there is no thought that exhausts the potentiality of the mind.
There is, however, a strange tendency (in minds of a certain order) to keep advancing toward some unknown point in an unknown firmament.
There is the insatiability of the understanding and the constructive faculty. . . .
The incomprehensibility of death is here proposed as its essential nature—death being presented as a nonproblem.
I mean the death of each as envisaged in each. Death in the other or biological sense forms an indispensable part of life, *and as such is comprehensible, a property without*

which the functioning of life must be incomprehensible.

The psychic equilibrium is maintained (if at all) by being reestablished at rather short intervals whenever the developing mental processes (attentions and associations) are interrupted by external sensations and perceptions.
We can find much of interest in the divagations of the mind, but these chance discoveries only take on value when brought into relation with the ordered system of acts and externalized stability.

things among which one is quite alone.

Just as music treacherously unites the freedom of dreams with a consecutive logic born of the closest possible concentration, and makes a synthesis of intimate states lasting only a moment, so the fluctuations of psychic equilibrium offer perceptions of aberrant modes of existence. Besides the ordinary forms of sensibility, we carry the seeds of other forms that cannot survive, although they may well be born. They are moments snatched from the implacable criticism of time. They cannot resist the complete functioning of our being: either we perish or else they are dissolved. But they are monsters full of lessons, these monsters of the understanding, these transitory states—gaps in which the known laws of continuity, connection, and movement have been altered; domains where light is associated with pain; fields of force in which we follow strange circuits between the poles of fear and desire; matter composed of time; abysses literally of horror, love, or quietude; regions bizarrely welded to themselves; non-Archimedean realms that defy movement; perpetual sites in a lightning flash; surfaces that cave in as they couple with our nausea, bend with our slightest intentions. . . . We cannot say that they are real and neither can we deny their reality. The man who has never traversed such states does not know the value of natural light or of the most common-place surroundings; he does not recognize the true fragility of the world, which does not depend on the alternative of being and nonbeing; that would be too simple; the wonder is not that things are, but that they are *what* they are, and not something else. *The pattern of this world* belongs to a family of patterns, of which, without knowing it, we possess all the elements of the infinite group. That is the secret of inventors.

As the consciousness emerges from such intervals and from the personal divagations into which it might be led—not only by physical weakness or the presence of poisons in the nervous system, but also by the strength and subtlety of its attention, by the most exquisite logic, or by a cultivated mysticism—it comes to suspect that all accustomed reality is only one solution, among many others, of

Here is a consideration that seems to merit some reflection

—although the reflection could hardly lead to definite conclusions.

Cognition and its objects are in some measure reciprocal. But this reciprocity is not at all strict, since it leaves room for a certain unspecified generality, or liberty with regard to all objects or contents. The needs of life do not exhaust all the intellectual and sensual resources that life sustains.

universal problems. It is convinced that things could be *sufficiently* different from what they are without its being *very* different from what it is. It dares to regard its "body" and its "world" as almost arbitrary restrictions imposed on the scope of its functions. It sees itself as responding or corresponding not to a *world*, but to some system of a higher order, the elements of which are worlds. It is capable of a greater number of mental combinations than are needed for survival, and of more rigor than any practical situation demands or tolerates; it judges itself to be deeper than the very abyss of animal life and death. Moreover, this attention paid to its own condition cannot react on consciousness itself, so far has it drawn aside from all things, so great are the pains it has taken *never to be part of anything it might conceive, or of any answer it might find*. It is reduced to a dark mass that absorbs all and gives nothing back.

Deriving a perilous courage from these exact observations and inevitable pretensions; strong in the sort of independence and invariableness it is forced to grant itself, at last it comes forward as the direct heir and counterpart of that being without a face, without a beginning, on whom the cosmic venture depends and devolves. . . . A little more, and consciousness will admit the necessary existence of only two entities, both essentially unknown: Oneself and X. Both abstracted from everything, implicated in everything, implying everything. Equal and consubstantial.

The man who, drawn forward by the demands of the tireless mind, is led to this contact with living shadows, to this point of pure presence, now sees himself as destitute and bare, reduced to the supreme poverty of a force that has no object; a victim of simplification, yet also a fulfillment, a masterpiece of dialectics. His state is comparable to that attained by the richest thought when it has become assimilated to itself, and recognized, consummated in a little group of words and symbols. The labor we devote to an object of reflection, he has expended on the subject that reflects.

He exists without instincts, almost without images, and he no longer has a purpose. He resembles no one. I say *man*, and I say *he*, by analogy and for lack of words.

He is no longer concerned with choosing or creating; with preserving himself or increasing himself. There is nothing to be surmounted, and there is not even the possibility of self-destruction.

All "genius" is now consumed. It could be of no further use, for it was only a means of attaining the final simplicity. There is no act of genius that is not *less* than the mere act of being. A magnificent law creates and informs the imbecile; the keenest mind finds nothing better in itself.

If we could fully understand the inner mechanism of an idiot and that of a man of genius, perhaps the difference between them, immense as it often seems to us, would be reduced to insignificant differences in their inherent *structures and modes of functioning—by comparison with which the great external differences would be* mere *accidents.*

Such is the state of a perfected consciousness. It feels compelled to define itself by the sum total of things, as the *excess* over that totality of its own power of perception. In order to affirm itself, it had to begin by denying an infinite number of elements an infinite number of times, and by exhausting the objects of its power without exhausting that power—with the result that it differs from nothingness by the smallest possible margin.

The image it brings to mind spontaneously is that of an invisible audience seated in a darkened theater—a presence that cannot observe itself and is condemned to watch the scene con-

This image of a theater serves to

fronting it, yet can feel nevertheless how it creates all that breathless and irresistibly directed darkness. A complete and yet a devouring darkness, secretly organized, all compounded of creatures that press against and limit one another; a compact night in which the shadows are alive with organs that throb and pant with excitement, while each in its own fashion defends its place and function. Facing this rapt and mysterious assembly, moving and glittering in a closed frame, are all things perceptible, all things intelligible, all things possible. Nothing can be born or perish, exist in some degree, possess a time, a place, a meaning, a figure—except on this definite *stage*, which the fates have circumscribed, and which, having separated it from who knows what primordial chaos, as light was separated from darkness on the first day, they have opposed and subordinated to the condition of *being seen*. . . .

If I have led you into this solitude, and even to this state of desperate clarity, it is only because the idea I formed of an intellectual power had to be carried to its ultimate consequence. The characteristic of man is

juxtapose and contrast the deep organic life with the superficial life that we call " the mind." The first is by nature regular and periodic, and manifests itself in the second only when undergoing functional disturbances—indeed, not always then, for there are extremely serious disturbances that remain concealed. It is as if by chance that the others become perceptible or even unbearable, without any proportion to their importance in the organic life.

consciousness; and that of consciousness is a perpetual emptying, a process of detachment without cease or exception from anything presented to it, whatever that thing may be. An inexhaustible act, independent of the quality as of the quantity of things presented; an act by which the *man of intellect* must finally reduce himself, deliberately, to an indefinite refusal to be anything whatsoever.

All phenomena being thus regarded with a sort of equal repulsion, rejected successively and, as it were, by an identical gesture, appear in a certain state of equivalence. Even thoughts and feelings are included in this uniform condemnation, which extends to all perceptible things. It must be understood that nothing escapes this rigorous process of exhaustion, and that our mere awareness of them puts our inmost feelings on a plane with exterior objects and events; the moment they are observable, they go to join the multitude of observed things: color and sorrow; memories, expectations, and surprise; that tree, and the fluttering of its leaves, and its yearly transformation, its shadow like its substance, its accidents of shape or position, and the distant images it recalls to my wandering mind—*all those things are equal*.... Anything can be substituted for anything else—might that not be the definition of *things*?

It is inevitable that the mind should be impelled by its own activity to this extreme and elementary act of consideration. Its multitudinous impulses, its inner debates, perturbations, analytical reactions—do these leave anything unchanged? If so, what is the changeless element? What is it that resists the fascination of the senses, the dissipation of ideas, the fading of memories, the slow variation of the organism, the incessant and multiform action of the universe?—It is consciousness alone, in its most abstract state.

Even our *personality*, which we crudely mistake for our most intimate, our deepest characteristic and our sovereign good, is only a *thing*, both changeable and accidental, in comparison with this naked *me*. We can think of our personality, calculate its interests, and sometimes even forget them. It is only a psychological deity of the second rank, which lives in our looking glass and answers to our name. It belongs to the order of Penates. It is

The personality is composed of memories, habits, inclinations, responses. In short, it is the sum total of the prompt responses of the organism, even when that promptness assumes the form of a tendency to postpone. Now, all this can be regarded as accidental by comparison with consciousness pure and simple, which has only one property: to be. Consciousness is perfectly impersonal.

subject to pain, greedy for incense like any false god and, again like false gods, it is a temptation to worms. It blossoms under praise. It does not resist the power of wine, the delicacy of words, or the sorcery of music. It is full of self-love and therefore is docile and easy to lead. It is squandered in the carnival of madness and is strangely distorted by the anamorphoses of dreams. And still worse: it is forced to acknowledge, with annoyance, that it has equals, and even to admit that it is *inferior* to certain others. For the personality, that is a bitter and puzzling experience.

Everything helps to persuade it, moreover, that in itself it is only a simple event; that it must appear in graphs and statistics, along with all the accidents of the world; that its beginning was a seminal chance and a microscopic incident; that it has run billions of risks, has been shaped by a quantity of coincidences, and is in short—however admirable or determined or definite or brilliant it may be—the result of an incalculable disorder.

Each person being a "sport of nature," *jeu de l'amour et du hasard*, it follows that the highest ambitions and

even the deepest thoughts of this improvised creature inevitably savor of
their origin. His acts are always relative, his masterpieces are casual. He
thinks perishably, he thinks as an
individual, he thinks by lucky flukes;
and he blunders on the best of his ideas
by secret accidents that he hesitates
to confess. Besides, he is not even sure
of being positively *someone*; he dis-
guises and denies his nature more
readily than he affirms it. Deriving a
few resources and a great deal of self-
esteem from his own inconsistency, he
finds his favorite activity in fictions of
all sorts. He lives on romances and is
legally wedded to a thousand fictional
characters. His hero is never himself.

Finally, he devotes nine-tenths of
his time to that which is to come, to
that which formerly was, and to that
which cannot be—with the result that
our true *present* has nine chances in
ten of never existing.

Meanwhile in each of our individual
lives, at the depth where treasures are
buried, there is the fundamental permanence of a consciousness that depends on nothing. Just as the ear loses
and recovers a grave and continuous
sound that has never ceased to echo

through the vicissitudes of a symphony, though at moments it ceases to be heard, so the pure *I*, that unique and monotonous element of each being, is lost and recovered by itself, but inhabits our senses eternally. It is the basic *tone* of our existence, and, as soon as one listens to it, it dominates all the complicated circumstances and varieties of existence.

The central but secret task of the greatest intellect—is it not to isolate this substantial awareness from the struggling mass of ordinary truths? And the man of intellect—must he not come to define himself, as against all things, in terms of this pure and unchanging relationship of any and all objects? It is a definition that confers on him an almost unimaginable breadth of scope and, as it were, carries him to the same power as the corresponding universe. But what he raises to this high degree is not his precious personal *self*, since he has renounced his personality by making it the object of his thought, and since he has given the place of *subject* to that unqualifiable *I* which has no name or history, which is neither more tangible nor less real than the center of gravity of a ring or that of a planetary system

—but which results from the whole, whatever that whole may be.

A moment ago the ostensible aim of this marvelous intellectual life was still. . . . to wonder at itself. It was engrossed in the process of bringing forth offspring to admire; it confined itself to whatever was fairest, sweetest, brightest, and most substantial; and it felt discomfort only when compared with other mental organisms that were its rivals. In this connection it was faced with the strangest problem one could possibly propound, but a problem actually propounded by the existence of others in our likeness: quite simply it consists in the possibility of other intelligences, in the plurality of the singular, in the contradictory co-existence of mutally independent durations—as many of these as there are persons, *tot capita, tot tempora*—a problem comparable with that of *relativity* in physics, though incomparably more difficult. . . .

But now, carried away by his zealous desire to be unique, guided by his ardor for omnipotence, this same being has gone beyond all creations, all works, and even beyond his own lofty designs; while at the same time he has left behind all tenderness for himself and all preference for his wishes. In an instant he immolates his individuality. He feels that he is pure consciousness; two of these cannot exist. He is the *I*, the universal pronoun, the appelation of that which has no connection with a body. How his pride has been transformed, and what a strange goal he has reached without seeking it! What a moderate reward is he granted for his triumphs! Such a firmly directed life, which had treated all the objects it might propose to itself as obstacles to be either avoided or overturned, deserved to reach an inexpugnable conclusion, not a conclusion of its duration, but a conclusion in itself. . . . Pride has conducted it to that point, and there pride is consumed. Its directing pride abandons it, astonished, bare, infinitely simple, at the summit of its resources.

The pride in question does not seem to be that which says to itself, "I am better than you." Rather it is the pride that says, "What I want is better than what you want."
My desire, my model, my impossible aim goes beyond and obliterates yours.

There is no mystery in these ideas. One could put it quite abstractly, that the widest range of our transformations, including all sensations, all ideas, all judgments, everything that is manifested *intus et extra*, admits of an *invariable*.

I have allowed myself to go beyond all limits of patience and clarity, having given way to ideas that occurred to me while speaking of my task. In a few words more I shall finish this somewhat simplified picture of my state of mind; there are still some moments to pass in 1894.

Nothing is so strange as lucidity at grips with inadequacy. Here roughly is what happens, had to happen, and did happen to me.

I was in the predicament of having to invent a character capable of producing a great diversity of works. My mania was that I cared only for the functioning of persons, and in works of art I cared only for their genesis. I knew that the works are always falsifications or contrivances; fortunately the *author* is never the *man*. The life of one is not the life of the other; no matter how many details we accumulate on the life of Racine, they will not teach us the art of writing his verse. All criticism has been dominated by the outworn principle that the man is *cause* of the work—as in the eyes of the law a criminal is *cause* of his crime. Much rather, they are the effects of it in each case! But the pragmatic principle lightens the task of judges and critics; biography is simpler than analysis. About what interests us most,

Nor is the life of the author ever the life of the man he is.

105

it tells us absolutely nothing. Less still!
A man's true life, which is always ill-defined even for his neighbors, even for himself, cannot be utilized in an explanation of his works, except indirectly and by means of a most laborious analysis.

Consequently, no mistresses, no creditors, no anecdotes, no adventures! One is led to adopt a more honest method, that of disregarding such external details and of imagining a theoretical being, a psychological *model* more or less approximate, but representing in some sort one's capacity for reconstructing the work that has to be explained. Success is doubtful at best, but one's efforts will not be wasted: if they do not resolve the insoluble problems of intellectual parthenogenesis, at least they *state* the problems with admirable clarity.

In the circumstances, that conviction was my only positive asset.

The necessity in which I was placed, as well as the total elimination of all solutions antipathetic to my nature, including erudition and the resources of rhetoric—one dismissed and the other scorned—had left me in a state of despair. In the end, it must be

That is the problem. It consists in trying to conceive what another in fact conceived, and not in trying to picture, with the help of documents, the hero of the novel.

confessed that my only solution was to attribute my own agitation to the unfortunate Leonardo, transporting the disorder of my mind into the complexity of his. I inflicted all my desires on him, presenting them as aims he had realized. I ascribed to him many of the difficulties that haunted me at the time, as if he had met and surmounted them. I transformed my perplexities into his supposed power. I dared to consider myself under his name and make use of my person.

It was a subterfuge, but there was life in it. A young man who is curious about a thousand things: might he not, after all, bear a rather close resemblance to a man of the Renaissance? Even his ingenuousness may well represent the sort of relative ingenuousness *created* by four hundred years of discoveries, to the disadvantage of the men of that time. And besides, I said to myself, Hercules had no more muscles than we have, but only bigger ones. I cannot even move the rock he carried away, but there is no difference in the structure of our machines; I correspond to him bone by bone, fiber by fiber, act by act; and our likeness enables me to imagine his labors.

A brief reflection is enough to show that there is no other course to follow. A writer must put himself deliberately in the place of the being who occupies his thoughts. And when we are trying to summon up a shade, who but ourselves can respond? Such are never to be found except in oneself. It is our own functioning, and *nothing else*, that can teach us anything about anything. Our knowledge, in my opinion, has for limits the consciousness we can have of our own being—and perhaps of *our bodies*. Whatever X may be, if my idea of X is carried far enough, it tends toward myself, whatever I may be. One may acknowledge the fact or ignore it; one may submit to it or grasp it eagerly; but there is no escaping it, no other exit. The *purpose* of our every thought is in ourselves. It is out of our own substance that we imagine and give shape to a stone, a plant, a movement, an *object*; any given image is no more, perhaps, than a beginning of ourselves. . . .

Who was it wrote these words? We can read pensate *or* penate. *What intimacy. . . .*

lionardo mio
O lionardo che tanto penate. . . .

As for the true Leonardo, he was what he was. . . . Yet this myth, which is stranger than any other, gains immensely when it is taken from the realm of fable and put back into history. The farther we go, the more definitely he increases in stature. The experiments of Ader and the Wrights have bathed his treatise *On the Flight of Birds* in a sort of retrospective glory. The germ of Fresnel's optical theories is to be found in certain passages of the manuscripts preserved at the Institut de France. During the last few years, the researches of the lamented M. Duhem on the *Origins of Statics* have made it possible to attribute to Leonardo the fundamental theorem of the parallelogram of forces, and a very clear—though incomplete—notion of the principle of virtual work.

So a stranger's hand was to inscribe a tender message on these learned pages.

Leonardo and the Philosophers

[1929]

A Letter to Leo Ferrero

INVOKING Leonardo da Vinci almost at the beginning of your career, you have set his name at the head of a treatise and meditation on pure aesthetics. Many philosophers have finished (and even perished) in this field of speculation. Nothing could be nobler than your undertaking, or more venturesome.

With remarkable precision and subtlety you have examined some of the most delicate points in the endless researches that aim to render the Beautiful more or less intelligible and to give us reasons for being moved by it to a superior degree.

But you are venturing into still more dangerous territory when you ask me to introduce your work to the public.

It is not that I have failed to encounter problems of the sort on many divergent paths, or failed to reflect on them at sufficient length; it is rather that my reflections have echoed one another and that my lights have been confined and confused as if between parallel mirrors. Between nature and artifice, between the delight of seeing and the delight of creating, the exchanges are infinite. Analysis is soon lost among them. Intelligence, which undertakes and continually resumes the task of reorganizing that which exists, while arranging the symbols of all things in order round itself as the unknown center, grows weary and loses hope in this realm where answers precede questions, where caprice gives birth to laws, where we are privileged to take the symbol for the thing and the thing for the symbol, playing with this liberty to the point of attaining thereby an inexplicable sort of rigor.

Uncertain though I am, you still ask me to prepare the minds of others for your dialectic. All I can offer them is the notion I have not very clearly formed on the speculations concerning the Beautiful.

It must be confessed that aesthetics is a great and even irresistible temptation. Almost everyone with a strong feeling for the arts has something more than that feeling; he cannot escape the need to search deeper into his enjoyment.

How can we bear to be mysteriously beguiled by some aspect of nature or by certain works of men without trying to explain this accidental or contrived delight? On the one hand it seems to be independent of the intelligence—*although it may be the principle and hidden guide of the intelligence*—while on the other hand it seems to be quite distinct from our ordinary feelings—*although it may include and transfigure their variety and depth.*

Philosophers could not fail to be puzzled by emotions of this curious type. Moreover, they had a somewhat less naïve and more systematic reason for examining such emotions and for searching out their causes, operation, meaning, and essence.

The tremendous undertaking of philosophy, as viewed in the philosopher's own heart, consists, after all, in *an effort to transmute everything we know into what we should like to know*, and the operation has to be effected, or at least presented, in a certain *order*.

Philosophies are characterized by the order of their questions, for, in a philosophic mind, questions do not and

We might define the philosopher as a specialist *in the* universal, *his function being expressed by a sort of contradiction. Moreover, this* universal *appears only in a* verbal *form.*
These two considerations naturally lead to our classifying the philosopher under the species artist. But *this artist will not admit to his being one—and here begins the drama, or the comedy, of Philosophy.*
Whereas the painters and the poets have

cannot exist in complete and sub-stantial isolation. On the contrary, what one finds in such a mind, as a sort of ground bass, is the feeling or fundamental tone of a latent though more or less close interdependence among all the ideas it contains or could ever contain. Awareness of this deep coherence imposes order; and the order of questions necessarily leads to a sovereign question, which is that of knowledge.

Now, as soon as a philosopher has postulated or founded or justified or depreciated knowledge (whether he has exalted and developed it *ultra vires* by potent logical or intuitive calcula-tions, or whether he has measured knowledge and, as it were, reduced it to its own limited dimensions by criticism), he always finds himself led onwards to *explain*—that is, to express in his system, which is his personal *order* of comprehension—human acti-vity in general, of which intellectual knowledge is only one of the modali-ties, although it stands for the whole.

Here we come to a crucial point in any philosophy.

A system of thought that was just now so pure and central, one that was

only their rank *to quarrel about, philo-sophers quarrel with one another about their* existence.

Does the philosopher think that an Ethics *or a* Monadology *is something more serious than a suite in D minor? It is true that certain questions presented by the mind to the mind are more general and* natural *than most works of art, but there is nothing to prove that the questions are not silly ones.*

pursuing in the real (whatever its contents and conclusions might have been) the ideal of a *uniform* distribution of concepts round a certain attitude or characteristic preoccupation of the thinker, is now obliged to try to recover the diversity, irregularity, and unexpectedness of other manners of thinking; and its order must regiment their seeming disorder.

It must reconstitute the plurality and autonomy of other minds as a consequence of its own unity and sovereignty. It must legitimize the existence of things it had convicted of error and thus undermined; it must recognize the vitality of the absurd, the fruitfulness of contradictions; and at times it must even acknowledge that in itself, for all its sense of being informed with the universality from which it seems to proceed, it is no more than a particular production, or the individual tendency of a certain person. With this a kind of wisdom sets in, and likewise the twilight of a philosophy.

The truth is that *other* existences are always disturbing to the splendid egotism of a philosopher. He cannot fail, however, to come against the great riddle presented by the inconsequence of others. The thoughts, the feelings, the actions of another always seem to us arbitrary. The partiality we always show to what is ours is fortified by our feeling that we are agents of necessity. But the *other* does exist, and the riddle is forced upon us. It harasses our minds under two forms; one consisting in the different types of conduct and character, the great variety of decisions and attitudes in all that touches on the preservation of the body and its possessions; the other manifested by the diversity of tastes, expressions, and creations of the sensibility.

Our Philosopher cannot make up his mind not to absorb into his own light all those realities he would wish to make his own or reduce to possibilities that might be his. He wants to *comprehend*, that is, to comprehend them all in the full meaning of the word. So he will meditate how to build himself a science of the values of action, and another science of the values of expression or of creating emotions—an ETHICS and an AESTHETICS—as if his Palace of Thought would be imperfect without these two symmetrical wings, in which his omnipotent and abstract

—which are invariably the weak points of a philosophy.

In my opinion, every philosophy is a question of form. *It is the most comprehensive form that a certain individual can give to the* whole *of his internal and external experience—and this* without respect to the learning and acquirements he might possess. *In his search for this form, the closer he comes to finding a more individual expression, one better adapted to his own nature, the more foreign will seem the* deeds *and* works *of* others.

Leonardo is one of the founders of Europe as a distinct entity. He resembles neither the ancients nor the moderns.

self might imprison action, passion, emotion, and invention.

Every philosopher, when he has finished with God and the Self, with Time, Space, Matter, the Categories, and the Essences, turns back toward men and their works.

Just as our Philosopher had invented the *True*, so he invented the *Good* and the *Beautiful*. Just as he had invented rules to harmonize thought in isolation with itself, so he undertook to prescribe other rules designed to harmonize action and expression with precepts and models shielded from everyone's caprices and doubts by the consideration of a unique and universal Principle, which must first of all, and *irrespective of any particular experience*, be defined or designated.

Few events in the history of thought are more remarkable than this introduction of Ideals, in which may be seen an essentially European achievement. The decline of ideals in men's minds coincides with that of the virtues typical of Europe.

But just as we are still rather firmly attached to the idea of a pure science rigorously developed on the basis of *local* evidence, having properties that may be extended indefinitely from identity to identity, in the same fashion we are still half convinced of the existence of a single *Morality* and a single *Beauty*, both independent of times, places, peoples, or persons.

Each day, however, the ruin of this noble edifice grows more evident. We are witnessing an extraordinary phenomenon: the very development of the sciences is tending to weaken the concept of Knowledge. I mean that a seemingly impregnable area of science, one that it shared with philosophy (in other words, with faith in the intelligible and belief in the inherent value of mental acquisitions) is gradually yielding ground to a new fashion of conceiving or evaluating the function of cognition. No longer can the effort of the intellect be regarded as converging toward an intellectual limit, toward the *True*. A moment of self-examination is enough to reveal in ourselves this modern conviction: that any form of *knowledge*, unless it corresponds to some effective *power*, has only a conventional or arbitrary importance. The value of any knowledge consists only in its being the description or the formula for exercising a

It is clear that the Good *and the* Beautiful *have gone out of fashion.* As for the *True, photography has shown us its nature and limits. The recording of phenomena purely by means of the effects of phenomena, with as little human intervention as possible— such is "our Truth." This is what I find to be happening.*

verifiable power. From this it follows that any metaphysical system and even any theory of cognition, whatever these may be, are ruthlessly cut off and set apart from what is regarded more or less consciously *by all* as the only real knowledge—*payable in gold.*

By the same process and of their own accord, ethics and aesthetics are dissolving into problems of legislation, statistics, history, or physiology... and into lost illusions.

If Aesthetics could really be, the arts would necessarily vanish before it— that is, before their own essence.

Moreover, what excuse could we offer for making and elaborating plans to "create an Aesthetics"?—A science of the Beautiful?...Do modern people still use this term? It seems to me that they only pronounce it tongue-in-cheek—or else when they happen to think of the past. Beauty is a sort of corpse. It has been supplanted by novelty, intensity, strangeness, all the *shock values.* Raw excitement is the sovereign mistress of recent minds, and works of art are at present designed to tear us away from the contemplative state, the *motionless delight,* an image of which was at one time intimately connected with the general notion of the Beautiful. Art is more and more penetrated by the most immediate and unstable moods of psychic and sensual life. The *unconscious*, the *irrational*, the *instantaneous*—which are, as their names indicate, privations or negations of the willed and sustained forms of mental activity—have replaced the models *expected by the mind*. Seldom do we encounter anything produced by a desire for "perfection." Let us observe in passing that this antiquated desire was bound to be destroyed by the obsession with the insatiable thirst for *originality*. The ambition to perfect a work of art comes close to being a project for making it independent of any era; but the effort to be new is also an effort to make the work of art a remarkable event by virtue of its contrast with the passing moment. The former ambition admits and even requires *heredity*, imitation, or tradition, these being stages in an ascent toward the absolute beauty it dreams of attaining. The latter rejects them, while insisting on them still more rigorously—for its essence is to *differ from*.

In our days a "definition of the Beautiful" has become scarcely more than a historical or philological document. This illustrious word has lost its ancient richness of meaning. Soon

It must be admitted that a positive or practical conception of life leads inevitably to a search for immediate effects and to the end of craftsmanship. We are living in the Twilight of Posterity.

the numismaticians of language will put it away in their cabinets, with many another verbal coin that has passed from circulation.

Nevertheless, certain problems remain, and certain others might well arise, that cannot be assigned to any of the well recognized scientific disciplines and have no connection with any particular technique. They have also been neglected by the philosophers, although they keep reappearing— however vaguely or strangely they may be expressed—in the gropings and uncertainties of artists.

There is nothing more surprising to the innocent mind than certain problems that philosophers insist on placing foremost— unless it be the absence of other problems that the innocent mind would regard as being of fundamental import- ance.

Take, for example, the general problem of composition (that is, of the *different types* of relationship between the whole and the parts); or take the problems resulting from the multiple functions of each element in a work; or the problems of *ornament* that border simultaneously on geo- metry, physics, and morphology with- out finding a definite center—although they permit us to glimpse an indefin- able kinship between the forms of equilibrium of physical objects, the figures of musical composition, the decorative shapes of living creatures, and the half-conscious or fully conscious productions of human activity when it endeavors to fill an empty space or time, as if in obedience to something like a horror of the void.

Questions of this sort do not obtrude themselves on abstract thinking. They take rise and acquire their strength from the creative instinct, at a moment when the artist has gone beyond the point of setting down what first occurs to him. He begins to look for solutions in a process of meditation that appears to be speculative, even assuming a philosophic form, and which he hopes will determine the form and structure of a concrete creation. He may well want to go back (following the same path as the philosopher for a time) to first principles that may justify and confirm his intentions by giving them more than a merely personal authority; but what he achieves is only a biased sort of philosophy, one that aims beyond his principles at a set of particular consequences for the work in hand. Whilst the true philosopher regards *what is* as the goal to be attained and the object to be recovered at the limit of his mental excursions and operations, the artist goes further, into the possible,

I mean that when an artist undertakes to produce a work so vast or complicated, or so new to him, that his plans and his means for realizing them are not immediately determined by their mutual compatibility, he often starts by inventing a theory that appears to have a general application. He explores the resources of abstract language to find an authority against itself, one that will simplify his task under pretense of subjecting it to universal conditions.
Anyone who has lived a little among artists and listened to what they say must have noticed this, and have heard many a precept.

and becomes the agent of *what is to be*.

The clearest difference between the aesthetics of a philosopher and the reflections of an artist is that the former proceeds from a system of thinking that regards itself as foreign to the arts and of another essence than the thinking of a poet or a musician—in which respect it may well be mistaken, as I hope to show later. To the philosopher's mind works of art are accidents, or particular cases, or the effects produced by a busy sensibility as it gropes blindly toward a principle that Philosophy sees as a whole and possesses as an immediate and pure concept. The practice of the arts does not seem *necessary* to the philosopher, since its supreme object is one that should belong immediately to philosophic thought, should be directly accessible to it, by way of the study which philosophers apply to understanding the understanding, or to a system that jointly explains the perceptible world and the intelligible world. The philosopher does not feel the particular necessity of artistic activity; he cannot appreciate the concrete methods, the means and values of execution and the importance of materials, since he instinctively tends to distinguish these from the *idea*. He finds it distasteful to think of an incessant, intimate, and even-handed exchange between the desired and the possible, between what he judges to be accident and what he judges to be essence, between "form" and "content," between consciousness and automatism, between circumstance and design, between "matter" and "spirit." Now, it is precisely the practiced habit, the acquired freedom of making such exchanges; it is the existence in the artist of a concealed standard of measurement applying to elements of radically different natures; it is the inevitable and indivisible collaboration, the coordination *at every moment*, in all his acts, of the arbitrary and the necessary, of the expected and the unexpected, of his body, his materials, his decisions, and even his fits of absence—it is all this that finally enables him to add something to nature considered as a practically infinite source of subjects, models, means, and pretexts, to create some *object* that cannot be simplified and reduced to an abstract idea, since it owes its origin and its effect to an inextricable system of independent conditions. *We cannot summarize a poem as we might summarize... a "universe."* To summarize a thesis is to preserve what is essential in it. To summarize a work of art, or replace the work with a diagram, is to lose what is essential. When we grasp the implications of this principle, we can see how the aesthetician's analysis is largely illusory.

The fact is that we cannot extract from an object, or from a natural or artificial arrangement, any group of aesthetic characteristics that can be found elsewhere and subsequently used as the basis of a general formula for things of beauty. Such an attempt has often been made, but those who make it are unaware that the method applies only to things "already found." Moreover, the object under consideration cannot be reduced to a few of its traits without losing its intrinsic emotive power.

It is hard for a philosopher to understand that the artist passes almost without distinction from *form* to *content* and from *content* to *form*; that a *form* may occur to him before the meaning he will assign to it; or that *the idea of a form* means as much to him as *the idea that asks to be given a form.*

In short, if aesthetics could really exist, the arts would melt away before it, that is, *before their own essence*.

What I have just said does not apply to technical studies which are concerned only with methods or particular solutions, whose more or less direct purpose is the production or classification of works of art, but which in no sense aim at attaining the Beautiful *by paths that lie outside its proper domain*.

The truth may be that we cannot form a clear conception of anything unless we might also have invented it. Pascal tells us that he would not have invented painting. He could not *see* the need for duplicating the most insignificant objects by making laborious images of them. And yet how often this great artist in words took pains over his *design*, to make a speaking portrait of his thoughts! It is true that he seems to have ended by including all desires *save one* in the same gesture of rejection, and by regarding everything but death as a painted thing.

What was Immanuel Kant really doing when he based his Ethics and his Aesthetics on a myth of universality,

It is quite easy to demonstrate by a certain chain of reflection that all is vanity. Pascal was finding new words to dress up a commonplace of the pulpit. What lies behind it is usually no more than a feeling of revulsion that is purely physiological in origin, or a resolve to make a resounding impression at no great expense.
It is as easy to evoke a horror of life, to picture its fragility, its hardships, and its folly, as it is to arouse erotic ideas and

sensual appetites. All one needs is a different vocabulary. (But it is to be assumed that the first is a nobler form of exercise.) I might add (if only for some) that the determination not to let oneself be manipulated by words is not without relevance to what I have termed, or what I mean by the term pure Poetry.

on the latent presence of an infallible and unanimous feeling about the universe presiding in the soul of every man coming into this world? And what about all the other philosophers of the Good and the Beautiful? The answer is that they were creators in spite of themselves, creators who believed that they were merely substituting a more exact or complete notion of reality for a crude or superficial one, when, on the contrary, *they were inventing*—one by subtle division, another by an instinct for symmetry, and all by a profound desire, a love for *that which might be.* What did they do but create when they added problems to problems, entities to entities, and new symbols, new forms and formulas of development, to the existing store of intellectual pastimes and arbitrary constructions of the mind?

Philosophy had set out to take over the artist, to *explain* what the artist feels and does; but the opposite is what proves to have taken place. Far from enveloping and assimilating the whole domain of creative sensibility into the concept of the Beautiful; far from becoming the mother and arbitress of aesthetics, what really happens is

that philosophy proceeds from aesthetics and can no longer find its justification, the answer to its qualms of
conscience, or even its real *depth* save
only in its constructive power and its
freedom as abstract poetry. An aesthetic
interpretation and that alone can shield
the venerable monuments of metaphysics from the collapse of their more
or less hidden postulates or from the
destructive effects of semantic and
logical analysis.

At first it may seem quite difficult
for philosophers to approach certain
problems *as artists* when they were
accustomed to thinking about them
as seekers of truth, or to regard the
products of their utmost sincerity as
beautiful lies and inherent fictions.
"What a splendid past," they will say,
"and what a sad present!" They
should set their minds at rest about this
change, which after all is only a change
in customs. I do not look on it as
anything more than a reform demanded by the course of events, one
for which a sort of model can be
found in the early history of the plastic
arts. There was a time when the likeness of a man or an animal, even if
people had seen the craftsman making
it, was regarded not only as a living

thing, motionless and crude though it was, but as being endowed with supernatural powers. Many of the gods fashioned out of stone or wood did not even resemble men, yet people nourished and venerated these images that were scarcely images at all. The more formless they were, the more they were adored—a remarkable fact that is also to be observed in the relation of children to their dolls and of lovers to the beloved; it appears to be a deeply significant trait. (Perhaps we believe that the more life we are obliged to give to an object, the more we receive from it.) But little by little, as this communicated life grew weaker and was withdrawn from such rude images, *the idol became beautiful*. Impelled by criticism, it lost its imaginary power over events and persons in order to gain a real power over men's eyes. Sculpture became free, and became itself.

Without shocking or cruelly wounding philosophic feelings, might I compare its idolized truth—its Principles, its Ideas, its Being, its Essences, its Categories, its Noumena, its Universe, the whole tribe of concepts that seemed indispensable each in its turn—with the idols of which I

Yes, all these abstractions of traditional philosophy seem to me the work of

was speaking? Today we might ask ourselves what sort of philosophy would stand in the same relation to traditional philosophy as that of a Greek statue of the fifth century B.C. to the faceless divinities of earliest times.

I sometimes think that little by little, as it becomes possible and permissible to compose with ideas—to make abstract constructions without having illusions about them and without recourse to hypostasis—it may become evident that this type of untrammeled philosophy is more fruitful and more *true* than the type that attached itself to a primitive belief in explanations, as well as more human and appealing than the type demanded by a rigorous critical attitude. Perhaps it will then be possible to resume—in a new spirit and with quite different ambitions—the speculative work that was undertaken by the great metaphysicians, whose goals, in the course of time, have been sadly undermined by criticism. Long ago mathematics made itself independent of every aim that was alien to the concept of itself created by the pure development of its technique and by its awareness of the intrinsic value of that development.

Primitives. *There is—if I dare say so—a certain innocence in these notions and in the problems they express. In particular, the philosophic notions of* reality *and* causality *impress me as rudimentary. To introduce abstract words without giving them a clear-cut and strictly formal definition seems to me far from commendable.*

In the freest sort of constructions, produced in the fullest consciousness of their arbitrary nature, mathematics has found the surest way of

developing its art
of the necessary.

Today everyone knows to what
extent its freedom as an art, which had
promised to carry it far from reality
into a world of pastimes, difficulties,
and useless elegance, has made it
marvelously flexible, besides equip-
ping it to come to the aid of the
physical scientists.

An art of ideas—an art of the order
of ideas, or of the multiple orders of
ideas—is that a wholly vain conception? I find it permissible to think that
all architecture does not exist in space,
that not all music is a matter of sounds.
There is a certain feeling for *ideas* and
their analogies that seems to me capable
of acting and of developing in the
same fashion as a feeling for sound or
color; and I might even be inclined, if
I had to propose a definition of the
philosopher, to make it depend on the
predominance in him of this mode of
sensibility.

*This is why the
teaching of philo-
sophy—unless it also
teaches that every
mind is free not only
with regard to
doctrines but even
with regard to the
problems themselves
—impresses me as*

I also believe that one is born a
philosopher, as one is born a *musician*
or a *sculptor*, and that this innate gift,
which has always taken the pursuit of a
certain *reality* or *truth* as its theme and
pretext, might henceforth rely more
on itself and, instead of merely pursuing, might create. The philosopher
would then expend in full liberty the

forces he had acquired through discipline; and in an infinite number of ways, under an infinite number of forms, he would be able to exploit the vigor and the faculty proper to his nature, that of giving life and movement to abstract things.

Thus it would become possible to *save the noumena* by way of sheer delight in their intrinsic harmonies.

Finally I might say that there exists an excellent demonstration of what I have so far been proposing in a tentative way. It was no more than a possibility, but we have only to consider the fate of the great philosophic systems to find it already realized. In what spirit do we read the philosophers, and who consults them in the true hope of finding anything else than enjoyment or an exercise for the mind? When we now set out to read them, is it not with a feeling that we are accepting for a time the rules of an admirable game? What would happen to these masterpieces of unverifiable discipline if it were not for these conventions we adopt out of love for an exacting pleasure? If we refute a Plato or a Spinoza, will nothing remain of their astonishing constructions? Absolutely nothing—*unless it be a work of art.*

being antiphilosophical.

The thing is to create the need for enjoying philosophical activity.

For that matter, what else could be hoped for by thinkers of this great species?

Nevertheless, quite apart from philosophy, yet in certain areas of the search for understanding, there have appeared a few extraordinary beings of whom we know that their abstract thought, highly developed as it was and capable of the greatest subtlety and depth, never lost its concern for figurative creations or tangible applications and proofs of its concentrative power. They seem to have possessed some indefinable inner aptitude for effecting continual interchanges between the *arbitrary* and the *necessary*.

Leonardo da Vinci is the supreme type of these superior individuals.

What could be more remarkable than the absence of his name from the list of recognized philosophers, grouped as such by tradition?

Nor is Montaigne in that list.
He would give the same answer, " I do not know," to all the questions in a philosophical catechism; therefore he could not be called a philosopher.
And yet...

Doubtless the lack of finished texts of a specifically philosophic nature might pass as a reason for this exclusion. Moreover, the quantity of *notes* he left behind is a simultaneous mass of observations that leaves us in doubt regarding the order of questions in his thinking. One hesitates to say which of his curiosities and intentions stood first or last, since Leonardo himself seems to have lavished his ardor on the greatest variety of subjects, depending on circumstances and the mood of the hour—so much so that he gives the not unpleasant impression of being a sort of condottiere in the service of all the Muses turn by turn.

But, as has already been said, the visible existence of a certain order of ideas is characteristic of the recognized philosophers whose qualities permit them to figure in the History of Philosophy (a history that can be written only with the help of certain conventions, including first of all a *necessarily arbitrary* definition of philosophy and the philosopher).

It follows that Leonardo would be excluded for lack of an explicit order in this thinking, and—let us not be afraid to say—for lack of an *easily summarized* statement that would enable us to classify his essential conceptions and compare them with other systems, problem by problem.

But I should like to go further and distinguish him from the philosophers by more tangible characteristics and for more substantial reasons than these purely negative considerations. Let us see—or imagine—in what respects his intellectual activity differs sharply from

Let us not forget that the broadest fame demands the sort of merit that can be called to mind in a few words.

theirs, while closely resembling it at moments.

The philosopher, to the eyes of an observer, has a very simple purpose: *to express in speech or writing the results of his meditations*. He tries to constitute a body of *knowledge* that is completely expressible and transmissible by *language*.

But for Leonardo, language is not all. Knowledge is not all; perhaps he regards it only as a means. Leonardo designs, computes, builds, decorates; he makes use of all the concrete methods and materials that are subject to ideas, serve as a test for them, and give them an opportunity to rebound in an unexpected fashion, since the materials offer an alien resistance to ideas and provide the conditions of another world that no previous knowledge or degree of foresight would make it possible to encompass in a purely mental elaboration. *Knowledge* is not enough for this strong-willed and many-sided nature; what matters to him is *power*. He does not separate understanding from creating. He does not care to distinguish theory from practice, or speculative thought from an increase in external power, or the true from the verifiable, or the true, again, from that modification of the verifiable manifested in the construction of works of art and machines.

In that respect, this man is an authentic and immediate ancestor of science as it exists today. Who does not see that science is coming more and more to identify itself with the acquisition and possession of power? Hence I would venture to define it in this fashion— for the definition *is within us*, however we may protest. *Science consists, I would say, of the total sum of formulas and processes that are invariably successful*, and it is coming progressively closer to being *a table of correspondences between human actions and phenomena*, an always longer and more definite table of such correspondences, recorded in the most precise and economical systems of notation.

Infallibility in prediction is, in simple fact, the only characteristic that modern man regards as having more than a conventional value. He is tempted to say, "All the rest is literature"; and the rest would include all explanations and *theories*. It is not that he fails to recognize their utility, even their necessity, but rather he has learned to consider them as means and

Science in the modern sense of the word consists in making knowledge depend on power. And it has reached the point of subordinating the intelligible to the verifiable. Our confidence in science is entirely based on the assurance that a certain phenomenon will be produced again or observed again as a result of certain well defined acts. As for the manner of describing the phenomenon— of explaining it— that is the arguable, changeable, and perfectible part of the development or exposition of science.

instruments, intermediate operations, steps in the dark, provisional methods that furnish him with logical formulations, with combinations of signs and images, in order to clear the way for the final decisive perception.

In the course of a few decades he has seen the successive and even simultaneous reigns of contradictory theses that proved equally fruitful; of doctrines and methods opposed in principle and making theoretical demands that canceled one another, while all of them produced positive results to be added to his stock of acquired powers. He has heard *laws* described as more or less helpful *conventions*; and he also knows that a great number of those laws have lost their pure and essential character by being reduced to the modest rank of simple probabilities— in other words, to rules that are valid only at the level of our observations. Finally, he can now appreciate the increasing and already almost insuperable difficulties that inhere in any attempt to represent a "world" that we surmise; a world that imposes itself on our minds, but—revealed as it is in a roundabout fashion by a series of relays and indirect effects on the senses; constructed by a process of analysis with disconcerting results when these are translated into common language; excluding any sort of images (since it must be the substance of their substance) and in a sense, blending all the categories—is something *that exists and does not exist*. But all these terrifyingly indeterminate principles, these inhuman hypotheses, this knowledge incompatible with the knower, nonetheless leave behind them an ever increasing and incorruptible capital of achievements and modes of producing achievements—in other words, of *powers*.

All the labors of the mind can thus no longer have as their object a final contemplation, even the idea of which has lost its meaning (or comes closer and closer to being a theological concept, demanding a contemplator different in essence from ourselves); but, on the contrary, these labors appear to the mind itself as *an intermediate activity connecting two experiences or two states of experience*, the first of which is *given* and the second *foreseen*.

Knowledge of this sort is never separated from action or from instruments of execution and control, without which, moreover, *it has no meaning*—whereas if it is based on them, if

Such is the foundation of what we regard as true knowledge. The propositions of this true knowledge should be simply directions for performing certain acts: do this, do that. All this amounts to power, *in other words, to an assured external transformation that depends on a conscious internal modification.*

137

it refers back to them at every moment, it enables us to deny meaning to knowledge of any other sort, and specifically to that which proceeds from words alone and leads only toward ideas.

What then becomes of philosophy, besieged and obsessed as it is with discoveries so unexpected as to arouse the greatest doubts concerning the virtues or values of all the ideas and deductions put forward by a mind reduced to its own resources and trying to encompass the world? What becomes of it when—in addition to feeling beset, overrun, and dismayed at every turn by the furious activity of the physical sciences—it is also disturbed and menaced in its most ancient, most tenacious (and perhaps least regrettable) habits by the slow and meticulous work of the philologists and semanticists? What becomes of the philosopher's *I think*, and what becomes of his *I am*? What becomes, or rebecomes, of that neutral and mysterious verb TO BE, which has had such a grand career in the void? From those modest syllables, released to a peculiar fortune by the loss or attrition of their original meaning, artists of great subtlety have

This is an age when metaphysics has been overtaken by the sudden changes in science, some of which have produced a truly comic dismay. Hence it has sometimes occurred to me that, if I were a philosopher, I should apply myself to making my philosophic thought independent of all forms of knowledge that might be overturned by some new experiment.

drawn an infinite number of questions and answers.

If, then, we take no account of our habitual thinking and confine ourselves to what is revealed by a glance at the present state of intellectual affairs, we can easily observe that philosophy as defined by its product, which is *in writing*, is objectively a particular branch of literature, characterized by its choice of certain subjects and by its frequent use of certain terms and certain forms. This very special type of mental activity and verbal production nevertheless aspires to a supreme place by virtue of its universal aims and formulas; but—since it is lacking in any objective verification, since it does not lead to establishing any *power*, and since the very universality it invokes cannot and must not be regarded as a transitional state, as a means of obtaining or expressing verifiable results—we are forced to assign it a place not far from poetry. . . .

—*but demands to be taken as an* end in itself.

But the artists of whom I was speaking fail to recognize themselves as artists and do not wish to be such. Doubtless their art, unlike that of the poets, is not the art of exploiting the sound values of words; it speculates on a certain faith in the existence of an absolute value that can be isolated from their meaning. "What is reality?" the philosopher asks, or likewise, "What is liberty?" Setting aside and ignoring the partly metaphorical, partly social, and partly statistical origin of these nouns, his mind, by taking advantage of their tendency to slip into indefinable meanings, will be able to produce combinations of extreme depth and delicacy. Not for him to solve his problem with the simple history of a word through the ages, with a detailed account of all the misunderstandings, figurative uses, and idiomatic expressions thanks to the

It seems to be characteristic of the greatest philosophers that they add problems of interpretation to the immediate problems raised by observation.

Each of them imports a terminology, and there is no case in which the terms they introduce are properly defined.

number and incoherence of which a mere word becomes as complex and mysterious as a living person, arouses an almost anguished curiosity as a person might do, eluding any sort of definite analysis, and—a chance product of simple needs, an age-old device to facilitate social intercourse and the immediate exchange of impressions— is elevated to the lofty destiny of calling forth all the interrogatory power and all the resources for finding answers of a marvelously alert mind. This word, this nothing, this chance device created anonymously, distorted by anyone, is now transformed by the meditation and dialectic of a few individuals into an instrument designed to torment the whole group of groups of ideas; it has become a sort of key that can wind all the springs of a powerful intellect, opening infinitely expectant vistas to the passion for conceiving everything that exists.

Now, the whole function and process of an artist consists in making something out of nothing. But what could be more truly *personal*, more significant of a person and his separateness as an individual, than what is done by a philosopher when he inserts a thousand difficulties into a common expression in which those who invented the expression could see none whatever; or when he creates doubts and perturbations, discovers paradoxes, and disconcerts the minds of others by overawing them with an imposing interplay of substitutions. . . . Could there be anything more personal under the appearance of being universal?

The word, that means and end of the philosopher; the word, that base matter into which he breathes life, which he troubles to its depths, was for Leonardo only the least of his resources. We know that he even regarded mathematics, which, after all, is essentially a language with exact rules, as little more than a provisional device. "Mechanics," he said, "is the paradise of the mathematical sciences." The idea is already quite Cartesian, as is also his unending concern with the physics of physiology.

By this route he proceeded on the path in which our minds are now engaged.

The idea of the animal as a machine, expressed by Descartes and forming a remarkable element of his philosophy, appears much more forcefully in Leonardo, who reveals it not only in word but in act. I doubt whether anyone before his time had thought of observing persons with the eye of a mechanical engineer. For him the support of the body, its propulsion, and its respiration were problems in mechanics. He was more the anatomist and more the engineer than Descartes. The dream of creating a mechanical man and hence of achieving knowledge by construction was paramount in his thinking.

But he belonged to an age less inclined or less accustomed than ours to confusing the useful, or the comfortable, or the exciting with *that which induces a state of resonance and of harmonic reciprocity among sensations, desires, impulses, and thoughts.* What seemed most desirable to men of Leonardo's day was not at all the need to increase the comfort of the body, save it time, and spare it from fatigue; nor to surprise and disturb merely the soul of the senses; rather it was something that multiplied sensuous enjoyment by means of intellectual artifice and calculation, while crowning this voluptuous enjoyment with the introduction of a certain contrived and delectable *spirituality.* Between the faun and the angel, the Renaissance had mastered the art of making very human blends.

And that brings me to the most difficult point for me to explain, one that may also prove the hardest to convey.

Here, then, is what seems to me most extraordinary in Leonardo, something that both opposes him and joins him to the philosophers in a much stranger and deeper fashion than anything I have so far asserted of him or of them. Leonardo was a painter: *I mean that painting was his philosophy*. The fact is that he said so himself, and he talked painting as others talk philosophy, which is to say that he made everything depend on it. He formed an excessively high opinion of this art, which seems so specialized in comparison with abstract thought and so far from being able to satisfy the whole intelligence; he regarded painting as a final goal for the efforts of a universal mind. So it was in our own time with Mallarmé, who held the curious notion that the world was made to be expressed, that all things would eventually be expressed, through the medium of poetry.

For it was a condition of his painting that he should make a minute preliminary analysis of the objects he planned to represent, one that was not in the least confined to their visual properties, but went deep into their organic life, involving questions of physics, then physiology, then psychology—so that finally his eye would, as it were, expect to perceive the visible accidents resulting from the hidden structure of the model.

Benvenuto Cellini tells us that Leonardo was the first to admire the adaptation of organic forms to mechanical functions. He revealed the special type of beauty possessed by certain bones (the shoulder blade, for example) and articulations (like that of the arm with the hand).
A very modern system of aesthetics is based solely on this principle of functional adaptation. The Greeks had thought only of optical effects, and they did not isolate

To paint, for Leonardo, was an operation that demanded every form of knowledge and almost all the scientific disciplines: geometry, dynamics, geology, physiology. A battle to be portrayed involved a study of vortices and clouds of dust, and he refused to depict such phenomena before observing them in a scientific spirit, with eyes that had been impregnated, so to speak, with understanding of their laws. A human figure was for him a synthesis of researches extending from dissection to psychology. With exquisite precision he noted the bodily attitudes according to age and sex, as he also analyzed the movements proper to each trade. All things were as if equal before his will to perceive and grasp forms through their causes. It seems to have been the outward appearance of objects that set his mind in movement; then he reduced, or tried to reduce, their morphological features to systems of forces; and only after those systems had been learned—*felt* —and reasoned out did he complete or, one might better say, resume the movement by executing the drawing or painting, as a result of which act he reaped the harvest of his toil. In this manner he projected or recreated an aspect of his subjects by means of analyzing all their properties in depth.

But what part did language play in this process? It served him only as an instrument, just as numbers did. It was no more than an accessory means, a working auxiliary, one that advanced his passionate enterprises in much the same way that sketches in the margin sometimes help *those who write* to sharpen a phrase.

In short, Leonardo found in a painting all the problems that could be offered to the mind by an effort to make a synthesis of nature—and other problems besides.

Then was he or was he not a philosopher?

If it were merely a question of the word!...But there is much else involved besides the choice of a rather vague appellation. What stops me at the point where the high title of philosopher might or might not be conferred on one whose name was rendered illustrious by so many works *not in writing* is the problem of the connection between the total activity of a mind and the mode of expression it adopts—the connection, that is, of the mind with *the sort of work that gives it the most intense sensation of its power*

the pleasure resulting from the virtual function of forms. Yet the men of every age have created perfect weapons and utensils.

When circumstances led me to consider da Vinci, I approached him as the archetype of those who perform each task so consciously that it becomes both art and science, inextricably mingled; as the exemplar of a system of art founded on universal analysis and demanding that every particular work should be created only out of verifiable elements.
As a result of Leonardo's analysis, his desire to paint led to a curiosity about all phenomena, whether or not they

were visual; he felt that nothing was alien to the art of painting, which in turn seemed precious to knowledge as a whole.

Another characteristic of Leonardo is the extraordinary reciprocity between making and knowing, as a result of which the former is guaranteed by the latter. This reciprocity stands opposed to any purely verbal science and has become dominant in the present era—to the great detriment of philosophy, which now appears to be something incomplete.

and with *the forms of external resistance it accepts.*

The particular case of Leonardo da Vinci offers one of those remarkable coincidences that demand a reconsideration of our intellectual habits and something like a rebirth of awareness in the midst of ideas we inherited.

It can be affirmed of him, I think with some degree of assurance, that the place occupied by philosophy in the life of other minds—the profound need to which it bears witness, the generalized curiosity that accompanies it, the hunger for facts to be retained and assimilated, and the constant search for causes—*is the exact place occupied in Leonardo by his steadfast preoccupation with painting.*

Here is something that offends in us some of our long-standing distinctions, that troubles both philosophy and art under the forms in which they had figured separately in our thinking.

Compared with what we are used to seeing, Leonardo appears to be a sort of monster, a centaur or a chimera, because of the hybrid species he represents to minds too intent on dividing our natures, on considering philosophers as lacking in hands or eyes, and artists with brains too small for anything but instincts. . . .

We must make an effort, however, to grasp what is implied by this strange adoption of the cult of a plastic art as a substitute for philosophy. Let us start by observing that there can be no question here of arguing about the more *subjective* states or occurrences, since, in the intimate or instant moment of psychic life, the differences between the philosopher and the artist are plainly indeterminate or even nonexistent. We must therefore have recourse to what can be seen and distinguished *objectively*; and at this point we again meet with the essential problem of the part played by language. If philosophy is inseparable from its expression in words, and if that expression is the goal of every philosopher, then Leonardo, whose goal is painting, is not a philosopher in spite of his meeting most of the other requirements. But having offered this judgment, we are obliged to accept all its consequences, some of which are far-reaching. I shall try to suggest what they might be.

The philosopher *describes* what he has thought. A system of philosophy can

Logic has only a limited value when it employs ordinary language, that is, a language without absolute definitions.

be reduced to a classification of words or a table of definitions. Logic is only our method of using such a table, and the form of its permanent properties. We take this condition for granted, and as a result of it we cannot but accord a quite special and central place in our intellectual life to articulated language. There can be no doubt that the place is deserved and that language, although composed of innumerable conventions, is almost *ourselves*. We can scarcely "think" without it, nor can we direct, preserve, or recapture our thought, or above all . . . *foresee* it in any great degree.

But let us look a little more closely; let us consider within ourselves. The moment our thinking starts to go deeper—that is, when it comes closer to its object, trying to operate on things in themselves (so far as its activity creates the equivalent of things), and no longer on signs that merely suggest the superficial notions of things—the moment when we start to live our thinking, we feel that it is drawing apart from any conventional language. No matter how closely woven into our lives the language may be; no matter how *densely* its *chances* are distributed; however sensitive this acquired organization may prove in ourselves, however quick it may be to intervene, still we can contrive, by a process of *enlargement*, or under the pressure of *continued attention*, to separate it from our mental life of the moment. We feel that words are lacking, and we know there is no reason why words should be found to answer us, that is... *to replace ourselves*; for the inherent power of words, from which comes their utility, is to carry us back *into the neighborhood* of states already experienced; to systematize, or to establish, *repetition*; whereas at this point we are penetrating into a mental life *that never repeats itself*. Perhaps that is the real nature of *thinking deeply*, which does not mean thinking more usefully, accurately, or totally than we usually do; it is simply thinking far, *thinking as far as possible from verbal automatism*. We feel at such moments that vocabulary and grammar are alien gifts: *res inter alios actas*. We have the direct perception that language, organic and indispensable as it may be, can fully express *nothing* in the world of thought, where *nothing* can arrest its transitional nature. Our attention distinguishes it from ourselves. Our rigor and our fervor both set us against it.

It also consists in reconsidering the values of our thinking as originally given—by extending the conscious duration of the given thoughts.

149

The philosophers, notwithstanding, have tried to bring language into a closer relation with their deepest feelings. They have tried to reorganize it, adding new words and meanings to meet the needs of their solitary experience, so as to make language a more subtle instrument, better adapted to *cognizing and recognizing their cognition*. We might picture philosophy as the attitude of concentration and restraint owing to which someone, at moments, thinks his life or lives his thinking in a sort of equivalence, or in a reversible state, between *being* and *knowing*— while he tries to suspend all conventional expression and waits eagerly for a combination much more precious than the others to take shape and reveal itself, a combination of the reality he feels impelled to offer with the reality he is able to receive.

All thinking involves taking one thing for another: a second for a year.

But the nature of language is quite opposed to the happy outcome of this great endeavor to which all the philosophers have devoted themselves. The strongest of them have worn themselves out in the effort to *make their thoughts speak*. In vain have they created or transfigured certain words; they could not succeed in transmitting their inner reality. Whatever the words may be—Ideas or Dynamis or Being or Noumenon or Cogito or Ego—they are all *ciphers*, the meaning of which is determined solely by the context; and so it is finally by a sort of personal creation that their reader— as also happens with readers of poetry —gives the force of life to writings in which ordinary speech is contorted into expressing values that men cannot exchange and that do not exist in the realm of spoken words.

There is not a single problem in philosophy that can be stated in such a form as to banish all doubt concerning the existence of the problem.

It can be seen that by basing all philosophy on verbal expression, and at the same time refusing it the liberties and even the... restrictions proper to the arts, we run the risk of reducing it to the varieties of eloquence or invocation offered by a few splendid and solitary figures. Moreover, we have never known, nor can we even imagine, two philosophers compatible with each other, or a doctrine open at all times to only one interpretation.

There is still another point to be noted about the relation between speech and philosophic activity, a simple matter of fact I should like to mention.

Merely by looking about us we can

observe that the importance of language is steadily diminishing in every field of activity in which we also observe an increasing degree of precision. Common speech will doubtless continue to serve as the initial and general instrument for establishing relations between external and internal life; it will always be the means of teaching us the other languages that have been consciously created; it will adjust these potent and accurate mechanisms to the use of still unspecialized minds. But gradually, by contrast, it is coming to be regarded as a first crude means of approximation. Its function is being restricted by the development of purer systems of notation, each better adapted to a single purpose, and every further degree of this contraction leads to a further shrinking of the ancient horizons of philosophy.... Everything that becomes more precise, in a world where everything tends toward precision, escapes from its primitive means of expression.

Today, in a number of truly remarkable cases, even the expression of things by means of discrete signs, arbitrarily chosen, has given way to lines traced by the things themselves, or to transpositions or inscriptions directly

Although it must be observed that the accommodation is often very far from being satisfactory— as note the definitions of point, line, relation, etc.

There has been no philosophy (thus far) that could withstand a precise examination of its definitions.

derived from them. The great invention that consists in making the laws of science visible to the eyes and, as it were, readable on sight has been incorporated into knowledge; and it has in some sort overlaid the world of experience with a visible world of curves, surfaces, and diagrams that translate properties into forms whose inflexions we can follow with our eyes, thus by our consciousness of this movement gaining an impression of values in transition. The *graph* has a continuity of movement that cannot be rendered in speech, and it is superior to speech in immediacy and precision. Doubtless it was speech that commanded the method to exist; doubtless it is now speech that assigns a meaning to the graphs and interprets them; but it is no longer by speech that the act of mental possession is consummated. Something new is little by little taking shape under our eyes; a sort of ideography of plotted and diagramed relations between qualities and quantities, a language that has for grammar a body of preliminary conventions (scales, coordinates, base lines, etc.), and for logic the relative size of figures or portions of figures and their relative situations on a chart.

—as well as a system of analogies.

An altogether different system of representation, but one that has certain analogies with that of graphs, is offered by the art of music. We know what an untold depth of resources exists in the *universe of sounds*; we know what *immediate presence* of all the affective life—what intuitions of the labyrinthine patterns, interminglings, and superpositions of memory, doubt, and affective impulses; what forces, what fictive lives, and deaths—are communicated, are imposed on us, by the skills of the composer. Sometimes the design and modulation are so in accord with the inner laws of our changing moods that they make us dream of their being exact *auditive formulas* of those moods, capable of serving as models for an objective study of the most subtle subjective phenomena. In this type of research, no verbal description could approach the effects produced by these auditive images, for they are transformations and restitutions of the vital states they transmit, even if they are presented—*since we are dealing with an art*—as the arbitrary creations of an individual.

There is much to be said about the arbitrary.
Everything we do that is arbitrary in our

From such examples we see that simultaneous groups and continued series of auditive sensations can be linked with what are supposed to be the *deepest* modes of thought—that is to say, those furthest from the language of philosophic thought. And we see how the most precious part of all that the latter may contain or perceive—the part it communicates so imperfectly—is if not transmitted at least suggested by what are not in the least its traditional methods.

Philosophy has always sought, however, and will put forth greater and greater efforts, to protect itself against *the danger of seeming to have a purely verbal aim. Consciousness of the self,* which, under various names, is its principal means of existence (as well as an ever present occasion for skepticism and self-destruction), keeps reminding philosophy of its inner vigor and necessity, but also of all the weakness it owes to its dependence on speech. That is why almost all philosophers insist, in their different manners, on distinguishing their thoughts from any accepted convention. Some, being particularly sensitive to what is produced and continually transformed in their inner worlds, are concerned with a region on *the hither side of language,*

own eyes—as, for example, letting the hand make random designs on a scrap of paper—is a more or less separate activity of some organ. We close our eyes in order to draw a card from a hat at random. Such acts, analogous to lapses of attention, are the opposite of our consciously controlled activities. All this can be expressed by the simple proposition that the degree of consciousness required by an act can be measured by the number of independent conditions imposed on it.

They have never done so, however—

155

or not to my know-
ledge—by starting
with an analysis of
language that would
reduce it to its
statistical nature, and
hence would permit
them not to attribute
verbal creations
(including problems)
to the essence of
things—*when their*
origin lies in the
ingenuousness, the
poetic sentiment, or
the gropings and
fumblings of genera-
tions.
A disregard of these
humble beginnings is
doubtless the pre-
condition of more
than one philosophic
problem.
In particular the
existence of notions
capable of being inter-
preted in different
fashions, or the
accidental coexistence
of terms created
independently of one
another, opens the
way for antinomies
and paradoxes that
favor a rich develop-
ment of highly

where they discover the nascent inner form that can be described as *intuition* —for our apparent or real spontaneity includes among its other contributions a number of sudden *illuminations,* instantaneous solutions, unexpected impulses and decisions. Other philosophers, less inclined to consider the changing than intent on *that which endures,* try to entrench their attitudes of thought in the language itself. They put their trust in formal laws, finding in them the very structure of the intelligible; and they hold that this is the source from which any language borrows its discontinuity and the typical forms of its propositions.

The first sort, if they further developed their tendency, might imperceptibly be carried toward the art of time and sound; they are the musicians of philosophy. The second sort, who impute to language a framework of reason and a sort of well-defined ground plan; who contemplate, one might say, all its implications as though they were simultaneous and who try to rebuild it as a substructure, or to complete as a personal superstructure this product of everyone and no one—these philosophers might be compared with architects.

I do not see why both sorts should not adopt our Leonardo, for whom painting held the place of philosophy? *"philosophic" misconceptions and subtleties.*

NOTE

This essay was written to serve as preface to a first book by Leo Ferrero, and I cannot let it be reprinted here without saying, to those who never knew the young writer, how much his loss must mean to Letters. While he was making a long trip abroad, a motor-car accident deprived us of that precious life. I have known few minds as precocious as his, and very few more subtle, quick, or sensitive. Depth, with the Italians, is not at all incompatible with liveliness and high spirits. That combination of qualities—not so much opposed to each other as they are rarely united in certain cultures—was strongly developed in Leo's case. He had a thorough-going knowledge of our language and an intuitive understanding of French authors and French ways of thought. Paris was adopting him as a son, when misfortune would have it that he must visit America, and there he was overtaken by death—of which he had written, "It is something that happens only to others."

P.V.

POE

On Poe s *Eureka*

To Lucien Fabre

I WAS TWENTY and believed in the might of human thought.
I found it a strange torment to be, and not to be. At times I
felt I had infinite forces within me. They collapsed when
faced with problems, and the weakness of my effective
powers filled me with despair. I was moody, quick, tolerant
in appearance, fundamentally hard, extreme in contempt,
absolute in admiration, easy to impress, impossible to con-
vince. I had faith in a few ideas that had come to me; I took
their conformity with my nature, which had given them
birth, to be a sure sign of their universal value. What seemed
so definite to my mind seemed also to be incontrovertible;
convictions born of desire are always the clearest.

I guarded these ghosts of ideas as my state secrets. I was
ashamed of their strangeness; I feared they might be absurd;
I knew they were absurd, and yet not so. They were futile in
themselves, but powerful by virtue of the remarkable force
which I drew from keeping them hidden. My jealous watch
over this mystery of weakness filled me with a sort of vigor.

I had ceased writing verse and almost given up reading.
Novels and poems, in my opinion, were only impure and
half-unconscious applications of a few properties inherent in
the great secrets I hoped some day to discover, basing this
hope on the unremitting assurance that they must necessarily
exist. As for the philosophers, I had read little of their work
and was irritated by that little, because they never answered
any of the questions that tormented me. They filled me only

with boredom, never with the feeling that they were communicating some verifiable power. Then too, it seemed to me useless to speculate about abstractions without first defining them. Yet what else can we do? The only hope for a philosophy is to render itself impersonal. We must still wait for this great step to be taken, shortly before the end of the world.

I had dipped into a few mystics. One can hardly speak ill of them, for what one finds in their work is only what one brings to it.

This was the point I had reached when *Eureka* fell into my hands.

My studies under drab and dismal instructors had led me to believe that science was not love; that its fruits might be useful but its bark was terribly rough and its leafage full of thorns. I consigned mathematics to a species of tiresomely exact minds, incommensurable with my own.

Literature, on the other hand, had often shocked me by its lack of discipline, coherence, and necessity in handling ideas. Frequently its object is trifling. French poetry ignores, or even fears, all the tragedies and epics of the intellect. When it sometimes ventures into that territory, it becomes bleak and boring. Neither Lucretius nor Dante was French. We simply have no poets of knowledge. Perhaps our feeling for the separation of literary genres—in other words, for the independence of the different activities of the mind—is such that we cannot tolerate the works in which they are mingled. If something can do without song, we are unable to make it sing. But our poetry, for the last hundred years, has revealed such a wealth of resources, such a rare power of renewal, that perhaps the future will not be slow to grant it some of those works, grand in style, noble in their severity, that dominate both senses and intellect.

In a few moments, *Eureka* introduced me to Newton's law, the name of Laplace, the hypothesis he proposed, and the very existence of speculations and researches that were never mentioned to adolescents—for fear, I suppose, that we might be interested, instead of measuring out the amazing length of an hour with yawning and dreaming. In those days, whatever was likely to stimulate the intellectual appetite was placed among the arcana. It was a time when thick text-books of physics had not a word to whisper about the law of gravity, or Carnot's principle, or the conservation of energy; instead they were addicted to Magdeburg hemispheres, three-branched faucets, and the tenuous theories to which they were laboriously inspired by the problem of the siphon.

And yet, would it be a waste of academic time to give young minds at least a hint of the origins, the high goal, and the living virtue of the dry calculations and barren theorems that are now inflicted on them in no logical order and even with a remarkable degree of incoherence?

These sciences, so coldly taught, were founded and developed by men with a passionate interest in them. *Eureka* made me feel some of that passion.

I confess that I was astonished and only half persuaded by the vast pretensions and ambitions of the author, the solemn tone of his preamble, and the extraordinary discussion of method with which the volume opens. Those first pages, however, brought forward a ruling idea, while presenting it in a mysterious fashion that suggested partly a feeling of helpless awe and partly a deliberate reserve, the reluctance of an enthusiastic soul to reveal its most precious secret. All this was not calculated to leave me cold.

To attain what he calls the *truth*, Poe invokes what he calls *consistency*. It is not easy to give a definition of that consistency. The author does not do so, although he must have had a clear conception of its meaning.

According to him, the *truth* he seeks can be grasped only by immediate adherence to an intuition of such nature that it renders present, and in some sort perceptible to the mind, the reciprocal dependence of the parts and properties of the system under consideration. This reciprocal dependence extends to the successive phases of the system; causality becomes symmetrical. To a point of view that embraced the totality of the universe, a cause and its effect might be taken one for the other, might be said to exchange their roles.

Two remarks at this point. The first I shall merely indicate, for it would lead us far, both the reader and myself. The doctrine of final causes plays a capital part in Poe's system. The doctrine is no longer fashionable, and I am neither able nor eager to defend it. But we must admit that our notions of cause and adaptation lead almost inevitably in that direction (not to speak of the immense difficulties, and hence of the temptations, that are offered by certain facts, such as the existence of instincts, etc.). The simplest course is to dismiss the problem. Our only resources for solving it are those of pure imagination, which might better be applied to other tasks.

Let us pass to the second remark. In Poe's system, *consistency* is both the means of discovery and the discovery itself. Here is an admirable conception: an example and application of reciprocal adaptation. Poe's universe is formed on a plan the profound symmetry of which is present, to some degree, in the inner structure of our minds. Hence the poetic instinct should lead us blindly to the truth.

Fairly often one meets with analogous ideas among the mathematicians. They come to regard their discoveries not as "creations" of their mathematical faculties, but rather as booty seized by their attention from a treasure house of preexistent and natural forms, one that becomes accessible only through a rare conjunction of disciplined effort, sensibility, and desire.

All the consequences developed in *Eureka* are not deduced with the precision, or explained with the degree of clarity, that one might desire. There are dark places and lacunae. There are interventions inadequately explained. There is a God.

For a spectator of the drama and comedy of the intellect, nothing is more interesting than to observe the ingenuity, the insistency, the trickery and anxiety of an inventor at grips with his invention. He is admirably aware of all its defects. Necessarily he would like to display all its beauties, exploit its advantages, conceal its poverty, and at any cost make it the image of what he desires. A merchant dresses up his merchandise. A woman improves herself in front of the mirror. Preachers, philosophers, politicians, and, in general, all those who undertake to propound uncertainties, are always a mixture of sincerity and reticence (on the most favorable assumption). What they do not like to consider, they do not wish us to see. . . .

The fundamental idea of *Eureka* is nonetheless a profound and sovereign idea.

It would not be exaggerating its scope to recognize, in Poe's theory of consistency, a fairly shrewd attempt to define the universe in terms of its *intrinsic properties*. There is a proposition to be found in Chapter Eight of *Eureka*: *Each law of nature depends at all points on all the other laws.* Is this not a formula for generalized relativity, at least the expression of a will toward it?

That this tendency approaches recent conceptions becomes evident when, in the *poem* under discussion, we find an affirmation of the symmetrical and reciprocal relationship of matter, time, space, gravity, and light. I emphasize the word symmetrical, for *the essential characteristic of Einstein's universe is, in effect, its formal symmetry.* Therein lies its beauty.

But Poe does not confine himself to the physical constituents of phenomena. He introduces life and consciousness into his plan. How many things this brings to mind! The time is past when one could easily distinguish between the material and the spiritual. Formerly all discussion was based on the complete knowledge of "matter" that we claimed to possess; in a word, it was based on *appearance*.

The appearance of matter is that of a dead substance, a *potentiality* that becomes *activity* only through the intervention of something exterior and entirely foreign to its nature. From that definition, inevitable consequences used to be drawn. But the look of matter has changed. Our former picture of it was derived from pure observation; experiments have led to a wholly different conception. By creating, as it were, *relays* for our senses, modern physics has persuaded us that our ancient definition had no absolute or speculative value. We find that matter is strangely diverse and endlessly surprising; that it is an assemblage of transformations which continue on a smaller scale until they are lost in smallness, in the very abysses of smallness; we learn that perpetual motion is perhaps realized. There is an eternal fever in substances.

At present we no longer know what a fragment of any given substance may or may not contain or produce, now or in the future. The very idea of matter is distinguished as little as you will from that of energy. Everything at a deeper level consists of agitations, rotations, exchanges, radiations. Our own eyes, our hands, our nerves, are made of such things; and the appearances of death or sleep at first presented by matter, by its passivity and surrender to external forces, are conceptions built up in our senses, like the shadows obtained by a certain superposition of lights.

All this can be summarized in the statement that the properties of matter seem to depend only on the order of size in which we place the observer. But it follows that the classical attributes of matter—its lack of spontaneity, its essential difference from movement, and the continuity or homogeneity of its texture—are merely superficial and can no longer be absolutely contrasted with such concepts as life, sensibility, or thought. Within the category of size in which rough observations are made, all former definitions prove incorrect. We are certain that unknown properties and forces are exerted in the *infra-world*, since we have discovered a few that our senses were not designed to perceive. But we can neither enumerate those properties and forces nor assign a definite number to the increasing plurality of chapters in the science of physics. We cannot even be sure that most of our concepts are not illusory, when transported into the realms that limit and support our own. To speak of iron or hydrogen is to presuppose entities the existence and permanence of which can only be inferred from experiments of very limited extent and duration. Moreover, there is no reason to believe that our space, our time, and our causality preserve any meaning whatever in those realms where the existence of our bodies is *impossible*. Naturally the man who attempts to picture the inner reality of objects can only apply to it the ordinary categories of his thinking. But the more he pursues his researches and, in some measure, the more he increases his ability to record phenomena, the farther he travels from what might be called the *optimum* of his perceptions. Determinism is lost among inextricable systems, with billions of variables, where the mind's eye can no longer trace the operation of laws and come to rest on some durable fact. When discontinuity becomes the rule, the imagination, which was once employed in giving final form to a truth guessed at by one's perceptions and woven into a single piece by one's reasoning, must confess to being helpless. When *averages* become the objects of our judgments, we are ceasing to consider events in themselves. Our knowledge is tending toward power and has turned aside from a coordinated contemplation of things; prodigies of mathematical subtlety are required to restore some degree of unity to it. We have stopped talking about first principles, and physical laws have become mere instruments, always capable of being improved. They no longer govern the world, but are matched with the weakness of our minds; we can no longer rely on their simplicity; always, like a persistent point, there is some unresolved decimal that brings us back to a feeling of uneasiness, a sense of the inexhaustible.

One can see from these remarks that Poe's intuitions regarding the general nature of the physical, moral, and metaphysical universe are neither proved nor disproved by the extremely numerous and important discoveries made since 1847. Some of his views might even be incorporated, without too much effort, into fairly recent conceptions. When he measures the duration of his Cosmos by the time necessary to realize all possible combinations of the elements, one

thinks of Boltzmann's theories and his estimates of probability as applied to the kinetic theory of gas. Carnot's
principle—the second law of thermodynamics—is also foreshadowed in *Eureka*, and is the representation of that principle
by the mechanics of diffusion. The author seems to have been
a precursor of those bold spirits who would rescue the
universe from certain death by means of an infinitely brief
passage through an infinitely improbable state.

Since it is not my present intention to make a complete
analysis of *Eureka*, I shall have very little to say about the
author's use of the nebular hypothesis. When Laplace
advanced the theory, his object was limited. He proposed
only to reconstitute the development of the solar system. He
assumed the existence of a gaseous mass in the process of
cooling. The core of the mass had already reached a high
degree of concentration, and the whole rotated on an axis
passing through its center of gravity. He assumed the existence of gravity, as well as the invariability of mechanical
laws, and made it his sole task to explain the direction of
rotation of the planets and their satellites, the slight eccen-
tricity of their orbits, and the relatively slight degree of
inclination. In these conditions, being subjected to centrifugal force and the process of cooling, matter would flow
from the poles toward the equator of the mass and, at the
points where gravity and centrifugal acceleration balanced
each other, would be disposed in a zone. Thus a nebulous
ring was formed; it would soon be broken, and the fragments
of the ring would finally coalesce to form a planet. . . .

Readers of *Eureka* will see how Poe has extended the application of both the nebular hypothesis and the law of gravity.
On these mathematical foundations he has built an abstract

poem, one of the rare modern examples of a total explanation of the material and spiritual universe, a *cosmogony*.

It belongs to a department of literature remarkable for its persistence and astonishing in its variety; cosmogony is one of the most ancient literary forms.

One might say that the world itself is not much older than the art of making the world. Had we a little more learning and much more intellectual brilliance, we might employ these books of genesis, whether they come from India, China, or Chaldea, whether they belong to the Greeks, to Moses, or to the late Svante Arrhenius, as standards to measure the intellectual innocence of each historical era. We should find, beyond a doubt, that the naïveté of the conception is a constant, but we should have to confess that the art varies exceedingly.

Just as tragedy touches on history and psychology, so does the cosmogonic form touch on religion, with which it is confused at many points, and on science, from which it is necessarily distinguished by the absence of experimental proof. It includes sacred books, splendid poems, outlandish narratives full of beauty and nonsense, and physico-mathematical researches often so profound as to be worthy of a less insignificant object than the universe. But it is the glory of man to waste his powers on the void, and it is something more than that. Often such crack-brained researches lead to unforeseen discoveries. The role of the non-existent exists; the function of the imaginary is real; and we learn from strict logic that *the false implies the true*. One might say that the history of thought could be summarized in these words: *It is absurd by what it seeks, great by what it finds*.

The problem of the totality of things, and of the origin

of this whole, arises from a very simple state of mind. We want to know what came before light; or perhaps we try to find whether one particular combination of ideas might not take precedence over all others and engender the system which is their source, meaning the world, and their author, who is ourselves.

Whether we dream of an infinitely imperious Voice, somehow shattering eternity, its first cry announcing Space, like tidings that grow ever more pregnant with consequences as they are carried toward the uttermost limits of the creative will, and the divine Word making a place for essences, for life, for liberty, for the fatal contest between law and reason, between law and chance; or whether (if we hesitate to launch ourselves from pure nothingness toward any imaginable state) we find that the first era of the world is a little easier to contemplate in the vague idea of a mixture of matter and energy, composing a sort of substantial but neutral and powerless mud, which endlessly awaits the act of a demiurge; or finally, whether, more profound, better equipped but no less eager for marvels, we invoke the aid of all the sciences to reconstruct the earliest possible condition of the system that is the subject of every science—in any case our idea of the origin of things is never more than a daydream based on their present disposition, in some sort a degeneration of the real, a variation on what is.

What do we actually need before we can think of this origin?

If we need the idea of nothingness, the idea of nothingness is nothing—or rather it is already something: it is a pretense of the mind, which plays a comedy of silence and perfect shadows, in the midst of which I know that I lie hidden and ready to create, simply by relaxing my attention; I feel myself to be present, and indispensable, and endowed with will, so that I may preserve, by a conscious act, this ephemeral absence of all images and this apparent nullity. But it is an image and it is an act; I call myself *Nothingness* by a momentary convention.

Or, if the idea I choose to place at the origin of all things is that of an extreme disorder, extending to the smallest particles of existence, I can easily see that the inconceivable chaos is ordained by my purpose of conception. I jumbled the cards myself, for the joy of arranging them later. And besides, to define a disorder so confused that one could neither discover the slightest trace of order nor substitute another chaos more thorough and more advanced would be a masterpiece of art and logic. A confusion that truly lies at the beginning of things must be an infinite confusion. But in that case we cannot derive the world from it, and the very perfection of the chaos renders its use forever impossible.

As for the idea of a beginning—I mean an absolute beginning—it is necessarily a myth. Every beginning is a coincidence; we must picture it as some sort of contact between all and nothing. In trying to think of it, we find that every beginning is a consequence—every beginning *completes* something.

But principally we need the idea of that Whole we call the universe, the beginning of which we desire to know. Even before we start to puzzle over the problem of its origin, let us see whether the very notion of a universe, which seems to impose itself on our minds, and which we find so simple and inevitable, will not disintegrate under our eyes.

We imagine vaguely that the *Whole* is *something* and, imagining *something*, we call it the *Whole*. We tell ourselves that it began as all things begin, and that the beginning of the

Whole, which must have been much stranger and more impressive than that of the parts, must also be infinitely more important to know. We form an idol of totality, and an idol of its origin, and we cannot refuse our assent to the reality of a certain body of nature, whose unity corresponds to another unity of which we are firmly assured—our own.

Such is the primitive, almost childish, form of our idea of the universe. It is very natural, in other words, very impure. We must examine it more closely and ask ourselves whether this notion could be part of any but a misleading chain of argument.

I shall observe in myself what I think under this head.

A first sort of universe is offered to me by the aggregation composed of all the things I see. My eyes guide my vision from place to place and everywhere find impressions. My vision stimulates the mobility of my eyes, by which it is continually sharpened, broadened, and deepened. There is no movement of the eyes that encounters a region of invisibility; there is none that does not give rise to colored effects. All the movements are mutually connected and prolonged, they absorb or correspond to one another, and they enclose me, as it were, in my own power of perceiving. All the diversity of my visual perceptions is harmonized in the unity of my directing consciousness.

I acquire the general and constant impression that a sphere of simultaneity is attached to my presence. It moves along with me, and its content is indefinitely variable; but through all the substitutions it may undergo, it preserves its fullness. I may change my place, or the bodies that surround me may give way to different bodies, but the unity of my total representation, and the property it has of enclosing me, are in no wise altered. It is useless to flee from myself or attempt to escape in any direction; I am always enveloped by all the *seeing-movements* of my body, which are transformed one into another and which irresistibly take me back to the same central situation.

Thus I see a *whole*. I say that it is a Whole because in a manner it takes up all my capacity for seeing. My vision is confined to this enclosed form and to the juxtaposition that surrounds me. All my other sensations have reference to some spot within the circle, of which the center thinks and speaks.

Such is my first Universe. I am not sure that a man blind from birth could have an equally clear and immediate notion of a sum of all things, for I am convinced that the particular properties of ocular perception are essential to the formation, *by myself*, of an entire and complete domain. Sight in some measure assumes the function of simultaneity, in other words, of unity as such.

But the unity that is necessarily formed of everything I can see in an instant, this aggregation of figures or blotches reciprocally joined, from which I later disentangle depth, matter, movement, and event, this whole which I scrutinize in order to distinguish the attractive objects from the harmful ones—inspires me with the first idea, the model and, as it were, the germ of the total universe which I believe to exist around my sensations, both disguised and revealed by them. Irresistibly I imagine that an immense and hidden system supports, penetrates, nourishes, and reabsorbs every actual and sensible element of my duration, forcing it to exist and to be resolved; and that hence every moment is the focus of an infinite number of roots that plunge to an unknown depth in an *implicit space*—in the past—in the secret structure of this our machine for perceiving and combining, which returns incessantly to the *present*. The present, considered as a permanent relation among all the changes that touch me, suggests the image of a solid to which all my perceptive life is attached, as is a sea anemone to its bit of shingle. On this little stone, how am I to raise a structure outside of which nothing could exist? How am I to pass from a limited and instantaneous universe to one that is complete and absolute?

The problem would now be one of conceiving and constructing, around a real germ, a figure that would meet with two essential conditions. First, it must admit all things, be capable of all things, and represent to us all things; second, it must satisfy our intelligence, lend itself to our reasonings, and make us a little better acquainted with our situation, a little more the masters of ourselves.

But merely to specify these two needs of the intellect, to set them side by side, is enough to reveal all the insurmountable difficulties that are inherent in the slightest effort to give a workable definition of the Universe.

Universe, therefore, is only a mythological expression. The movements of our thought around the word are perfectly irregular, entirely independent. As soon as we leave the bounds of the moment, as soon as we try to increase and extend our presence outside of itself, we exhaust ourselves in our liberty. We are surrounded by all the disorder of our knowledge, of our faculties. We are besieged by what is remembered, what is possible, what is imaginable, calculable, all the combinations of our ideas in all degrees of probability, in every phase of precision. How can we form a concept of something that is opposed to nothing, rejects nothing, resembles nothing? If it resembled something, it would no longer be the whole. If it resembles nothing... And, if this totality is equivalent in power to one's mind, the mind has no hold over it. All the objections that rise against an active infinity, all the difficulties encountered when one attempts to draw order out of multiplicity, here assert themselves. No proposition can be advanced about this *subject* so disordered in its richness that all *attributes* apply to it. Just as the universe escapes intuition, in the same way it is transcendent to logic.

As for its origin—IN THE BEGINNING WAS FABLE. It will be there always.

Some Fragments from Poe's *Marginalia*

I do not know in what circumstances Poe was led to publish the Marginalia. It is not hard for me to imagine. The preamble in which he introduces them breathes the embarrassment of the author and seems to be a kind of excuse, or special plea, for a publication he would probably not even have thought of undertaking, had not some critical phase in his hapless fortunes forced him, in spite of himself, to print and give to the public these crumbs of his thought.

He scattered them at diverse periods in the Messenger, the Philadelphia Democratic Review, Graham's Magazine. . . .

Publications of this kind make me think of the story of a man whose sled is being pursued by a pack of starving wolves. To gain time and distance he throws them everything he has with him. He begins with the least precious. . . .

POE'S *MARGINALIA*

I HAVE been always solicitous of an ample margin; this not so much through any love of the thing in itself, however agreeable, as for the facility it affords me of penciling suggested thoughts, agreements, and differences of opinion, or brief critical comments in general. Where what I have to note is too much to be included within the narrow limits of a margin, I commit it to a slip of paper, and deposit it between the leaves; taking care to

One may see in these preliminary explanations the seed of a theory of notes. Although not in the margins of my books, and almost never concerning what I have read, I have spent my life noting down what has come to my mind, above all what has seemed to me the most prevail-

*ing and most import-
ant observations
about the mind itself,
that is to say, my
own mind's func-
tioning.
Many people write
down their thoughts
and recollections, and
make of their note-
books a memorandum,
a confidential friend,
a mirror, a shedding
process. Often a
chance succession of
events or some per-
sonal accident yields
up strange treasures.
Astonishing confes-
sions, impressions of
amazing sincerity or
perversity are brought
to light. There are
men who dare to
write what they
almost dare not think.*

*This sketch of a
theory of form would
require rigorous*

secure it by an imperceptible portion
of gum-tragacanth paste.

All this may be whim; it may be
not only a very hackneyed, but a very
idle practice; yet I persist in it still;
and it affords me pleasure. . . .

This making of notes, however, is
by no means the making of mere
memoranda—a custom which has its
disadvantages, beyond doubt. "Ce
que je mets sur papier," says Bernardin
de St.-Pierre, "je remets de ma
mémoire, et par conséquent je
l'oublie";—and, in fact, if you wish to
forget anything on the spot, make a
note that this thing is to be remembered.

But the purely marginal jottings,
done with no eye to the Memorandum
Book, have a distinct complexion, and
not only a distinct purpose, but none at
all; this it is which imparts to them a
value. They have a rank somewhat
above the chance and desultory comments of literary chitchat—for these
latter are not unfrequently "talk for
talk's sake,". . . while the *marginalia* are
deliberately penciled, because the mind
of the reader wishes to unburthen
itself of a *thought*—however flippant,
however silly, however trivial—still a
thought indeed, not merely a thing

that might have been a thought in time, and under more favorable circumstances. In the *marginalia*, too, we talk only to ourselves; we therefore talk freshly, boldly, originally, with *abandonnement*, without conceit, much after the fashion of Jeremy Taylor, and Sir Thomas Browne, and Sir William Temple, and the anatomical Burton, and that most logical analogist, Butler, and some other people of the old day, who were too full of their matter to have any room for their manner, which, being thus left out of question, was a capital manner indeed—a model of manners, with a richly marginalic air.

The circumscription of space, too, in these pencilings, has in it something more of advantage than inconvenience. It compels us (whatever diffuseness of idea we may clandestinely entertain) into Montesquieu-ism, into Tacitus-ism...or even Carlyle-ism....

During a rainy afternoon, not long ago, being in a mood too listless for continuous study, I sought relief from *ennui* in dipping here and there at random among the volumes of my library—no very large one certainly, but sufficiently miscellaneous; and, I flatter myself, not a little *recherché*.

discussion.
The artist moves between spontaneousness and elaboration. The former does not always have the virtues which common opinion attributes to it a priori.
Moreover, he who in unguarded moments and in his impromptu talk is favored with happy discoveries, and invents forms and models of an original nature—is generally the same *as he whose pains and prolonged attention will finally produce at least the* same *effects.*
A powerful mind seeks to obtain from itself by conscious labor the results that are analogous to those it has sometimes been able to produce by *the very fact that it was not concerned to attain them.*

Perhaps it was what the Germans call the "brain-scattering" humor of the moment; but, while the picturesqueness of the numerous pencil-scratches arrested my attention, the helter-skelter of their commentary amused me. I found myself at length forming a wish that it had been some other hand than my own which had so bedeviled the books, and fancying that, in such case, I might have derived no inconsiderable pleasure from turning them over. From this the transition-thought... was natural enough—there might be something even in *my* scribblings which, for the mere sake of scribbling, would have interest for others.

The main difficulty concerned the mode of transferring the notes from the volumes—the context from the text—without detriment to that exceedingly frail fabric of intelligibility in which the context was imbedded. With all appliances to boot, with the printed pages at their back, the commentaries were too often like Dodona's oracles—or those of Lycophron Tenebrosus—or the essays of the pedant's pupils in Quintilian, which were "necessarily excellent, since even he (the pedant) found it impossible to

There are many works whose true value lies in the notes that accompany them.
One might observe in this regard that the attentive reading of a book is really a

comprehend them": what, then, would become of it—this context—if transferred? if translated?...

I concluded at length to put extensive faith in the acumen and imagination of the reader—this is a general rule. But, in some instances, where even faith would not remove mountains, there seemed no safer plan than so to remodel the note as to convey at least the ghost of a conception as to what it was all about. Where, for such conception, the text itself was absolutely necessary, I could quote it; where the title of the book commented upon was indispensable, I could name it. In short, like a novel-hero dilemma'd, I made up my mind "to be guided by circumstances," in default of more satisfactory rules of conduct.

As for the multitudinous opinion expressed in the subjoined farrago—as for my present assent to all or dissent from any portion of it—as to the possibility of my having in some instances altered my mind—or as to the impossibility of my not having altered it often—these are points upon which I say nothing, because upon these there can be nothing cleverly said.

continuous commentary, a succession of notes that emanate from the inner voice. Marginal notes represent part of the notations of pure thought.

The value of a work for a given reader is commensurate with the importance of these parallel reactions to his reading. The work may finally be judged a very bad one; if the notes in question have been numerous and explicit, the book has proved its value as a stimulant.

Poe stops at the very moment when he was about to develop the most interesting

*reflections of his
preamble.
The multitude of
disordered thoughts,
the purposeful glance
which confirms some,
dissolves others,
abolishes or goes
deeper here and there
into the present effect
of a number of
previous moments
that have been
recorded one by one
—no subject is more
stimulating for the
mind. The essential
object of the mind is
the mind. What it
pursues in its analyses
and its construction of
worlds, what it tracks
down in heaven and
on earth, can only be
itself. It seeks out an
idea of itself that will*
saturate it, *equal it,
exhaust all its
powers, or reflect its
true image. But
nothing informs it
more clearly of the*
transcendence *of its
desire and its nature,*
which is desire, *than
the immediate*
spectacle *of its
contradictions and of*

the infinite ways it possesses of considering and classifying the same subject.

Concerning Expression

SOME FRENCHMAN—possibly Montaigne—says: "People talk about thinking, but for my part I never think except when I sit down to write." It is this never thinking, unless when we sit down to write, which is the cause of so much indifferent composition. But perhaps there is something more involved in the Frenchman's observation than meets the eye. It is certain that the mere act of inditing tends, in a great degree, to the logicalization of thought. Whenever, on account of its vagueness, I am dissatisfied with a conception of the brain, I resort forthwith to the pen, for the purpose of obtaining, through its aid, the necessary form, consequence, and precision.

How very commonly we hear it remarked that such and such thoughts are beyond the compass of words! I do not believe that any thought, properly so called, is out of the reach of language. I fancy, rather, that

This observation is simply a disguised definition of logic. On reflection this whole passage is imprecise. At times the unformulated thought is opposed to the thought that is expressed in words; at others, the un-written thought is opposed to the written thought. It would

perhaps be worth examining whether the same *can exist in both spheres— whether it is the same thought that is found again after being verbally treated.*

The author's assertion about logic would also need to be verified.

There is no logic without some language. But there is no logic of a language that has been formed by chance. Now ordinary language is a language formed by chance *which is not logically usable except in particular cases— cases that are particularly simple and remarkably rare.*

Logic is only rigorous if, among other conditions, every subject *can be wholly replaced by a finite, explicit group of* attributes.

Ordinary language is far from this state.

where difficulty in expression is experienced, there is, in the intellect which experiences it, a want either of deliberateness or of method. For my own part, I have never had a thought which I could not set down in words with even more distinctness than that with which I conceived it; as I have before observed, the thought is logicalized by the effort at (written) expression.

There is, however, a class of fancies, of exquisite delicacy, which are *not* thoughts, and to which, *as yet*, I have found it absolutely impossible to adapt language. I use the word "fancies" at random, and merely because I must use some word; but the idea commonly attached to the term is not even remotely applicable to the shadows of shadows in question. They seem to me rather psychal than intellectual. They arise in the soul (alas, how rarely!) only at its epochs of most intense tranquillity—when the bodily and mental health are in perfection—and at those mere points of time where the confines of the waking world blend with those of the world of dreams.

In reality, writing generally obliges us to observe in our expression the conventional forms of language, to organize in the manner of propositions the words that confusedly and concurrently occur to our minds. Now the object and effect of this method seems to me designed to determine the action of one word on another; and it obliges us in many cases to be more precise than our primitive mental production was, or needed to be. And it forces us to this very determination even when it is grossly inexact; for example, when it imposes a convergence of terms, which our inner sense suggested were only parallel.
We substitute a melody for a harmony or a dissonance. To what we have felt and intuitively formed or verified we add what

we need for that immediate psychological product to be negotiable in common linguistic values. We ourselves change into interhuman *currency what our "inner lives," that is to say, our* inhuman, extrahuman, subhuman *lives have brought forth for us. . . .*

One must never let pass an occasion to underline how poor our vocabulary is in psychological terms. Although the English language is a little less impoverished than our own in this regard, it does not allow a nicer distinction of what we would like to differentiate, what we try to designate by words like psychic, mental, intellectual. . . .

I am aware of these "fancies" only when I am upon the very brink of sleep, with the consciousness that I am so. I have satisfied myself that this condition exists but for an inappreciable point of time—yet it is crowded with these "shadows of shadows"; and for absolute thought there is demanded time's endurance. These "fancies" have in them a pleasurable ecstasy, as far beyond the most pleasurable of the world of wakefulness, or of dreams, as the heaven of the Northman theology is beyond its hell. I regard the visions, even as they arise, with an awe which, in some measure, moderates or tranquillizes the ecstasy—I so regard them, through a conviction (which seems a portion of the ecstasy itself) that this ecstasy, in itself, is of a character supernal to the human nature, is a glimpse of the spirit's outer world; and I arrive at this conclusion, if this term is at all applicable to instantaneous intuition, by a perception that the delight experienced has, as its element, but *the absoluteness of novelty*.

I say the absoluteness; for in these fancies—let me now term them psychal impressions—there is really nothing even approximate in character to impressions ordinarily received. It is as if the five senses were supplanted by five myriad others alien to mortality.

Now, so entire is my faith in the *power of words*, that at times I have believed it possible to embody even the evanescence of fancies such as I have attempted to describe. In experiments with this end in view, I have proceeded so far as, first, to control (when the bodily and mental health are good) the existence of the condition—that is to say, I can now (unless when ill), be sure that the condition will supervene, if I so wish it, at the point of time already described—of its supervention, until lately, I could never be certain even under the most favorable circumstances. I mean to

This whole fragment is remarkable for there is nothing more remarkable in the field of criticism than the absence of research and reflections about the essential question of expression. Critical judgments about literary works never take into account the difficulties that are inherent in the object which the author has striven to evoke for his readers or those with which he has contended by the very form he has chosen. The result is that the notion of technical value in literature is generally ignored. Edgar Allan Poe, who let nothing stand

187

in his mind without disturbing it with his precise questions, could not fail to touch on the essential problem of the passage from thought to language—and from formlessness to form. The rule is to resolve this problem without stating it— to resolve it by the work itself.

say, merely, that now I can be sure, when all circumstances are favorable, of the supervention of the condition, and feel even the capacity of inducing or compelling it—the favorable circumstances, however, are not the less rare, else had I compelled already the heaven into the earth.

If it were possible to realize Poe's experience and, afterwards, to be sure one had achieved it, one would then have experienced a quasi-reversible state, *a state of equilibrium between two very distinct states, and one could at will, by giving some kind of very slight impulse to* oneself, *rise towards*

I have proceeded so far, secondly, as to prevent the lapse from *the point* of which I speak—the point of blending between wakefulness and sleep—as to prevent at will, I say, the lapse from this borderground into the dominion of sleep. Not that I can *continue* the condition—not that I can render the point more than a point—but that I can startle myself from the point into wakefulness, *and thus transfer the point itself into the realm of Memory*; convey its impressions, or more properly their recollections, to a situation where (although still for a very brief period) I can survey them with the eye of analysis. For these reasons—that is to say, because I have been enabled to accomplish thus much—I do not altogether despair of embodying in words at least enough of the fancies in question to convey to certain classes of intellect a shadowy conception of their character. In saying this I am not to be understood as supposing that the fancies or psychal impressions to which I allude are confined to my individual self—are not, in a word, common to all mankind—for on this point it is quite impossible that I should form an opinion—but nothing can be more certain than that even a partial record of the impressions would startle the universal intellect of mankind, by the *supremeness of the novelty* of the material employed, and of its consequent suggestions.

fullness of knowledge or descend to unconsciousness.
Poe affirms that, finding himself at the critical point where consciousness enjoys the combined advantages of waking and dreaming, he obtains glimpses of another world in which the number of sense-dimensions is extraordinarily greater than the norm.
Here the question of truthfulness—of the value of the observation, of the effects of drugs or hypnotic substances—arises.
That there are rare *states, as there are rare metals, is a fact one cannot think of disputing.*
What can they teach us? My feeling is that they are negligible in themselves, precisely because they are rare and because those who explore them declare to us that they concern a wholly different world.

*But if such accounts
are faithful, if they
are precise, these
experiences of the
extreme poles of
consciousness can
give us some rather
valuable insights into
the conditions of
normal consciousness.*

*This final sentence
demolishes our belief.
The man of letters
appears and deval-
uates the visionary.*

In a word—should I ever write a paper on this topic, the world will be compelled to acknowledge that, at last, I have done an original thing.

Fatal Superiority

*I find a dubious
point in these pro-
found observations. It
does not appear to me
certain that a man of
supreme intelligence
must necessarily
manifest the con-
sciousness of his own
superiority, or at
least in such a way
that it irritates the
temperate intelligence
of those who are his
near equals. The
hypothesis of a mind's*

I have sometimes amused myself by endeavoring to fancy what would be the fate of an individual gifted, or rather accursed, with an intellect *very* far superior to that of his race. Of course, he would be conscious of his superiority; nor could he (if otherwise constituted as man is) help manifesting his consciousness. Thus he would make himself enemies at all points. And since his opinions and speculations would widely differ from those of *all* mankind—that he would be con- sidered a madman is evident. How horribly painful such a condition! Hell could invent no greater torture than that of being charged with abnormal weakness on account of being abnormally strong.

In like manner, nothing can be clearer than that a *very* generous spirit —*truly* feeling what all merely profess —must inevitably find itself misconceived in every direction, its motives misinterpreted. Just as extremeness of intelligence would be thought fatuity, so excess of chivalry could not fail of being looked upon as meanness in its last degree: and so on with other virtues. This subject is a painful one indeed. That individuals *have* so

general superiority implies the ability to foresee the fatal consequences of its manifestation. This very great mind would be able to hide within itself. It would easily know moreover that superiority of a purely mental kind is also purely subjective. It is external power alone which permits us to distinguish between two theories *that are equally distant from common opinion. I do not believe that the psychiatrists of today choose their madmen from among those whose* ideas *differ from the ideas of the average. The enterprises of science have made common sense into a system of provisional naïvetés. The developments of literature have accustomed us to consider incoherence as a simple fact which at times can be put to use. A statement, the terms of which are*

drawn by lot: such
is the elementary
form of every mind.
A madman is not
defined by the contents
of his thoughts but
by the judgment he
makes about the
value of these con-
tents, by the illegiti-
mate powers a thought
usurps.
This idea is essen-
tially "romantic,"
cf. the English
Romantics, the
Stendhal who con-
ceived Lamiel,
Balzac, Sue, Dumas,
Hugo, Mérimée, etc.
Vautrin, Monte
Cristo, Quasimodo,
Valjean...
It is nevertheless
"popular." No one
is more popular,
more romantic, than
a great criminal. As
for madmen, they
have had an immense
role in history. They
raised the Pyramids,
and brought about a
few other grandiose
achievements. Not
all of them ended as
wretchedly as Poe
asserts.

soared above the plane of their race is scarcely to be questioned; but, in looking back through history for traces of their existence, we should pass over all biographies of "the good and great," while we search carefully the slight records of wretches who died in prison, in Bedlam, or upon the gallows.

192

The Place of Baudelaire

BAUDELAIRE'S fame is now at its height.

The small volume of *Les Fleurs du mal*, containing less than three hundred pages, stands as high in literary esteem as the most celebrated and imposing works. It has been translated into most European languages: this is a fact on which I shall dwell for a moment since it is, I believe, without parallel in the history of French literature.

French poets are generally little known and appreciated abroad. We are more readily given the advantage in prose; but poetic power is sparingly and reluctantly allowed us. The order and the kind of strictness that have ruled our language since the seventeenth century, our particular accentuation, our strict prosody, our taste for simplification and immediate clarity, our fear of overstatement and bathos, a sort of modesty of expression and an abstract tendency of mind have created a poetry which differs considerably from that of other nations and to which foreigners most often remain insensitive. La Fontaine seems to them insipid. Racine is forbidden ground: his harmonies are too subtle, his design too pure, his language too elegant and finely shaped for those who lack an intimate and native knowledge of our tongue. Even Victor Hugo's name has scarcely spread beyond France except for his novels.

But with Baudelaire, French poetry at last has gone beyond our frontiers. It has come to be read throughout the world; it has taken its place as the true poetry of modernity; it has provoked imitation, it has nurtured many minds. Men like Swinburne, Gabriele d'Annunzio, and Stéfan George bear splendid witness to the widespread influence of Baudelaire.

I can therefore say that, although there are French poets who are greater and more richly gifted than he, there is none who is more *important*.

What explains this extraordinary importance? How could a man who was so peculiar, so far from the average, engender so extensive a movement?

His great posthumous reputation, his spiritual richness, his fame now reaching its highest period, must depend not only on his own value as a poet but also on exceptional circumstances. Critical intelligence allied to the gift of poetry is one such circumstance. To this rare combination Baudelaire owes a capital discovery. He was born sensuous and precise; his demanding sensibility led him to pursue the most refined experiments in form; but these gifts would doubtless have made him no more than a rival of Gautier, or an excellent Parnassian, had his curiosity of mind not earned him the good fortune of discovering in Edgar Allan Poe a new intellectual world. The daemon of lucidity; the genius of analysis; the inventor of the newest, most seductive combinations of logic and imagination, of calculation and mystical fervor; the psychologist of the exceptional; the literary engineer who had studied and utilized all the resources of art: thus Poe stood revealed to him and filled him with wonder. So many original views and extraordinary promises bewitched him; his talent was transformed, his destiny splendidly changed.

I shall return shortly to the effects of this magic confrontation of two minds. But now I must consider a second remarkable circumstance in the making of Baudelaire.

He reached manhood at a time when the star of Romanticism was at its height; a dazzling generation had appropriated the empire of Letters. Lamartine, Hugo, Musset, Vigny were the masters of the moment.

Let us put ourselves in the place of a young man who is about to begin writing in 1840. He has been brought up on artists whom an imperious instinct commands him to blot out. His literary vocation has been awakened and nourished by them, inspired by their glory, shaped by their works, yet his survival necessarily calls for the denial, overthrow, and replacement of these same men who appear to him to occupy the whole expanse of fame: one who appears to exclude him from the world of form, another from that of feeling, a third from the picturesque, a fourth from depth of meaning.

He has to make himself distinct at any cost from a group of great poets, all vigorously flourishing in the same period, who have been brought together by an exceptional stroke of chance.

Thus Baudelaire's problem might have—indeed, must have—posed itself in these terms: "How to be a great poet, but neither a Lamartine nor a Hugo nor a Musset." I do not say that these words were consciously formulated, but they must have been latent in Baudelaire's mind; they even constituted what was the essential Baudelaire. They were his *raison d'État*. In the domain of creation, which is also the domain of pride, the need to come out and be distinct is part of life itself. Baudelaire wrote in the preface he planned for *Les Fleurs du mal*: "Illustrious poets had long shared among themselves the most abundantly flourishing provinces of the domain of poetry...*I shall therefore do otherwise....*"

In short, he was led, constrained by his state of mind and

the given conditions, to come into increasingly direct conflict with the system, or lack of system, called Romanticism.

I shall not define the term. To attempt to do so would mean dispensing with all sense of precision. My present concern is merely to evoke the most probable reactions and intuitions of our poet in his "nascent state," when faced with the literature of his age. Baudelaire received from it a certain impression that we may reconstitute without much trouble. Indeed, thanks to the passage of time and to later literary developments—thanks even to Baudelaire, to his work and its success—we have a sure and simple means of bringing a little precision to our necessarily vague, at times conventional, at times completely arbitrary idea of Romanticism. *This means consists of observing what followed Romanticism*, what modified it, corrected and contradicted it, and finally took its place. It is sufficient to consider the movements and works that came after it, in opposition to it, and which inevitably, automatically, were *exact responses* to what it was. Considered in this light, Romanticism was, then, what Naturalism contradicted and the forces of the Parnassians rallied against; likewise it was what determined Baudelaire's particular attitude. It was what roused almost simultaneously against itself the will to perfection—the mysticism of "art for art's sake"—the demand for observation and the impersonal expression of things; *the desire*, in a word, *for a denser substance*, and for *a subtler, purer form*. Nothing tells us more about the Romantics than the whole complex of programs and tendencies of their successors.

Perhaps the vices of Romanticism are only the excesses that always accompany self-confidence?...The puberty of innovation is always presumptuous. Wisdom, calculation and, in a word, perfection only appear when resources must be sparingly used.

However this may be, a period of scrupulousness began about the time when Baudelaire was a young man. Gautier had already protested and reacted against the relaxation of formal requirements and the meager resources of language or its improper use. Soon, each in his own way, Sainte Beuve, Flaubert, and Leconte de Lisle were to react against impassioned facility, inconsistency of style, bizarre and puerile excesses.... Parnassians and Realists agreed to surrender the outward show of intensity, abundance, oratorical impetus for greater depth, truth, and technical and intellectual quality.

To sum up, I would say that the displacement of Romanticism by these various "schools" may be seen as the substitution of spontaneous action by consciously considered action.

Romantic compositions, *in general*, stand up rather badly to a close reading which subjects them to the recalcitrance of a refined and fastidious reader.

Baudelaire was such a reader. Baudelaire had the greatest interest—a vital interest—in observing, recording, exaggerating to himself all the weaknesses and failings of Romanticism that he observed at close hand in the works and personalities of its greatest men. *Romanticism is in its prime*, he might have told himself, *so it is mortal*; and he was able to consider the gods and demigods of his time with the estranged eyes of Talleyrand and Metternich when, about 1807, they looked on the master of the world....

Baudelaire considered Victor Hugo; and it is not impossible to imagine what he thought of him. Hugo was enthroned; over Lamartine he had the advantage of infinitely more powerful and more precise *materials*. The vast range of his vocabulary, the diversity of his rhythms, the super-abundance of his images, overwhelmed all rival poetry. But his work was sometimes compromised by vulgarity, and spent itself in orphetic eloquence and endless apostrophe. He flirted with the crowd, he exchanged dialogues with God. The simplicity of his philosophy, the excess and incoherence of his developments, the frequent contradiction between marvels of detail and rickety themes, and the inconsistency of the whole, in short everything that might scandalize, and thereby instruct and guide a pitiless young observer in the way of his own future art: all these things Baudelaire must have recorded in his mind, distinguishing the admiration forced upon him by Hugo's wonderful gifts from the impurities, the imprudences, the vulnerable points of his work—that is to say, the chances for life and fame that so great an artist left behind him to be gleaned.

By applying a little more mischief and a little more ingenuity than is called for, it would be only too tempting to compare Victor Hugo's poetry and Baudelaire's, with a view to showing how exactly the one is *complementary* to the other. I shall not labor the point. It is sufficiently clear that Baudelaire sought to do what Hugo had not done; that he refrained from all the effects at which Hugo was unsur-passable; that he returned to a less free prosody scrupulously removed from prose; that he pursued and almost always succeeded in achieving a *continuous sensuous charm*, that inestimable and, as it were, transcendent quality of certain poems—yet a quality seldom found, and then rarely in a pure state, in Hugo's immense output.

Moreover, Baudelaire did not know, or scarcely knew, the later Victor Hugo, the poet of extreme lapses and supreme beauties. *La Légende des siècles* appeared two years after *Les Fleurs du mal*. As for Hugo's later works, they were published long after Baudelaire's death. With regard to their technique, I ascribe to them an infinitely greater importance than all Hugo's other poems. This is not the place, nor have I the time, to expand this statement. I shall merely sketch a possible digression. What strikes me in Victor Hugo is his incomparable vitality. Vitality is a combination of longevity and capacity for work—longevity *multiplied by* capacity for work. For more than sixty years this extraordinary man was at his desk every day from five o'clock until noon! He unremittingly called up new combinations of language, willed them, waited for them, and had the satisfaction of hearing them respond to his call. He wrote one or two hundred thousand lines of poetry and acquired by that uninterrupted exercise a curious manner of thinking which superficial critics have judged as best they could. But, in the course of this long career, Hugo never tired of perfecting and fortifying himself in his art. Doubtless he sinned more and more against the need to select, he increasingly lost the feeling for proportion, he swelled up his verse with an indeterminate, vague, and vertiginous vocabulary; and so abundantly and facilely did he employ the abyss, the infinite, the absolute, that these monstrous terms lost the very appearance of profundity which usage had given them. Nevertheless, what extraordinary poems he wrote in the last period of his life—poems wholly incomparable for scope, internal organization, resonance, and amplitude! In *La Corde d'airain*, in *Dieu*, in *La Fin de Satan*, in the piece on the death of Gautier, this seventy-year-old artist—who had outlived all his rivals, who saw his work give rise to a whole generation of younger poets, and even profited from the invaluable lessons that pupils could give their masters if their masters survived—attained in his illustrious old age the pinnacle of poetic power and of the noble science of versification.

Hugo never ceased to learn through practice; Baudelaire, whose life was barely more than half as long as Hugo's, developed in quite a different way. One might say he had to compensate for the probable brevity, the prescience of this lack of time in the short life he had to live, by the use of that critical intelligence of which I have just spoken. A score of years were granted him to reach the peak of his own perfection, to determine his particular field, and to define a specific form and attitude that would bear and preserve his name.* He had not, would not have time to pursue at leisure the high goal of the creative will by means of the greatest number of experiments and a multiplicity of output. He had to choose the shortest road, to put a limit on his gropings, to avoid repetitions and divided enterprises: he had therefore to seek analytically what he was, what he was capable of, and what goal he wished to attain; and to unite the spontaneous virtues of a poet with the sagacity, the skepticism, the consciousness, and the reasoning skill of a critic.

In this sense Baudelaire, although a romantic in origin, and even in taste, can sometimes appear to be a *classic*. There are infinite ways of defining a classic, or to believe we are defining one. For today, we shall adopt the following: *a*

---

* *Je te donne ces vers afin que si mon nom*
  Aborde heureusement aux époques lointaines....

  I give you these verses so that if my name
  By some happy chance should reach a far distant time....

  [*Spleen et Idéal*, XLI]
  [P.V., as all footnotes in this section.]

classic is a writer who carries within him a critic whom he associates intimately with his work. In Racine there was a Boileau, or an image of Boileau.

After all, to *select* from Romanticism and discern in it good and bad, falsity and truth, weakness and virtue, means quite simply treating the authors of the first half of the nine-teenth century as the men of the age of Louis XIV treated the authors of the sixteenth. *All classicism presupposes a romanticism that went before.* All the advantages that are attributed to "classical" art, all the objections that are made to it, are related to this axiom. *The essence of classicism is to come after. Order* implies a certain disorder it has come to control. *Composition*, which is artifice, follows some primitive chaos of natural intuitions and developments. *Purity* is the result of endless labors on language, and care for *form* is nothing but the considered reorganization of the means of expression. "Classical" then implies conscious, voluntary acts which modify "natural" production in conformity with a *clear* and *rational* conception of man and art. But, as the sciences show us, we can only carry out rational work and build in orderly fashion by means of a system of *conventions*. Classical art is recognized by the existence, the clarity, the imperative character of these conventions; whether it be the three unities, prosodic precepts, verbal restrictions, these apparently arbitrary rules constituted its force and its weak-ness. Little understood today, difficult to defend and almost impossible to observe, they nevertheless have their origin in an ancient, subtle, and deep understanding of the conditions of *unadulterated* intellectual pleasure.

In mid-Romanticism Baudelaire makes us think of a classic—but he does no more than make us think of one. He died young, and he shared moreover the wretched impression left on men of his time by the unhappy survival of the old classicism of the Empire. There was no question whatsoever of breathing life into what was quite dead, but of rediscovering, perhaps by other means, the spirit that was no longer to be found in the corpse.

The Romantics had neglected practically everything that requires an effort of concentration and deduction. They sought the effects of shock, enthusiasm, and contrast. Neither measure nor rigor nor depth preoccupied them excessively. They were averse to abstract thought and reasoning, not only in their works, but also in the preparation of their works, which is infinitely more serious. One might have thought that the French had forgotten their analytical talents. It should be noted here that the Romantics were reacting against the eighteenth century much more than the seventeenth, and readily brought charges of superficiality against men who were infinitely more learned, more curious of facts and ideas, more solicitous of precision and thought on a grand scale than they ever were themselves.

At a time when science was about to experience extraordinary developments, Romanticism manifested an antiscientific state of mind. Passion and inspiration were persuaded that nothing was needed beyond themselves.

But, under quite another sky, among a people that were wholly concerned with their material development, still indifferent to the past, organizing their future and allowing the most complete freedom for experiments of every kind, there lived about this same time a man who had considered the things of the mind, including literary production, with a precision, a sagacity, a lucidity such as had never to this degree been encountered in a head gifted for poetic invention. Before Poe the problem of literature had never been examined in its premises, reduced to a psychological problem, and approached by means of an analysis that deliberately used logic and the mechanics of effect. For the first time the relationship between the work and the reader was made clear and proposed as the actual foundation of art. His analysis—and this circumstance assures us of its value—can be applied and just as clearly verified in every kind of literary production. The same observations, the same distinctions, the same quantitative remarks, the same guiding ideas can be adapted with equal success to works meant to act powerfully and crudely on the sensibility and win an audience that likes strong emotions or strange adventures, as to the most refined types of literature and the delicate organization of the products of the poet's mind.

To say that this analysis holds good for both the tale and the poem, that it applies to the construction of the imaginary and the fantastic as it does to the reconstitution and literary representation of an apparent reality, indicates that its scope is remarkable. What distinguishes a truly general law is its fertility. To reach a point which allows us to dominate a whole field of activity necessarily means that one perceives a quantity of possibilities—unexplored domains, roads to be traced, land to be exploited, cities to be built, relations to be established, processes to be extended. It is therefore not surprising that Poe, possessing so effective and sure a method, became the inventor of several different literary forms; that he provided the first and most striking examples of the scientific tale, of a modern cosmogonic poem, of the novel of criminal investigation, of literature that portrays morbid psychological states; and that all his work presents on every page the act and exigency of an intelligence the like of which is not to be observed to the same degree in any other literary career.

This great man would today be completely forgotten if Baudelaire had not taken up the task of introducing him into European literature. Let us not fail to observe here that Poe's universal fame is dimmed or dubious only in his native country and in England. This Anglo-Saxon poet is strangely neglected by his fellow countrymen.

We may make a further observation: *Baudelaire and Edgar Allan Poe exchanged values.* Each gave to the other what he had, and received from the other what he had not. One communicated to the other a whole system of new and profound thought. He enlightened him, enriched him, determined his opinions on a number of subjects: the philosophy of composition, the theory of the artificial, the comprehension and condemnation of the modern, the importance of the exceptional and of a certain strangeness, an aristocratic attitude, mystical fervor, a taste for elegance and precision, even politics... Every aspect of Baudelaire was impregnated, inspired, deepened by Poe.

But, in exchange for what he had taken, Baudelaire gave Poe's thought an infinite expanse. He offered it to future generations. That transcendence which changes the poet into himself, as in Mallarmé's great line,★ this was what Baudelaire's action, his translations, his prefaces, assured for the miserable shade of Edgar Allan Poe.

I shall not go into everything that literature owes to the influence of this marvellous inventor. Whether we take Jules Verne and his disciples, Gaboriau and the like, or whether, at far more sophisticated levels, we recall the productions of

★ *Tel qu'en Lui-même enfin l'éternité le change....*

To what he was in himself eternity transforms him....

Villiers de l'Isle-Adam or of Dostoevsky, it is easy to see that the *Narrative of Arthur Gordon Pym, Murders in the Rue Morgue, Ligeia,* the *Tell-Tale Heart,* are models that have been abundantly imitated, thoroughly studied, and never surpassed.

I shall merely ask myself what Baudelaire's poetry, and more generally French poetry, may owe to the discovery of the works of Poe.

Some poems in *Les Fleurs du mal* derive their sentiment and their substance from Poe's poems. Some contain lines which are exact transpositions; but I shall ignore these particular borrowings, the importance of which is, in a way, merely local.

I shall concentrate on the essential, that is to say, the very idea Poe had formed of poetry. His conception, which he set forth in various articles, was the principal factor in the modification of Baudelaire's ideas and art. The ramifications of this theory of composition in Baudelaire's mind, the lessons he deduced from it, the developments it received from his intellectual posterity—and above all its great intrinsic value —require us to pause a little to examine it.

I will not deny that Poe's reflections are founded on a certain metaphysical system he forged for himself. But this system, if it directs and dominates and suggests the theories in question, by no means penetrates them. It engenders them and explains their generation; it does not constitute them.

His ideas on poetry are expressed in a few essays, the most important (and the one which least concerns the technique of English verse) being entitled "The Poetic Principle."

Baudelaire was so deeply moved by this essay, he received so intense an impression from it, that he considered its

contents—and not merely the contents but the form itself—
as his own property.

Men cannot help appropriating what seems so exactly
made *for them* that, in spite of themselves, they look on it as
being made *by them*. . . . They tend irresistibly to take over
what suits their own person so closely; and in the very word
good, language itself confounds the notion of what is adapted
to someone and satisfies him entirely with what is a man's
possessions.

Now although Baudelaire was enlightened and obsessed
by the theory contained in "The Poetic Principle"—or,
rather, just because he was enlightened and obsessed by it—
he did not include a translation of this essay in Poe's own
works, but introduced the most interesting part of it, scarcely
altered and with the sentence order changed, into the preface
he wrote for his translation of the *Tales*. This plagiarism
would be open to discussion if its author had not himself, as
we shall see, drawn attention to it: in an article on Théophile
Gautier★ he reproduced the whole passage in question, and
prefaced it with these very clear and surprising lines: "It is
on occasion permissible, I believe, to quote from one's own
writings in order to avoid self-paraphrase. I shall therefore
repeat. . . ." The borrowed passage follows.

What then were Poe's views on poetry?

I shall sum up his ideas briefly. He analyzes the psychological conditions of a poem. In the first rank he puts those
conditions that depend on the *dimensions* of poetical works.
He gives singular importance to the considerations of their
length. He also examines the very substance of these compositions. He easily establishes that there exist a great number
of poems concerned with notions for which prose would

★ Included in *L'Art Romantique*.

have been an adequate vehicle. Neither history, science, nor morality gains when it is expounded in the language of the soul. Didactic, historical, or ethical poetry, although exemplified and consecrated by the greatest poets, combines the alien materials of discursive or empirical knowledge with the creations of the secret sensibility and the forces of passion.

Poe saw that modern poetry was destined to conform to the tendency of an age which has witnessed an increasingly sharp distinction between the modes and provinces of human activity; and that it could now entertain claim to attain its true object and produce itself, as it were, in a *pure state*.

Thus, having analyzed the conditions for poetic enjoyment, and defined *pure poetry* by way of *elimination*, Poe was opening up a way, teaching a very strict and deeply alluring doctrine, in which a kind of mathematics and a kind of mysticism became one. . . .

If we now look at *Les Fleurs du mal* as a whole and take the trouble to compare this collection with other poetic works of the same period, we shall not be surprised to find that Baudelaire's work is remarkably consistent with Poe's precepts, and thereby remarkably different from Romantic productions. *Les Fleurs du mal* contains neither historical nor legendary poems: nothing that depends on narrative. There are no philosophical orations. Politics makes no appearance. Descriptions are rare, and always *relevant*. But all is enchantment, music, powerful yet abstract sensuality. . . . *Luxe, forme et volupté*.

In Baudelaire's finest poems there is a combination of flesh and spirit, a mixture of solemnity, warmth, and bitterness, of eternity and intimacy, the rarest possible alliance of strength of will with harmony, which distinguishes them clearly from Romantic verse as well as from that of the Parnassians. The latter were not excessively gentle with Baudelaire. Leconte de Lisle reproached him with sterility. He forgot that true fertility in a poet does not consist in the number of poems he writes but rather in the scope of their effect. It is only with the passing of time that they can be judged. Today we see after more than sixty years that the resonance of Baudelaire's unique and far from copious output still fills the whole poetic sphere, that it is still present in our minds, impossible to ignore, reinforced by a remarkable number of works that derive from it, that are not its imitation but its consequences; in justice, it would therefore be necessary to add to the slender collection of *Les Fleurs du mal* a number of works of the first rank and a body of the most profound and subtle experimentation that poetry has ever undertaken. The influence of the *Poèmes antiques* and the *Poèmes barbares* has been less diverse and less extensive.

It must be recognized, however, that Leconte de Lisle's influence, had it been exerted on Baudelaire, would perhaps have dissuaded him from writing, or from retaining, some very slack lines that are to be encountered in his book. Of the fourteen lines of the sonnet "Recueillement," which is one of the most enchanting pieces in the collection, I am always surprised to observe five or six that are undeniably weak. But the first lines and the last are so magical that we do not feel the ineptitude of the central part, which we are ready to consider as null and void. None but a very great poet can effect a miracle of this kind.

A short while ago I spoke of the production of "enchantment," and I have just now pronounced the word "miracle." These are doubtless terms which must be used with discretion because of the force they possess and the ease with which they are employed; but I could only replace them by an analogy which would be so long, and perhaps so debatable, that I will be forgiven for sparing both the one who would have to develop it, and those who would have to endure it. Let me remain vague, and confine myself to suggesting what it might be. One would have to show that language contains emotive resources mingled with its practical, directly significant properties. The duty, work, and function of a poet are to bring to light and to utilize these powers of movement and enchantment, these stimulants of the emotional life and the intellectual sensibility, which ordinary language combines with the signs and means of communication of everyday superficial life. The poet, then, dedicates and sacrifices himself to the task of defining and constructing a language within the language; and this operation, which is long, difficult, and delicate, which requires the most diverse qualities of mind, and which is never finished just as it is never scientifically achievable, tends to constitute the speech of a man who is purer, more powerful and profound in his thoughts, more intense in his life, more elegant and felicitous in his speech, than any real person. This extraordinary speech we perceive and recognize in the rhythm and in the harmonies that sustain it, and that must be so intimately and even so mysteriously bound to its origins that the sound and sense, no longer separable, inexhaustibly correspond each to each in our memory.

Baudelaire's poetry owes its survival, and the ascendancy it still enjoys, to the fullness and the unusual clarity of its timbre. At times this voice gives way to rhetoric, as happened a little too frequently in the poets of the period; but it almost always preserves and develops an admirably pure melodic line and a perfectly sustained sonority that distinguish it from all prose.

In this Baudelaire reacted happily against the tendency to prosaic expression which can be observed in French poetry from the middle of the seventeenth century. It is noteworthy that the same man to whom we owe this reorientation of our poetry toward its essence is also one of the first French writers to be passionately interested in music as such. I mention this taste, which found expression in the famous articles on *Tannhäuser* and *Lohengrin*, because of the later development of the influence of music upon literature. . . . "What was baptized Symbolism may be summed up very simply in the aim common to several groups of poets of taking back from music what belonged to them. . . ."

In order to make this attempt to explain Baudelaire's present importance less imprecise and incomplete, I should now recall his worth as an art critic. He knew Delacroix and Manet. He sought to weigh the respective merits of Ingres and his rival, just as he compared the quite different "realisms" of Courbet and Manet. For the great Daumier he conceived an admiration that posterity shares. Perhaps he exaggerated the value of Constantin Guys. But, in general, his judgments were always motivated and accompanied by the subtlest and most substantial considerations about painting, and remain models of that terribly easy, and therefore terribly difficult genre, art criticism.

But Baudelaire's greatest glory, as I suggested to you at the beginning of this lecture, is undoubtedly to have engendered a few very great poets. Neither Verlaine, nor Mallarmé, nor Rimbaud would have been what they were if they had not read *Les Fleurs du mal* at a decisive age. It would be easy to point to poems in this collection which, in their form and inspiration, foreshadow certain pieces of Verlaine, Mallarmé, or Rimbaud. But these correspondences are so clear, and your attention so nearly exhausted, that I shall not go into detail. I shall confine myself to noting that clearly present and recognizable in Baudelaire are the sense of intimacy, and the powerful, uneasy mixture of mystical emotion and sensuous ardor which are developed in Verlaine, just as one may discover Rimbaud's frenzy for departure, his gesture of impatience with the world, his deep consciousness of inner sensations and their harmonic resonance that give his brief, violent work so much energy and stimulus.

As for Stéphane Mallarmé, whose earliest poems might be confused with the most condensed and beautiful compositions of *Les Fleurs du mal*, he pursued to their most intricate and ingenious consequences the formal and technical experiments of which Poe's analyses and Baudelaire's essays and commentaries had conveyed to him the passion and taught him the importance. While Verlaine and Rimbaud have continued from Baudelaire in the way of feeling and sensuousness, Mallarmé extended his influence in the realm of perfection and poetic purity.

MALLARMÉ

The Existence of Symbolism

THE MERE NAME of *Symbolism* is already an enigma for many, as if it had been chosen expressly to torment the minds of mortals. I have known persons who attributed an imaginary depth to the little word *symbol*; they meditated on it day after day in the hope of defining its mysterious resonance. But a word is a bottomless pit.

Those without literary leanings were not the only ones to be puzzled by these innocent syllables. Scholars, artists, and philosophers have sometimes revealed the same embarrassment. But as for the men who were given and still bear the proud title of "Symbolists"—the men of whom one necessarily thinks in discussing Symbolism, whose lives and works would provide the clearest possible notion of Symbolism—they never adopted the name for themselves, and never used or abused it as people came to do in the time that followed their time.

I must confess that I too have tried to define the term (and perhaps have done so at different times in different fashions). Perhaps I shall go back to those efforts in a moment, for there is no greater temptation than that of trying to resolve the nebula presented to the mind by the meaning of any abstract word. The word *Symbolism* makes some people dream of obscurity, strangeness, and excessive refinement in the arts; others find in it some indefinable aesthetic spiritualism or correspondence of the visible world with the unseen; while others think of liberties and licenses that they regard as a threat to the language, as well as to prosody, form, and common sense. Still others...but there is no limit to the suggestive power of a word. In this realm all the arbitrary tendencies of the mind can be given free rein; nobody can either disprove or confirm these different values of the word Symbolism.

After all, it is only a convention.

Conventional names of the sort often lead to misunderstandings, and these in turn to rather diverting questions, of which I find a delightful example in an anecdote related somewhere or other by the eminent astronomer Arago.

About 1840 Arago was director of the Paris Observatory. He was approached one day by a messenger from the Tuileries—an aide-de-camp or a court chamberlain—who revealed the desire of an august personage (not otherwise identified by Arago) to visit the Observatory and there enjoy a somewhat closer view of the heavens. The visit took place at the appointed hour. Arago greeted the royal guest, conducted him to the great telescope, and invited him to look through the eyepiece at the finest star in the sky; he announced, "That, Monseigneur, is Sirius." After gazing for some time, the prince raised his head and, with the air of complicity and the sly smile of a man who cannot be imposed upon, who knows there is another side to everything, murmured to the astronomer, "*Between you and me, Monsieur le Directeur, are you quite certain that this magnificent star really calls itself Sirius?*"

And so in exploring the skies of literature, in a certain region of the literary universe, which is to say in France between 1860 and 1900 (if you will), we indubitably find something there, some clearly separate system, some mass (I dare not call it luminous, in case of offending various persons) of works and authors that are distinguished from others and form a group. It would appear that the aggregate is called "Symbolism"; but, like Arago's prince, I am not quite certain that this is its real name.

The men who lived in the Middle Ages did not suspect that they were medieval, and those of the fifteenth or six-teenth century did not have engraved on their calling cards, "Messer So-and-So, of the Renaissance." The same is true of the Symbolists. That is what they are called today, not what they were.

These few remarks might help us to recognize what we are doing at this moment: we are engaged in constructing Symbolism, as others have constructed a vast number of intellectual entities, which, if they have not achieved a bodily presence, have never lacked for definitions, since everyone was at liberty to present them with a definition of his choice. We are constructing Symbolism; we are announcing its birth today at the happy age of fifty, thus permitting it to dispense with the fumbling steps of childhood, the disorders and doubts of adolescence, the problems and anxieties of early manhood. It is being born with its fortune made—perhaps, alas, after its decease. Yes, to celebrate this fiftieth birthday in 1936 is to create an entity which will always be the Symbolism of fifty years before; and the creation depends not at all on the existence in 1886 of something that was then called Symbolism. Nothing written, nothing remembered by survivors, existed under that name at the date assigned. It is marvelous to think that we are celebrating the existence fifty years ago, of something that was absent from the universe of fifty years ago. I am happy and honored to take part in the generation of a myth, in broad daylight.

Let us set to work. Let us construct Symbolism and, to be rigorous in our task, let us consult the available documents and memories. We know that between 1860 and 1900 there was certainly, in the literary universe, something. How should we undertake to isolate that something? I assume that we have formed three clear or supposedly clear notions: one that permits us to distinguish a type of work we shall describe as classic; another that will more or less define a type we shall call romantic; a third that we shall declare to be realist. Proceeding on this basis to explore and ransack the shelves of libraries, to examine the books one by one, and then to place each of them on a pile containing others of its type—classic or romantic or realist—we shall find that certain works cannot be included in our three categories. There is no place for them in any of the piles. Either they reveal characteristics quite different from those we had foreseen in our definitions, or else they mingle characteristics we had tried to separate. For example, how should we classify the little volume of *Illuminations* by Arthur Rimbaud? And where should we place Mallarmé's *L'Après-midi d'un faune*? The former is like nothing else; the latter, in point of technique and invention, includes and surpasses everything done before its time.

We are therefore tempted to make a fourth pile for these refractory works—but on what principle? We can easily ascertain that the two works have nothing in common; or, to be accurate, nothing but the identical gesture that separates each of them from our first three piles. As we continue our investigation, we meet with still more puzzling questions. Verlaine, too, brings us his specific differences; and what is there in common between Verlaine and Villiers de l'Isle-Adam, or between Maeterlinck, Moréas, and Laforgue? Perhaps we might find more affinities among Verhaeren,

Vielé-Griffin, Henri de Régnier, Albert Mockel. But Gustave Kahn? And Saint-Pol Roux? And Dujardin?

I must go back to astronomy for the image of a nebula that, when seen through a telescope, can be distinguished from other celestial objects; it has been situated and even christened. But looking through a larger telescope that brings us a little nearer to this remote system, we find it to be composed of quite separate stars that differ greatly in color, size, and brilliance. So it is that the closer one looks at our future symbolists, the more they seem to be marked by total differences, by incompatibilities in their styles, methods, preconceptions, and aesthetic ideals. We are forced to this double conclusion, that almost no unity of theories, convictions, or techniques is to be found among these authors, but that they are nonetheless related to one another, held together by something not yet visible, or at least not revealed by mere inspection of their works; on the contrary, the inspection shows that these are mutually incomparable.

What, then, is the something that holds them together, if all their possible and positive features—their doctrines, methods, their manners of feeling and execution—seem rather to separate them from each other? We could hardly be content to explain this coalescence of talents by distance alone, by a simplification resulting from the passage of time and leading to the disappearance, after fifty years, of everything that divided these individualities, while everything that identified them was emphasized. No, there is indeed something. And we know, after comparing their works and recognizing their irreconcilable differences, that the something does not reside in the obvious qualities of their art. There is no aesthetic of Symbolism. Such is the result of our first operation.

We arrive at this paradox: an event in aesthetic history that cannot be defined in aesthetic terms. The secret of their cohesion lies somewhere else. I offer one hypothesis. I suggest that in all their diversity the Symbolists were united by some negation, and by one that was independent of their temperaments and their function as artists. This negation was all they had in common, but it was essentially marked in each of them. However different they were, they recognized themselves to be identically separated from the other writers and artists of their time. No matter how much they differed, opposing one another sometimes so violently that they hurled insults, excommunications, and even challenges to the field of honor, they continued to agree on one point, which, as I said, was foreign to aesthetics. *They agreed in a common determination to reject the appeal to a majority*: they disdained to conquer the public at large. And not only did they deliberately refuse to solicit readers in quantity or number (thereby distinguishing themselves from the realists, eager for statistical glory, who reveled in big printings and came to measure value by tonnage sold), but also they quite as sharply challenged the judgment of the groups or persons who were in a position to influence the most distinguished readers. They scorned the decrees and shrugged off the ridicule of those critics who were best established in the most imposing reviews; they inveighed against Sarcey, Fouquier, Brunetière, Lemaître, and Anatole France. By the same token, they spurned the advantages of public esteem, disparaged public honors, and, on the contrary, exalted their own saints and heroes, who were also their martyrs and the models of their virtues. Everyone they admired had suffered: Edgar Poe, dying penniless; Baudelaire, haled into court by a public prosecutor; Wagner, hissed down at the Opéra; Verlaine and Rimbaud, suspicious vagrants; Mallarmé ridiculed by the lowest journalist; Villiers, sleeping on the floor of a hovel, beside the little valise that contained his manuscripts and his titles to the Kingdom of Cyprus and Jerusalem.

As for our Symbolists of 1886, without support in the press, without publishers, without access to a normal literary career and its promotions in rank, its rights of seniority, they adapted themselves to this irregular existence; they created their own reviews, their own publishers, their own school of criticism; and step by step they created that little public of their own, which became an object of derision like themselves.

In this manner they effected a sort of revolution in the realm of values. For the notion of works that solicit the public, approaching it by way of its habits or inclinations, little by little they substituted the notion of works that create their public. Instead of writing to satisfy a need or a preexistent desire, they hoped to create the desire and the need; and they stopped at nothing that might rebuff or shock a hundred readers, if they judged it might win them a single reader of superior merit.

All this amounts to saying that they demanded a sort of active intellectual cooperation, something remarkably new and an essential feature of our Symbolism. Perhaps it would not be impossible or mistaken to deduce, from the attitude of renunciation and negation I have just described, first, the change that consisted in choosing as partner of the writer, as reader, an individual made elect by the intellectual effort of which he was capable; and then a second consequence, that this painstaking and refined reader could henceforward be offered texts in which there was no lack of the difficulties, the unexpected effects, and the prosodic or even graphic experiments that a bold and inventive talent might undertake to produce. A new path was open to inventors. Seen in this light, Symbolism is revealed as an era of inventions; and the simple process of reasoning I have just sketched out, starting with a consideration foreign to aesthetics, and fundamentally ethical, is one that guided Symbolism to the very principle of its technical activity, which is freedom of research, absolute adventure in the realm of artistic creation, at the risk and peril of the adventurers.

Thus, set free from the public at large, delivered from the usual type of criticism that is both guide and slave of the public, unconcerned about sales, and having no regard for the limitations and mental sluggishness of an average reader, the artist could dedicate himself without reserve to his experiments. Each artist could choose his own gods, his own ideals, and Heaven knows no one denied himself the privilege. Heaven knows the innovations of the period were numerous, varied, surprising, sometimes bizarre. Everything was laid under contribution by these prospectors in search of hidden literary treasures: not only philosophy and the sciences but music, philology, occultism, and foreign literatures.

At the same time, exchanges among the different arts, first introduced by the Romantics, but practiced spasmodically, became a recognized and sometimes excessively methodical procedure. There were poets who tried to borrow from music whatever they could entice from it by means of analogies; at times their works were arranged on the page like orchestral scores. Others, subtle critics of painting, tried to introduce into their style some imitation of the contrasts and correspondences of the system of colors. Still others did not hesitate to create words or to twist French syntax, which many tried forcibly to rejuvenate, while a few, on the contrary, restored some of the finery of its ceremonious past.

Never was a literary movement more learned or more preoccupied with ideas than this movement in all directions of minds whose common principle was the renunciation of any appeal to public preference. Everything I have seen produced in literature since that tormented era, in the way of audacities, ventures into an uncertain future, or brusque returns to the past, was indicated, or already attained, or prefigured, or rendered possible, if not probable, by the intense and disorganized efforts carried on at the time.

Around those authors gradually took shape a little community of disciples, analogous to the group that had formed around Wagner after the spectacular failure of *Tannhäuser* at the Paris Opéra. No doubt these disciples, "the happy few," were expected to be attentive, zealous, willing to sacrifice their habits, and disdainful of everything they had once been taught to admire—all this to a rather commendable degree; and no doubt the only reward for their fervor would be the ridicule of good society and the press, together with the handsome title of "snob" bestowed on them by scoffers with a smattering of English; but whether they appreciated or imitated, whether they explored and discovered or merely followed, they performed a genuine and useful function. Without such readers, what would have happened to how many artists of the first rank, and how many works among those of which the glory is now beyond dispute?

Let us continue our analysis. I now propose to assert that this resolution jointly adopted by men who were usually divided on all questions of art—this determination not to worship other truths than those deliberately chosen or discovered by themselves; to turn away from the idols of their era and from those who served the idols, at the cost of all the advantages that might have been offered by their assent to public judgment—entailed the creation of *an entirely new and singular state of mind*. This never developed to the point of revealing its full or imaginable potentialities, and its evanescence, which I deplore, might be assigned to the first years of the present century.

Renunciation, as we know, bears some resemblance to mortification. When we mortify ourselves, we are trying to regenerate and reconstruct ourselves by harsh and even painful methods that will raise us, we hope, to a state forejudged to be superior. The desire for such elevation, such *ascesis*, expressing itself in the domain of art, becoming a condition of the true artist's life and a prerequisite for masterpieces: such is the quite new development and the deepseated characteristic to be observed in all the authentic participants in this Symbolism that was still without a name.

I have explained that the unity we might agree to call Symbolism does not reside in any agreement about aesthetic principles: Symbolism was not a school. On the contrary, it included many schools of the most divergent types, and I have said: *Aesthetics divided them; Ethics united them*. It is from this point that we now advance toward another idea I should like to propose. The idea can be expressed in this fashion: at no other time did the powers of art, beauty, and form, or the virtue of poetry, come so close to providing a number of persons with the substance of an inner life that might well be called "mystical," since it proved to be sufficient in itself, and since it satisfied and sustained more than one heart *as effectively as a formal creed*. There is no doubt that some few

224

depended on this sort of religious faith to furnish the constant nourishment of their thoughts, the guiding principle of their conduct, and the strength to resist temptation; or that, in the most difficult circumstances, it inspired them to pursue projects that had as little chance of being carried out as they had of being understood if by any chance they were ever completed.

This I say advisedly: we had the impression, in those days, that a sort of religion might be born, whose essence would have been the poetic emotion. Could anything be more understandable, to those who study the period and try to reconstitute the conditions that prevailed in the world of the intellect?

But this sort of study is an especially living type of history, since the reconstitution of an intellectual experience is a history of isolable individuals, taken one by one and not in masses; it tries to restore singularities, not human units treated collectively in statistical forms, as men are treated in histories of the usual sort. It is also especially vivid in this respect, that what it regards as events are inner events and personal reactions: here an idea has the value of a battle in other histories; a man in very modest circumstances, almost unknown, assumes the stature of a hero, the power of a despot, the authority of a legislator. Hence everything takes place in the domain of the perceptible and intelligible, and is resolved into impressions, into thoughts, into those individual reactions I have just mentioned. But the impressions are more intense, the reactions stronger and more creative, when one observes them in a new and young person at the moment when he is entering his intellectual puberty. One morning he wakens with a fresh judgment of himself, a rigorous judgment that condemns his tastes and ideas of the day before.

These he suddenly finds childish; he says to himself that he has been merely accepting what he was taught, that he has been reflecting the opinions and assertions of those around him—in other words: *he now feels that he has been pretending to like what he did not like, and has been forcing himself not to like what attracts him.* He is on the point of separating himself from what had been the accepted system of his admirations, his evaluations, his borrowed ideals—and he tries to be himself, by means of himself.

But it is at the same age that he enters the world of real experiences. We know only too well what he finds there. It is seldom that he fails to suffer disappointments, to be revolted by the imperfections of the real, by all the assorted forms of ugliness that are the most frequently observable elements of reality—and these precisely were the favorite themes of the naturalistic school. . . .

I believe this to be the essential fact that will help us to reconstitute, by a sort of synthesis, the spirit of the time and of the group that would bear the name of Symbolists. How could I better explain the devotion to pure art that was proclaimed and developed for a dozen years, in all countries, by a few, than by presenting to your minds the state of soul of a young man fifty years ago—whose culture, whose sensibility, and whose character I assume to be of a high order to make him feel at every moment the need of a second life and the desire for every form of beauty?

What does he find on completing his formal education? We must note that he feels no regret at leaving his books behind; since they served a utilitarian purpose and were prescribed with a view to examinations by the academic authorities, they had long since revolted him. It is only natural that they should be regarded as corpses, unhappy authors wheeled in for dissection, or else as detached fragments, dried, injected with commentaries, and reduced to the state of anatomical specimens. He has rejected these remains, these residues of century-old admiration by others. But what then does he find that will now serve him as spiritual nutriment?

Necessarily he samples the current fashions. In 1886 (since we have chosen that year) the bookshop windows offer him (besides a quantity of the negligible books that are always being written and displayed), on one side, a pile of volumes in very active demand; the wrappers announce that a hundred, two hundred thousand copies have been printed. These are the novels of the Naturalists, thick volumes usually covered with canary-yellow paper.

On the other side, less patronized by customers and much less visible (for these are poets), he discovers the Romantics, from Lamartine to Hugo. Not far away, in miniature white tomes, are the fashionable rhymers: Parnassians of all dimensions. If he looks patiently, he can perhaps lay hands on a copy of *Les Fleurs du mal*.

But our young explorer of this stock of reading matter is not quite satisfied. What the realists present to him only too well, with cruel force and obstinacy, is the very world for which, having merely glimpsed it, he already feels abhorrence. Although their picture is laboriously exact and sometimes remarkably well painted, still it seems to him incomplete, since *he is not there in person*, and since he is unable or unwilling to recognize himself in this blemished humanity, burdened with hereditary evils, a bestial prey to these cruel observers. He does not choose to believe that men and women have more reflexes than thoughts, more instincts than depth of feeling. On the other hand, the Parnassian poets win his admiration for a little while, the time required by a nimble mind to assimilate their methods and conventions—by observing which, one can soon and with a fair degree of ease write verse that appears fairly difficult. But their system, which had the merit of being opposed to negligence in form and language, so obvious in many Romantics, kept tempting them into a factitious rigor, into a search for effects and "fine lines," into the use of rare words, foreign names, and an ostentatious splendor that obscured the poetry under arbitrary and lifeless decorations. Rich rhymes are to be admired if they are not in contrast with the poverty of the verse; they become unbearable as soon as they are sought at the expense of all other qualities, including the general unity of the poem. That is an absolute law. The "fine line" is often the enemy of the poem: a great deal of intelligence and art is required to construct a body of work from which one is not tempted to detach, here and there, an alexandrine that makes us forget the rest of the troupe—as leading ladies in the theater do.

Our young hero, who serves us as a touchstone, and whose sensibility helps to reveal the quality of the era in which we place him, finds little, then, in the productions of the time to fulfil his desire. He is not at all dazzled by the works that are in fashion. It might be added that all intellectual activity would cease if young people were ever satisfied with what *is*, at the moment when they first look around them and, emerging from the awkward age, come forward to take their places among men.

But works derive from ideas, and the prevailing ideas appeal to him no more and offer no better nourishment to an eager mind than do the books of the time. Neither pure criticism, which enjoys great prestige, nor the evolutionist metaphysic, which has been adopted by the naturalistic school and translated into fiction; neither dogmatic philosophy nor the orthodox creeds, which have long been under siege and against which positivism, determinism, and philosophy in general have directed so many assaults, can have any hold on him. He is inclined to reject indiscriminately everything that rests on a tradition or on texts—just as he is repelled by anything that depends on arguments and a more or less rigid dialectic, and just as he holds that every affirmation based on scientific knowledge, whether of physics, geology, or biology, must be eternally provisional and always premature, since it exploits the implications of such knowledge beyond the possibility of verification. He confronts all these doctrines; in each of them he sees only the strength of the arguments it brings forward against the others. He decides that the sum of them all is equal to zero.

What is left to him? How can he escape from this intellectual stalemate and the feeling of helplessness to which it gives rise? This much remains: that he is himself, that he is young, and that he is resolved to accept nothing unless he feels its real inner necessity, its existence foreshadowed in the depths of his being; to admit nothing unless it can be expressed in words of which the meaning is an immediate experience and a value represented in the treasury of his *affections*. Idols for idols, he prefers those fashioned from his own substance to those offered him by others. He interrogates himself. He makes a discovery. He finds that he still has one sure possession: *the feeling imposed on him by certain aspects of nature and life, and by certain productions of men.* These he recognizes by the singular joy he derives from them, and by the strange need he finds in himself for such moments or objects, which, although perfectly useless for the preservation of physical existence, still offer him precious sensations, endlessly varied ideas, a sometimes miraculous union of thought, sentiment, fantasy, and logic, and also delight mysteriously conjoined with energy. But is this not precisely that substance of an "inner life" of which I was speaking, as well as the nutriment I described as sustaining a devotion to pure art? The barest statement of this condition compels me to use terms only to be found in the vocabulary of religious ecstasy.

One circumstance of the period under consideration greatly intensified the quasi-mystical type of aesthetic feeling that was inseparable from Symbolism. Among all modes of expression and excitation, there is one in particular that imposes itself with unmeasured power: it dominates and devalues all the others; it acts upon our whole nervous being, overstimulates, penetrates, soothes and then shatters it, while lavishing upon it a wealth of surprises, caresses, illuminations, and rages; it is the master of our conscious time, our nervous ecstasies, our thoughts. That power is *Music*; and it so happened that the most powerful type of music was sovereign at the very moment when our fledgling Symbolist was about to enter his predestined path; he became intoxicated with the music of Richard Wagner.

As Baudelaire had already done at an earlier time, he sought every opportunity for hearing this music, which seemed to him both diabolical and sacred. It was his cult and his vice, his course of study and his poison, while it also performed the function of a liturgical office, by effecting the fusion of an entire audience, in which each member received the full force of the enchantment. Think of a thousand persons in the same hall, who, under the same compulsions, close their eyes, suffer the same transports, feel alone with themselves, and yet are identified by their personal emotions with so many of their neighbors, until these become truly their *counterparts*—here is the essence of a religious atmosphere, that is, a unity of sentiments in a living plurality.

All this could be observed and felt in 1886, on Sundays, at concerts in the Cirque d'Été. The concerts were indeed religious services, attended by all of Paris that was most elegant, profound, or enthusiastic—most original, as well as most imitative. The conductor mounted to the podium. One would have said that he mounted to the altar, that he assumed the supreme power, and indeed he did; he was about to promulgate the laws and manifest the power of the very gods of Music. His baton rose; everyone held his breath; all hearts were waiting.

But while the vibrant strings, the soft hoarse woodwinds, the all-powerful brasses were building up and tearing down the resounding edifice, the temple of marvelous transformations adumbrated by genius, there was one man overshadowed by a row of men seated on a bench in the gallery, an uncommon listener who submitted to the enchantment of this symphonic sovereignty with rapture, but also with that sublime pain that is born of exalted rivalries.

After the concert, the young enthusiast was waiting for him and sought his company. Mallarmé would greet him with the deep smile that everyone remembered for the infinite sweetness that emanated from an unyielding judgment. They would talk. The problem of Mallarmé's whole life, the perpetual object of his meditations, of his subtlest researches, was, as we know, how to win back for poetry the empire that had been seized by the great modern composers. I shall not attempt here to give any detailed idea of the development of his analyses or endeavors, of which his works remain as the successive vestiges. It is enough to say that beset and irritated, as it were, by the problem of power, Mallarmé had approached literature as no one before him had ever done: with a depth, a rigorous logic, a sort of instinct for deducing laws that made him akin—without the great poet's ever suspecting it—to some of those modern geometricians who transformed the basis of the science, giving it a new scope and power by a closer and closer analysis of its fundamental notions and necessary conventions.

After taking leave of the Master, and coming back to himself, the young man returning home, drunk on ideas, haunted by the echoing grandeur of the impressions he had just received from Music, as well as by the few admirable remarks he had been listening to, felt himself at once enlightened and crushed, with deeper insight and less power. In that state of mind he returned to the places where *everyday* life would take hold on him, break off his dreams, restore his self-possession, and give him little by little—in spite of the overwhelming impression left by works of genius—the audacity to conceive of other horizons, other paths to be taken, other ways of justifying oneself and of being an individual source of thoughts and expressions, an origin, a maker, a poet. . . .

He would go to one of those cafés—only a few have survived—that played such a great role in elaborating the countless literary schools of the period. A history of literature that failed to mention the existence or function of such establishments would be dead and valueless. Like the literary salons, the cafés were true laboratories of ideas, the scene of interchanges and collisions, the medium for groupings and differentiations, in which the greatest intellectual activity, the most fertile disorder, an extreme liberty of opinion, clashing personalities, wit, jealousy, enthusiasm, pitiless criticism, laughter, insults, all contributed to an atmosphere that was sometimes intolerable, always stimulating, and strangely miscellaneous.

Those still living who used to spend some of their evenings—if only a few—in such noisy gaslit caverns have not forgotten them. With nostalgia they can relive the hours spent between those mirrors where now vanished muses preened themselves or adjusted their little veils; among those tables now and forever haunted, where Verlaine here and Moréas over there would utter their shocking pronouncements, under thick streamers of smoke, in the clatter of saucers and spoons, the outbursts of the card players, and the shrieks of women squabbling with each other. Many a notion was being formed and formulated in these surroundings.

At a given moment there was a school and a dogma in each of these privileged haunts. A review would be founded on the spot, although nobody had the faintest idea of how to pay the printer's bill. But that was of little moment. First it was essential to choose a name for the review and draw up a manifesto; these were the big undertakings. It sometimes happened that the composition of the manifesto was enough to set the founders and the scheme at odds. Half of them would form a new school, and change to another café. . . .

One of the great disputes of the era was, as we know, the civil war about Vers Libre. The subject is such a thorny one that I hardly dare to grapple with it. The propriety, the opportunity, or the necessity of dispensing with the traditional rules of verse; arguments for and against; proofs that one side or the other was right according to theory, fact, phonetic laws, or history...but if I tried to deal with this inexhaustible topic, I should be asking you to display more patience, attentiveness, and courage than could be rewarded by anything I might say. Moreover, we should soon find ourselves entangled in other difficulties. Even the question of who invented free verse has been hotly argued. Battles of the sort go on forever. In our own time I should prefer not to rekindle a war that, like many others, could never be won.

But it would be impossible to discuss Symbolism, even in a summary fashion, without lingering a moment on this question of poetic technique. I shall merely indicate a few points of fact, keeping to what is incontestable.

Regular verse is defined by a certain number of restrictions conventionally imposed on our everyday manner of speaking. These might be compared, without our intending the least disparagement, to the rules of a game. They have as their combined effect the quite remarkable virtue of separating the particular language they govern from the language in ordinary use.

At every moment they remind the man who observes them, as they also remind those who listen, that his discourse does not resound in the world of action, in the domain of practical life. To provide its proper meaning, explain its form, there must be another world, a universe of poetry.

It is to be noted that although this restraint imposed on language is partly an external one, it also gives us liberties. If the form I employ is one suggesting at every moment that my discourse is outside the order of real objects, then the listener or the reader can anticipate and accept all the fantasies of a mind left to its own devices. On the other hand, the form is a continual admonition; it forewarns or should fore-warn us against the danger of lapsing into prose.

Another established fact: all poets from the beginning to the period now under consideration employed some conventional system of discipline. No need to speak of the ancients: Shakespeare's nondramatic works are sonnets and lyrics or narratives in rhymed stanzas. Dante wrote his poem in *terza rima*. Horace and Villon, Petrarch and Banville, all observed the rules of verse.

But a few years after 1870—that is, when the school that called itself the Contemporary Parnassus was at the height of its glory, and when, in reaction against Romanticism, it had adopted still more stringent rules than the classical poets—there began to be noted an insurrectional movement, of which the first tremors are to be found in some pages of Rimbaud and in the very un-Parnassian gait of the poems of Verlaine that followed his *Poèmes Saturniens*. Their free grace set them against the sculptural appearance and solid sonorities of Leconte de Lisle and his disciples. They introduced a simple and melodious form, sometimes inspired by folk poetry.

Still bolder innovators came forward a little later. Deliberately casting aside the conventions, they depended only on an instinct for rhythm and a delicate ear as guides to the cadence and musical substance of their verse. Some of the new experiments were the result of theoretical investigations that started with the study of phonetics or with recordings of the human voice. I cannot undertake to expound the various theories advanced at the time; but I note as a characteristic feature of Symbolism the long theoretical discussions, often developed in a scholarly manner, that accompanied or contributed to the artistic production of the period. In the years between 1883 and 1890, several rash spirits attempted to formulate a doctrine of art based on the new and fashionable science of psychophysiology. Studies of sense reactions in terms of physical science, investigations into the (hypothetical) correspondence of colors with sounds, and the energetic analysis of rhythm were other enterprises not without their effects on painting and poetry. These attempts to substitute precise data for the vague notions hitherto utilized by criticism and for the subjective opinions that artists are likely to hold, were doubtless premature and perhaps chimerical; but I confess that what I knew of them aroused my keen interest —less by their substance than by their tendency, and also by the contrast they offered with the a priori systems and vain affirmations of dialectical aesthetics.

The liberated poets of the time drew also upon scholarship, and discovered charming models in fifteenth- and sixteenth-century verse. Their borrowings from older French literature included such lyrical forms as the ode and the odelette, as well as many words that had disappeared from the language, although delightfully adapted to poetry. It so happened that these borrowings, which were suggested and carried out as a direct result of the liberties that poets were taking with the strict Parnassian forms, gradually led to a so-called *Romanesque* revival of traditional prosody. That might serve as a rather diverting example of recurrence and of our inability to foresee.

In still another quarter, very much opposed to that of the Romanesque poets, a remarkable enterprise was taking place: *l'Instrumentisme* made its appearance. The *Instrumentistes* preserved most of the rules for writing the classical alexandrine, but added rules of their own, in the shape of something like a table of correspondences between the sounds of the alphabet and the tones of orchestral instruments.

All this serves to illustrate the very active life of "Symbolism" and its fertility in all sorts of inventions, as well as revealing the inner diversity of the authors whom we now classify under the same label.

Meanwhile the *Enemy* was waking; in truth he had never slept. The literary ferment of which I have just given you a very incomplete picture was not allowed to continue undisturbed. The moment its existence was suspected by those who stand guard over the interests of the public (which they manage to confuse with their own), laughter, smiles, parodies, contempt, accusations—and sometimes invectives, reprobation, regrets at seeing so much talent wasted on ridiculous fancies—began their work of depreciation and demolition. I can still hear the worthy man who told me, "*Sir, I am a doctor of letters and a doctor of law, and I can't understand a blessed word of your Mallarmé. . . .*"

Little by little the counts of the indictment took shape. They have not changed in fifty years; they are always the same and always three. Those who pronounce them are not too inventive. Here are the three heads of this average Cerberus speaking in turn:

One of the mouths says to us: Obscurity.

Another says: Preciosity.

And the third says: Sterility.

Such is the motto inscribed on the frieze of the Symbolist temple.

What does Symbolism answer? It has two ways of exterminating the dragon. The first is to say nothing, but merely point to the number of copies sold, of editions of Mallarmé, Verlaine, and Rimbaud. The figures have grown larger every year from the beginning, and especially since 1900.

The second way consists in saying: You call us *obscure*? But does anyone force you to read us? If there were some decree that compelled you to do so on pain of death, one can imagine your indignation.

You call us *precious*? But the opposite of the precious is the commonplace. But you should praise us for that. If we are sterile, there will be that much less obscurity and preciosity in the world.

It must be confessed that Symbolism had other enemies than such criticisms, which disturb only those lacking in conviction. Its own virtues were also against it, as was its ascetic ideal. Moreover, the demands of everyday life, and the coming of middle age—which makes it more and more difficult, and sometimes more disheartening, to devote oneself single-mindedly to a cult that is too austere; the wish to broaden a reputation that had inevitably been circumscribed by the exquisite quality of works produced for the admiration of a few; and finally the coming of new generations which no longer received the same impressions or encountered the same set of circumstances, and which, by the inevitable need to exist and create in their turn, were constrained to deny or ignore the aspirations and motives and values of the "Symbolists"—all this was bound to lead to a dissolution, a corruption, and at certain points a vulgarization of the spirit I have tried to explain.

In any case the immense disruption of human affairs, so much in evidence since the beginning of the twentieth century, could scarcely have failed to demonstrate the utter impossibility of this attempt to create a separate culture, to preserve taste and refinement, to stand aloof from publicity, from the progress of statistical values, and from the agitation that increasingly jumbles together all the elements of life.

The chemistry of art no longer carries on the slow process of fractional distillation that produces pure substances, nor does it prepare the crystals that can be formed and enlarged only in perfect stillness. It now manufactures explosives and poisons.

How can we dedicate ourselves to long elaborations, how waste our time on theories and subtle distinctions, when events and manners hurry us as they do, when our days are divided between futility and anxiety, and when leisure, an assured livelihood, and the freedom to dream and meditate have become as rare as gold?

These are the circumstances that confer its present value on Symbolism, besides enhancing the value of its past—making it, in short, a *symbol*.

The conditions for the development of talents in depth, in subtlety, in perfection, in exquisite power, have disappeared. Everything is opposed to the possibility of an independent life of art. The complaints of poets uttered sixty years ago seem to us purely rhetorical as compared with the lamentations that would be forced from poets today, if they did not feel it was useless to complain in the midst of the universal hubbub, the tumultuous noise of machines and arms, the cries of the crowd and the crudely imposing harangues of those by whom it is subjugated or driven.

So let me conclude by observing that "Symbolism" is henceforth the symbol that names the intellectual qualities and conditions most opposed to those which reign, and even govern, today.

Never did the Ivory Tower seem quite so high.

Letter about Mallarmé

YOU THINK that a study of Mallarmé, even one as reverent, searching, and full of love as you have planned and carried out, should nevertheless open with a few pages in another hand than yours, and you have asked me to write these.

But what can I say on the threshold of this book that the book itself does not say, or that I have not said before, or that everyone has not said? What can I say that is not difficult for me to explain without going into minute details, and at length, without making it too abstract and laborious for the public to read?

Here and there I have had occasion to record certain memories of our Mallarmé, or reassert some of his intentions, or sometimes call attention to the astonishingly enduring resonance of his work in the thinking world, even now after all the years since his death. But I have never allowed myself, for a number of powerful reasons, to compose a work that was truly and exclusively concerned with him. I am too keenly aware that I could not go very far into the subject without speaking too much of myself. From my first glance at his work it became—as it has always remained for me— a subject for wonderment; and soon the system of thought behind his work was the secret object of boundless questions. He played such a great part in my inner history without knowing it; he changed so many of my values merely by existing; his simple *act of presence* assured me of so many things, confirmed me in so many things, and, even more, has been an inner law forbidding me so many things, that I can hardly distinguish what he was from what he was to me.

No word comes easier or oftener to the critic's pen than the word *influence*, and no vaguer notion can be found among all the vague notions that compose the phantom armory of aesthetics. Yet there is nothing in the critical field that should be of greater philosophical interest or prove more rewarding to analysis than the progressive modification of one mind by the work of another.

It often happens that the work acquires a singular value in the other mind, leading to active consequences that are impossible to foresee* and in many cases will never be possible to ascertain. What we do know is that this derived activity is essential to intellectual production of all types. Whether in science or the arts, if we look for the source of an achievement we can observe that *what a man does* either repeats or refutes *what someone else has done*—repeats it in other tones, refines or amplifies or simplifies it, loads or overloads it with meaning; or else rebuts, overturns, destroys and denies it, but thereby assumes it and has invisibly used it. Opposites are born from opposites.

We say that an author is *original* when we cannot trace the hidden transformations that others underwent in his mind; we mean to say that the dependence of *what he does* on *what others have done* is excessively complex and irregular. There are works in the likeness of others, and works that are the reverse of others, but there are also works of which the relation with earlier productions is so intricate that we become confused and attribute them to the direct intervention of the gods.

* In that respect *influence* is clearly distinguishable from *imitation.*
[P.V.]

(To go deeper into the subject, we should also have to discuss the influence of a mind on itself and of a work on its author. But this is not the place.)

It is when a book or an author's collected work acts on someone not with all its qualities, but with one or a few of them, that influence assumes its most remarkable values. The development of a single quality of one person by the full talent of another seldom fails to produce results marked by an *extreme originality*.

So it was that Mallarmé, developing in himself a few qualities of the Romantic poets and Baudelaire—selecting whatever they offered that was most exquisitely finished, making it his constant rule to obtain at every point the sort of results that in them were rare, exceptional, and produced as if purely by chance—little by little wrought out a highly individual *manner* from this obstinacy in choosing the best and this rigor in exclusion; and then went on to deduce from them a doctrine and problems that, in addition *to being completely novel, were prodigiously foreign to the modes of thinking and feeling known to his fathers and brothers in poetry*. For the direct desire, the instinctive or traditional (and in either case unreflecting) activity of his predecessors, he substituted an artificial conception, minutely reasoned and obtained by a certain sort of analysis.

One day I told him that he belonged to the family of the great scientists. I do not know whether the compliment was to his taste, for he did not have a conception of science that rendered it comparable to poetry. He tended rather to set them against each other. But for my part, I could not fail to draw what seemed to me an inevitable parallel between the construction of an exact science and, on the other hand,

Mallarmé's evident design of reconstructing the whole system of poetry with the help of pure and distinct notions isolated by the delicacy and soundness of his judgment and disengaged from the confusion usually created, in minds that reason about literature, by the multiplicity of functions served by language.

His conception necessarily led him to envisage and write combinations of words very different from those which common usage regards as having "clarity," and which habit makes it so easy for us to understand almost without having perceived them. The obscurity found in his work results from certain rigorously observed requirements, almost as it happens in the sciences that logic, analogy, and a regard for consistency result in a very different picture of things from the one made commonplace by immediate observation, and may even lead to *expressions* that deliberately go beyond our power of conception.

That Mallarmé, lacking as he was in scientific training or tendencies, should have risked himself in enterprises comparable with those undertaken by the artists of number and order; that he should have consumed his life in a marvelously solitary endeavor; that he should have drawn apart in his thoughts as anyone who tries to deepen or systematize his thinking draws away from other human beings, in drawing away from confusion and superficiality—all this testifies to the boldness and depth of his mind, as well as to his extraordinary courage in defying fate, ridicule, and the public during his whole life, when he had only to surrender a little of his force and determination in order to be recognized immediately for what he was—the first poet of his time.

It must be added here that the development of his personal principles, most of which were so precise, was retarded, embarrassed, and disturbed by the uncertain notions that prevailed in the literary atmosphere of the time and did not fail to reach him. For all that his mind was solitary and autonomous, it had still been impressed by the amazing and fantastic improvisations of Villiers de l'Isle-Adam, and had never quite detached itself from a certain metaphysic, or even from a certain mysticism, hard to define. But by a remarkable reaction of his essential nature, he could not but transpose those alien themes into the system of his authentic aims, and could not but adapt them to the highest of them, which was also the dearest of all and the closest to himself. So it was that he came to dream of giving the art of writing a *universal meaning*, a universal value, and to acknowledge that the supreme object of the world and the justification of its existence—so far as that existence might be conceded—was and could only be a *Book*.

At the still rather tender age of twenty, and at the critical point of a strange and thoroughgoing intellectual transformation, I suffered the impact of Mallarmé's work. I experienced amazement, an instantaneous inner shock, then dazzlement and a sense of breaking my ties with what had been my intellectual idols at that age. I felt myself becoming a sort of fanatic; I had to undergo the overwhelming progress of a decisive spiritual conquest.

To define the Beautiful is easy; *it is that which fills us with despair*. But we must bless the sort of despair that undeceives us, that enlightens us, and, as Corneille's elder Horace said, *qui vous secourt*, that brings us help.

I had written some verse; I loved the sort of poetry that one was supposed to love in 1889. The idea of "perfection" still had the force of law, although its meaning was becoming more subtle and less purely plastic than the too simple meaning that poets had given it ten or twenty years before. Nobody had yet dared to attribute *values*, and even infinite ones, to the immediate, unforeseen, unforeseeable, and— might I call them?—*haphazard* products of the movement. The principle was still to be put forward that *one can win on every throw*, and nothing counted then but the lucky hits, or those regarded as such. In a word, poetry was required to produce an image of itself quite opposed to the one that would become seductive a few years later—as might have been expected to happen.

But the revelation of even the least of Mallarmé's writings, what an intellectual—and moral—effect they had on us in those days!...There was something religious in the atmosphere of the time, when some fashioned for themselves a cult and adoration of that which they found so beautiful they could only call it superhuman.

The *Hérodiade*, *L'Après-midi d'un faune*, the *Sonnets*, the fragments we found in reviews and exchanged by mail so that they united the adepts scattered over France as the initiates of an ancient religion were joined at a distance by the exchange of tablets and leaves of beaten gold, constituted for us a treasury of incorruptible delights, inaccessible to barbarians and the profane.

A magic power resided in that strange and seemingly absolute work. By the mere fact of its existence it acted as a charm and a sword, dividing at a single stroke all the human tribe that could read. Its enigmatic appearance instantly irritated the vital node of literary communications. Immediately and infallibly it seemed to find the most sensitive point of any cultivated consciousness, to overstimulate the precise center at which men hold in reserve their boundless store of self-esteem, and to reveal the secret home of *that which cannot bear not to understand.*

The mere name of the author was enough to produce interesting reactions: amazement, irony, resounding rages, and sometimes sincere and comic examples of inadequacy. Many invoked our *great classical writers*, who never could have imagined the sort of prose in which they would one day be abjured. Others made a show of laughing or smiling, and (helped by those happy accidents of the facial muscles that reassure us of our liberty) quickly recovered all the immediate superiority that enables self-sufficient persons to live. Seldom do we meet with articulate beings who are not wounded by their inability to understand, but who simply accept it as they might accept their ignorance of algebra or a foreign language. One can live with it, after all.

Any witness of these phenomena enjoyed the spectacle of a notable contradiction: here was a profoundly meditated work, more consciously willed and executed than any other work in existence, and it released a quantity of *reflexes.*

The truth was that this remarkable work, from the moment it came under one's eyes, touched and shattered that fundamental convention of ordinary speech: *You would not read me unless you had already understood me.*

And now I am going to offer a confession. I grant and confess that all those respectable persons who protested and railed and did not perceive what we perceived were well within their rights. Their feeling was of a natural sort. We have to admit that the realm of letters is only a province in the vast empire of entertainment. We pick up a book, we give it up, and even when we cannot stop reading it we are aware that our interest depends on the accessibility of the pleasure it affords.

In other words, the very essence of his work requires that the creator of beauty and fantasy should exert himself to provide the public with pleasures that demand no exertion, or almost none. And he has to deduce from the public what it is that touches, moves, caresses, or enchants the public.

There are several publics, however, and among them it is not impossible to find someone who does not ask for a pleasure wholly without struggle, who does not like to enjoy without paying for his enjoyment, and who does not even feel happy unless the happiness has been achieved partly through his own efforts, of which he likes to remember the cost. It can happen, moreover, that a very special public takes form.

It was Mallarmé, then, who created in France the notion of a *difficult author*. He expressly introduced into art the necessity of making an intellectual effort. By that step he raised the standing of the reader, and, with an admirable sense of how to achieve true fame, he selected from the multitude that little number of individual enthusiasts who, once they had acquired a taste for his work, could never again bear to read poems that were impure, accessible, and without defenses. *Everything else seemed artless and slack after Mallarmé.*

His short and marvelously finished compositions imposed themselves as types of perfection, so unerring was the movement from word to word, from verse to verse, from rhythm to rhythm, and so strong was the sense each poem gave of being in some sort an absolute object, produced by an intrinsic equilibrium of forces, and preserved by some miracle of reciprocal combinations from those vague notions of correcting or improving that spontaneously occur during one's reading of most texts.

I was fascinated by the brilliance of those pure crystalline systems, polished as they were from every angle. Doubtless they have not the transparency of glass, but one's habits of thought are refracted against their facets and transformed in passing through their dense structure. What has been called their obscurity is more truly their *refringency*.

I would try to imagine the paths and labors of their author's thinking. I felt that this man had meditated on every word, had considered and enumerated all possible forms. Step by step I became interested in the operation of a mind so different from my own—more interested, perhaps, than in the visible results of its activity. I mentally reconstructed the constructor of such works. I felt that they must have been endlessly reconsidered in a mental enclosure from which nothing was permitted to emerge until it had *lived* for a long time in a world of presentiments, harmonic arrangements, perfect forms, and their correspondences; an initiatory world where everything met and collided and where chance itself was forced to linger and find a direction, until it finally crystallized in a chosen pattern.

No work can emerge from a sphere so rich in reflections and resonances except by a sort of accident that projects it from the world of thought. It falls from the reversible into irreversible Time. I concluded that Mallarmé must have an inner system to be distinguished from that of the philosopher and, in a different fashion, from that of the mystics, yet revealing some analogies with both.

I was not a little disposed by nature, or rather by a change in nature that had been taking place in me, to develop my impressions in a rather curious direction, derived as they were from poems so manifestly careful in their preparation that even their beauty paled beside the notion it gave me of the hidden labor to which it was owed.

A little while before I had thought out and innocently written down an opinion in the form of a resolution: *If I am to write, I should infinitely prefer writing something feeble that was produced in full consciousness and utter lucidity, rather than being carried out of myself to give birth in a trance to one of the greatest masterpieces in literature.*

I felt, as a matter of fact, that the world was full of masterpieces and that productions of genius were not so rare that there was much point in wishing to increase their number. I also thought, with a little more precision, that when a work was resolutely willed, and when it was pursued among the hazards of the mind with the help of a passion for order and a stubborn analysis of conditions defined and prescribed in advance, whatever might be the external value of the work produced, it could not fail to have an internal effect on its creator, forcing him to become aware of himself and, in some measure, to reorganize his personality. I said to myself, *It is not the finished work or the impression it makes on the world that can develop or complete us, but only the manner in which the work was performed.* Art and toil enhance us, but chance and the Muse only tempt us to take and leave.

In that respect I withdrew some degree of importance from the *work* and transferred it to the will and purposes of the *agent*. It does not follow that I was willing to see the work neglected, but rather the contrary.

The heinous train of thought—and a dangerous one for literature (though I have never abandoned it)—was combined in a contradictory fashion with my admiration for a man who, by following his own, had reached a point nothing short of deifying the written word. What I most admired in him was his fundamentally stubborn character and the absolutist tendency revealed by the extreme perfection of his

249

work. Painstaking work, in literature, is manifested and operates in terms of *refusals*. One might say that it is measured by the number of refusals. If it were possible to study the frequency and nature of these, we should have taken an essential step toward understanding the inner nature of a writer, since it would throw light on the secret dialogue that takes place, during the progress of a work, between the temperament, ambitions, and plans of the man and, on the other hand, the impulses and intellectual expedients of the moment.

The rigorousness of the refusals, the number of solutions rejected, and the sort of possibilities that an artist will not accept, reveal the nature of his scruples, the degree of consciousness attained, the quality of his pride, and likewise the reserves and the various fears he may entertain with regard to the future judgments of the public. *Here is the point at which literature enters the realm of ethics:* and here it confronts the struggle between the natural and the willed; creates its heroes and martyrs of *resistance to the facile*; manifests virtue, and hence also, at times, hypocrisy.

But it comes about that this will to reject everything not in accordance with the law one has chosen to respect may exercise such a degree of constraint upon the artist that his works, endlessly revised as they are and carried on without regard to toil or time, become exceedingly few. Soon, in spite of the density they acquire, the accusation of sterility is brought against the author who has become excessively self-exacting. Most printed things are so artlessly fragile, so arbitrary, and so much of the offspring of a personal monologue; the greater part of them can be so easily invented by anyone; they are so easy to transform, to invert, to deny, and even to render less negligible—and so much is printed—

that it is ridiculous to reproach an author for not having added enough to the immense aggregation of books, merely because he has taken the time to reduce his own to their essence. But what is most remarkable is that the reproaches do not come from the admirers of this self-limited work, who might justly complain that their pleasure was being measured out, but that, on the contrary, it is the others who are furious because the work exists at all and, in addition, because there is so little of it.

Almost with my first approaches to the art of writing, Mallarmé the sterile, Mallarmé the precious, Mallarmé the obscure—but also Mallarmé the most fully conscious, Mallarmé the most highly perfected, Mallarmé the most pitiless toward himself of all who have ever held the pen— provided me with an idea of writing that was in some way transcendent, a *limit-idea* or archetype of its value and power.

Making me happier than Caligula, he offered me one head in which was contained everything that troubled me in literature, everything that attracted me, everything that redeemed it in my eyes. That mysterious head had weighed all the possibilities of a universal art; had known and, as it were, assimilated all the joys and the various sorts of bitter-ness and the purest despairs that can be engendered by the extremes of spiritual desire; had eliminated the crude allusions from poetry; had judged and exterminated personal ambi-tions, during its long and profound silences, in order to reach the level at which it could conceive and contemplate a principle applying to all possible works; and had found at the summit of itself an instinct for dominating the *universe of words* that was in all respects comparable to the instincts of those greatest men of thought who, by a combined analysis and construction of *forms*, equipped themselves to master all possible relations of the *universe of ideas*, or that of numbers and orders of magnitude.

All this was what I attributed to Mallarmé, an asceticism which was perhaps too deeply colored by my judgment of Letters. I have always regarded literature with great doubts as to its true value. Since the magic spell it can exert on others implies—by the very nature of language—a quantity of errors in comprehension, and since those misunderstandings are so necessary that *the direct and perfect transmission of an author's thought*, if such a thing were possible, *would entail the suppression and almost the obliteration of the finest artistic effects*, it follows that anyone who reflects on this situation is likely to feel a certain distaste for spending his time in speculating about the inexact, or in trying to provoke others into having astonishing thoughts and emotions as little foreseen by ourselves as the consequences of a spontaneous act might be. Even when those incalculable reactions of the reader are favorable to our work, as sometimes happens, and infinitely sweet to our happily surprised vanity, still a deeper pride complains of being offended in its rigor. It wants nothing to do with a fame that is only an accidental and external attribute of the person, and it does not hesitate to make us feel all the wide distance that it places between *being* and *seeming*.

As a result of these curious reflections, I was no longer disposed to grant more value to the act of writing than that of a pure *exercise*, founded on the properties of language as redefined for the purpose and generalized with precision: a game that should tend to make us extremely free and sure in the use of language, while detaching us from the illusions created by its use—though literature is nourished by those illusions, and men as well.

Such was the resolution of a conflict that was doubtless implicit in my nature between a propensity for writing poems and the strange need for satisfying all my intellectual demands. I have tried to preserve one and the other.

As I said earlier..., I could not think of Mallarmé without *egotism*. Hence I must put an end to this mixture of reflections and memories, though it might have been of some interest to pursue the analysis of a particular case of *influence* in depth and detail, to show the direct and contradictory effects of a certain work on a certain mind, and to explain how a tendency towards one extreme is answered by another.

Stéphane Mallarmé

THE LIFE and destiny of Stéphane Mallarmé and the growth of his fame present one of the most felicitous conjunctures in the history of the mind. For those who study the spiritual universe, the drama of the intellectual life here provides an episode that is strictly *unique*.

A man leads an existence of the humblest; he is enslaved by work which bores him, but he continues to carry it out regularly and honorably until it terminates on his retirement. On the other hand, he produces a few rare writings that are difficult to read; so rare and so difficult that the majority of casual readers condemn them immediately (that is to say, they abolish, annul them) by way of this triple execration: *obscurity*, *preciousness*, *sterility*. There are, however, a small number, a very small number of men who love this work, impenetrable and hard to come by as it is. They set very high store by it, send it to one another in secret; they comment on it; they talk about it among themselves, but do not in the least seek to distribute it widely. Moreover they know that this would be attempting the impossible, and they consider it almost an impiety. They are casually looked upon as adepts and initiates.

For the public at large, and even for that part of it which takes itself more seriously than the rest, it is clear that this is merely a question of literary peculiarity without significance, of work that has come from a strange mind, that has been supported by the addiction of a few readers, or perhaps by a conspiracy of a few cronies. A little madness in it undoubtedly, and much pretentiousness; elements of pose; a kind of perversity and a very probable desire to mystify on the part of both master and disciples....

However, the man dies. Thirty-five years pass—thirty-five years in which, I take it, events were not lacking. Among these were a great number of rather signal literary events; schools, sensational works, novelties.... All this sequence of events, catastrophes, surprises of every nature, the number of successful books, of new works, has no doubt wholly obliterated the name, the poetic knickknacks, the small influence, as well as the mockers themselves and their laughter that, after all, constituted *the most apparent* part of Mallarmé's notoriety about 1895.

Well then, today, on January 17, 1933, someone is giving a lecture in Paris on this selfsame poet it seems! That is a very small fact, but it presupposes a certain survival. The poet has been dead for thirty-five years. It is not usual to offer the public a completely unknown name, a name already forgotten, meaning nothing to anyone.

But more than this: a very easy piece of research for anyone who would care to undertake it, in bookshops and in publishing houses, would show that the sales of this impenetrable work rose after the poet's death and have not ceased to hold their own, while the works of his poetic contemporaries, the most famous poets of his time, are found on the whole to have been relatively neglected. I do not want to quote any names, since in some cases the lack of favor is regrettable; in a few it is completely unmerited. But I shall stick to the facts: I refer to them alone. The *fact* is that the poetry of Mallarmé, once so little sought after and unknown to booksellers, today enjoys constant popularity and is the object of regular demand in the trade, while the works of the poets I mentioned (and whose names I do not quote) suffer a disfavor that is more or less justified.

That is one fact. Here is another: the number of studies, commentaries, works of every kind, whether biographical or critical, which have been published, not only in France but also abroad, on the poetry or ideas of Stéphane Mallarmé is quite as remarkable as the number of his books that are sold. The influence of this enigmatic author is clearly felt; on minds that belong to the most diverse families of mankind it is deep and incontestable. I could here mention translators or commentators among whom are eminent foreign names. Translations or studies of Mallarmé's works have appeared in English, in German, in Italian, and in Russian.

These incontestable facts are paradoxical. The glory of Mallarmé is almost as incomprehensible for many as was his method of writing. For others it is the subject for elevated reflections, almost an *edifying theme*. It also proposes a problem, which we shall now examine.

The truest, most sincere and, moreover, most tempting method of interesting other people in a poet one has known himself—whose influence one has been able to observe on oneself, whose action was at first uncertain and as it were latent, then increasing, then triumphant, until it finally reached its limits, which are the very limits of the finite expressions of a different mind—the best method, I say, of conveying the idea one has of such a poet undoubtedly consists in a simple recourse to memory. It is enough for me to recall to you my successive impressions of Mallarmé in order to give you all I know of him. I shall not go into detailed recollections, I shall not launch out into the positively abstract or theoretical parts of my reflections about these impressions; the time would be lacking for me to tell you everything and to tell it to you in the clearest way of which I am capable; but I shall follow this general method of covering my subject.

I came to know the name of Mallarmé about 1889, first of all by a few more or less ironical shafts that were directed against him in various publications. Mockery is a means of advertising that is not to be despised: on many occasions a sensitive reader turns the point of the shaft back in the other direction. After that, I obtained a rather less summary knowledge of the derided poet from two very short quotations inserted in J.-K. Huysmans' strange work *À Rebours*. This book was not without influence fifty years ago on one category of young men. I shall recall to you that the author describes therein the way of life of a sophisticated man who shuts himself up alone, fleeing from his numerous aversions, cultivating his few predilections. In particular, he chooses works of prose or poetry that were generally unknown to the public and hated by the masters of public opinion, and draws infinite pleasure from his collection of small books and literary rarities. Among them are certain of Mallarmé's poems that have been copied by calligraphers. In this chapter Huysmans quoted a few lines of *Hérodiade* and *L'Après-midi d'un faune* which held my attention. The very stimulating judgments accompanying these quotations gave me the keenest desire to acquaint myself more with Mallarmé.

I was then living in the provinces; the literary movement was known to me only through books that were intended for general sale and through the more established reviews, so that we perceived practically nothing of what was happening in secret, in the *finer structure* of the literary life of the time. The widespread publicity given to the least poetic pheno-menon, and to the least circumstances in the lives of the ıeast authors, was not yet organized as it is today. Yet the moment one became interested in literature with that degree of concern which confers some unknown sense of divination, one could suspect, from certain indications and signs of intellectual disquietude, that neither the Parnassians, nor the Naturalists, nor the Moderates, who held the most important places and the highest obvious positions in the republic of letters, enjoyed a prerogative in matters of quality. You could breathe in the air of the time some wholly new breath of strangeness. . . .

One day, a selection of poetry that I came across by chance revealed to me a few poems of Mallarmé, of whom I had so vague an idea. Nothing could be more astonishing than this small collection. I found in it first of all two or three poems that showed the author's admirable mastery by reason of their formal perfection and distinction, the fullness of their form, the will, maintained and rewarded, to construct and succeed in composing finished lines one could not possibly wish to change. . . .

On the other hand, there were certain sonnets that reduced me to a state of stupor; poems in which I could find a combination of clarity, brightness, movement, the fullest sound, but strange difficulties as well: associations that were impossible to solve, a syntax that was sometimes strange, thought itself arrested at each stanza; in a word, the most surprising contrast was evident between what one might call the *appearance* of these lines, their *physical* presence, and the resistance they offered to immediate understanding. I did not know how to imagine a poet capable of marrying so many beauties, so much charm and so many obstacles, so many lights and so much darkness. I was confronting the problem of Mallarmé.

258

I remember the ordinary, facile hypotheses of the reviewers of the time. I rejected them quickly enough. No, the texts I had in my hands were not those of a madman or a mystifier. Without doubt they were for me riddles in themselves and propounded to me the riddle of their author's intention. I myself had tried my hand at poetry and the few attempts (quite studied ones I admit) that I had made at writing it were enough to assure me that the work expended on this verse, the elaboration certainly required to compose these obscure lines, had been considerable; I was sure also they had demanded an activity, an energy, a strength of mind that were rare and absolutely incompatible with the mental state of a madman, just as they were incompatible with the aim of mystifying credulous readers. Mystification pushed to such a limit would be a true delusion; it would be comparable to the act of a thief or a swindler whose efforts expended on committing his crimes were infinitely greater than the gain he hoped to reap.

Moreover, if the meaning of these lines appeared to me to be very difficult to decipher, if I did not always manage to resolve these words into a complete thought, I nevertheless observed that verse was never more *clear* as verse, poetry was never more plainly poetry, speech was never more decisively or luminously musical than I found in the poems I was contemplating. Their poetic quality was manifest. And I could not help thinking that even in the greatest poets, if the *meaning* in most cases leaves no room for doubt, there are lines which are *dubious poetry*, which *we can read with the diction of prose without being forced to raise our voices to the point of song.*

Consequently the poetry of Mallarmé as I read it, with my imperfect understanding of what it said, impressed me with the existence of poetry itself, whether I understood it or not! First and foremost was not understanding, but the existence of the poetry.

That is not all. I could see that these same very obscure lines had a curious property: there was in them some necessity that engraved them in my memory; and I knew by my own sad experience at school and elsewhere that my verbal memory was remarkably weak. Never had I been able to learn a lesson *by heart*. Well, these lines of Mallarmé now came back effortlessly to my mind: I knew them after reading them once or twice, and I still know them. Moreover, as I repeated without any conscious effort this verse that was so difficult to understand, I observed that the riddles became less, that understanding became clearer. The poet became justified. Repetition caused my mind to be extended toward a limit, a perfectly defined meaning. I found that these bizarre combinations of words could very well be explained; that the difficulty one experienced in understanding came from the extreme contraction of the images, from the fusion of metaphors, from the rapid transmutation of extremely condensed images that had been submitted to a sort of *discipline of density* (if you will allow me the phrase) that the poet had imposed on himself and which was in harmony with his intention to keep the language of poetry always strongly, and almost absolutely, distinct from the language of prose. One would have said that he wanted poetry, which must essentially be distinguished from prose by phonetic form and music, to be distinguished also by the *form of the meaning*. For him, *the contents of the poem had to be as different from ordinary thought as ordinary speech is different from poetic speech.*

That was a point of capital importance.

In brief, I was little by little won over, little by little captivated. After being intrigued, I felt myself to be deeply involved: converted as it were. In vain I might protest at times, trying to break the charm; I could not manage it. And yet I heard people say so many incontrovertible things in criticism of this poetry and this poet! Someone buttonholed me one day and said to me, with a sort of grief and desperate indignation: "But sir, I am a doctor of letters and I cannot understand a word of it!"

I could give him no answer, holding as I did a mere bachelor's certificate.

What would he have thought if I had confided in him? If I had revealed to him what this hermetic poet made me feel?

I felt that there was in the work of Mallarmé *something more* than in other poetic works, and not merely *something else*; something that for me was important, more profound, which went directly to my soul and probably depended on the entire system of the mind. . . .I was well prepared to receive new gifts.

Up till then, as I have told you, I had known only a few fragments of the works of Mallarmé, very short passages that had been laboriously copied out or found in reviews. But I well deserved to be satisfied—and almost immediately I was. While I was still living in the provinces, chance had brought me into contact with Pierre Louÿs first of all, then with André Gide, and I promptly gained from their friendship precise information about the person and the life of Mallarmé; then I received from them precious copies of *Hérodiade* and *L'Après-midi d'un faune*. . . .

L'Après-midi d'un faune has a rather curious history.

Banville liked Mallarmé; he took an interest in his

affairs, which were in rather a bad way. As he was seeking to be helpful to the young poet, an event occurred which gave hope to the whole Parnassian community: the great success of François Coppée's *Le Passant* played by Agar and Sarah Bernhardt.

About the same time, Banville gave a few plays of his own to Constant Coquelin. It struck him that, perhaps by making a few sacrifices to public taste, his young friend Mallarmé could write a dramatic scene for Coquelin, whose career had just brilliantly begun, and that the possible success might well transform the poet's destiny. Mallarmé yielded to temptation and agreed to write a poetic dialogue that he probably never completed. A quite unknown fragment of this poem was rediscovered a few years ago in his father's papers by the son of Chausson, the celebrated composer, who brought it to me. My surprise was great to read this first draft of *L'Après-midi d'un faune*.

Nothing could be more interesting than the comparison of the two texts. They are marvelously different. While the known text presents a complex structure of sophistication, the original was quite simple and would not have caused the slightest stir if it had been produced on the stage of the Odéon. Although Mallarmé often told the story of his writing for Coquelin he never alluded to the first draft. He only said that he had envisaged a setting of reeds behind which he intended that his faun would mime and declaim his poem.

It is clear that, having abandoned the plan in its dramatic form, he later took up the motif and made of it *L'Après-midi d'un faune*, in which *only one line* of the first draft was retained.

The poem has become a sort of literary *fugue*, in which themes are intermingled with prodigious artistry; all the resources of the poetic art are employed to sustain a triple development of images and ideas. An extreme sensuality, an extreme intellectuality, an extreme musicality are combined, interwoven, or opposed in this extraordinary work, in which we find the most beautiful lines in the world:

> *Tu sais, ma passion, que pourpre et déjà mûre*
> *Chaque grenade éclate et d'abeilles murmure....*

But I do not wish to linger over it.

We shall therefore leave aside *L'Après-midi d'un faune*. I shall only say this one further thing—it is a curious and significant detail: Mallarmé was not very happy when Claude Debussy wrote a musical score for his poem. He believed that his own music was sufficient, and that even with the best intentions in the world, it was a veritable crime as far as poetry was concerned to juxtapose poetry and music, even if it were the finest music there is....

As for *Hérodiade*, this poem produced on me an effect of incomparable beauty. It was a marvelous union of a rather external kind of art—the art of the Parnassians—but of a most refined kind, and a *spirituality* whose origin can be found in the works of Edgar Allan Poe.

In *Hérodiade*, a poem that Mallarmé never finished (and to which he later returned toward the end of his life hoping to finish it), purity, virginity, sterility appear as the very conditions of beauty. Perhaps one must see in this apparently inhuman alliance, in this sort of crystalline vocation of a soul, the supreme expression of a whole aesthetic—or perhaps even an ethic....

Some forty years ago we had reached a critical point in the evolution of literature. The time was ripe for Mallarmé's influence. The young men of my generation rejected almost everything the intellectual horizon offered them. They stood aloof from the Parnassians, from Naturalism, and moreover from every tendency that was restricted to a technique. They sought not merely an art—this is the singular characteristic of the time—but an orientation of that art toward a new perfection, and even more than this, a veritable *direction* which I will not risk calling a moral one, for it was not a question of morality in the ordinary sense of the word. One must not forget that at this time people were talking both of the bankruptcy of science and the bankruptcy of philosophy. Some were following the doctrines of Kant, who had caused the ruin of all metaphysics; others reproached science with failing to keep promises it had not made. In this state, and since they lacked any faith that could satisfy them, some men held that the kind of certitude they felt in an ideal of beauty was the only one that could be relied on. How is one not to believe that one admires, when one admires; what can undermine the immediate feeling imposed on us by what we find beautiful? All this is sufficient explanation of the enormous influence acquired over a very small number by the difficult and perfect poet, the purest of characters, in whom we found the extreme rigorousness of artistic dogma and the extreme gentleness of a truly superior intelligence. One felt he represented something that was *positive enough*.

I shall emphasize this word—I want you to feel with what force a kind of poetry that had deliberately isolated itself, that sought to owe nothing to the seductions of the common images of life, could act on a few minds. To the point of appearing obscure, it was stripped of any claim to reproduce the sensible world—a claim that possessed the power of a superstition among the Realists and the Naturalists of that time; it was no less innocent of any explicit "metaphysical" preoccupation. It had, finally, almost eliminated the recourse to "feeling" (from which the most facile art draws its great effects). Everything naïve or vulgar was abolished, and replaced by a sort of faith in *pure* aesthetic expression.

Now these paradoxical and daring evaluations which we knew to be the fruits of a whole life given over to meditation won our sympathies and transformed us little by little, for they built on what we took to be the most unquestionable thing we knew. We found, in the impression certain works produced on us, absolute unimpeachability, conviction, power. Since all other truths—dogmas, doctrines, theses— were so vain and mortal, and since moreover there could hardly remain of them anything but what they sometimes contained in the way of *poetry* or *beauty*, we had to adhere to the single and supreme assurance, obey the unique private and personal light which leads each one of us towards our most exalted mode of being. The works that elevate us show us also *that which seeks to grow in us*, and the sense of our vital development in as much as it can be *a universal concern*. Thus it is that our feeling for the highest beauty can have some claim to guide our lives.

This interpretation of the kind of influence Mallarmé had may explain the depth of his influence on the very small number of adepts of whom I have spoken.

Doubtless such a growth in the value of the notion of poetry was opposed to the ordinary idea that is held of it, even among those who enjoy it. What appeared to be only the ornament of life became its essential object (and even its vindication). But many were shocked by the rigors which (as happens in other fields) were sometimes the effects of this imagined purity. In particular they could not admit that it was necessary to renounce the surest means of pleasing, the tender or touching effects which are directly obtained by a sort of provocation of the reader's memories or passions.

But the finest art can certainly not consist of arousing emotion by way of emotive objects. What is simpler than to make people shudder or wax tender by the artistic representation of death, grief, or tenderness? That is hardly *creation*. It is easy to captivate a public by a spectacle or a speech that goes straight to our weaknesses, that tortures or swells our hearts, making us live a fictional life by playing on our naïve energies. But art of this kind (which is called *human*) is therefore a *lie*. As for me, nothing so cools my emotions as to recognize the desire to manoeuvre me, and to see the simple mechanism of it.

But to move one's readers by forms and objects that are moving by nature of their art alone, to reject simulation, to found oneself neither on credulity nor silliness, to refuse to speculate on the most probable reactions, is to conceive the firmest and most profound design an artist can have. He is satisfied with only the most difficult tears and the most difficult joy, which seek *their own cause and discover it in no experience of life.*

An absolutely pure work of music, a composition of Johann Sebastian Bach, for example, owing nothing to sentiment but constructing a sentiment which has no *model*, and whose entire beauty consists in its combinations, in the construction of a separate intuitive order, is an inestimable acquisition, an immense value that has been wrenched from nothingness. . . .

Poetry is doubtless not as free as music in its means. Only with great difficulty can it order to its will the words, forms, and objects of prose. If it succeeded, it would be *pure poetry*. But that term has been strongly criticized. Those who have reproached me with it have forgotten that I wrote that pure poetry is only a limit situated at some infinite distance, an ideal of the power of linguistic beauty. But it is the direction that matters, the tendency toward a pure work. It is important to know that all poetry is oriented towards some *absolute poetry*. . . . Mallarmé meditated on its existence and tried at all costs to bring it closer by the development of his art.

The man who wrote *Hérodiade* (which he composed about the age of twenty-three, at Tournon) had already renounced (this is a remarkable thing) the career of a writer as it is commonly conceived. The glory most men covet was repugnant to his elevated ideal, for ordinary glory (which I call *statistical*) is measured by the number of people who know a name. Mallarmé was not concerned with an undistinguished mass of votes! He thought that the few men who could follow him in his labyrinth were worth a whole crowd that had been indiscriminately conquered. He wished to win over his adepts one by one. *Despite his magnificent gifts* he would therefore do everything possible for statistical glory not to encroach on him, *for it to respect him*. I think you will appreciate the full nobility of his refusal. But some people wish to see in this the insular tendency of a mind that wants to get away from the most common opinions. They will perhaps speak of schizophrenia, a strange name invented to designate the malady of isolating oneself from one's fellow men, for we are living in a time when everything demands, imposes, works towards the uniformity of individuals, as it does with cities, names, clothes, and pleasures. But on what did Mallarmé, in his solitude, lucidity, firmness of faith found his resolution?

Thanks to documents that have been quite recently published we know he made within himself, about his twentieth year, a remarkable discovery. A kind of revelation, a decisive intellectual illumination took place about which we have some knowledge from the publication, in *Le Journal des débats*, of documents given to M. André Mévil by the son of the famous Provençal poet Théodore Aubanel. Aubanel was a very close friend of Mallarmé. A teacher at the lycée of Tournon, Mallarmé was a regular habitué of the Félibrige group; he knew Mistral. With him he even conceived the curious plan of establishing a kind of free-masonry of artists which would have united throughout the world the loyal followers, the believers, the faithful of poetry and art. The idea of a spiritual cooperative is not new. In the seventeenth and eighteenth centuries it was in the air; Mallarmé was reviving a tradition. . . .

His relations with Aubanel were completely intimate and affectionate. He wrote to him rather often and it was in a few of his letters that he confided to his friend what he had found in his meditation. Here is a sentence I take from a letter of 1864:

Keystone or center, if you wish, so as not to confuse our metaphors, center of myself where I station myself as a spider does on the principal threads that have already *come out* of my mind and with the aid of which I shall weave *at the meeting points* a marvelous lacery which I can divine, which already exists in the heart of beauty.

And this:

My good Théodore, I have not yet found a minute to explain to you the enigmatic words in my letter, for I have no wish to be a logogriph for friends such as you; although I willingly employ this means to oblige others to think of me, it appears that I had forgotten to light my lantern, the one on which I used to hang myself. I mean simply that I have just laid the plans of my whole life's work, that I foresee it will take me twenty years for these five books which will compose my work, and that I shall wait, only reading fragments of it to friends like you, and laughing at glory as a frayed foolishness. What is relative immortality, often applying only in the minds of *fools*, when one thinks of the joy of contemplating eternity and enjoying it alive, within one's self?

In another letter:

My good Théodore,

I have laid the foundations of a magnificent work. Every man has a secret in himself, many die without finding it and will not find it because, when they are dead, it will no longer exist, nor will they. I have died and come to life again with the bejewelled key of my final spiritual casket; now it is for me to open it in the absence of any borrowed impression, and its mystery will emanate into a lovely sky.

These were the hopes and expectations of Mallarmé in 1865. Already strong and irrevocable in him was his decision to create out of solitude, and almost with a view to solitude. His resolution was the more admirable and virtuous in that he had already published in *Le Parnasse* and other reviews a few poems... which proved to his friends, and to readers of taste, the excellence of his poetic gifts. If he had then renounced his unlimited research in order to apply himself to conquering the favor of lovers of poetry, he would doubtless have appeared in a few years in the very first rank of French poets. His procedure was completely different. He withdrew into his own mind, communing with the endless analysis of his own insights. He considered language in a wholly personal way, and it became the center of his thoughts. I must add a capital point: his idea of it was remarkably *precise*. He reflected on the conditions of his art with a precision and a depth that are unparalleled in literature. His only *singularity* was that the subjects of his meditation were those on which no one ever thinks of meditating. He was unwilling to write without knowing what writing means and what that strange practice may signify. I should have great difficulty in telling you at this moment what a *sentence* or a *verse* is. You will find in the best books nothing but vague and valueless definitions of these terms. Mallarmé never ceased thinking of the nature and possibilities of language with the lucidity of a scientist and the conviction of a poet. We can only conjecture about the depth of a thought that was wholly occupied with the tax of extracting from language all its power and giving to the act of expression a higher meaning. From his reflections he drew formulas that constitute a singular metaphysics.

He would say that the world had only been made so as to end in a beautiful book, and that it could and must perish once its mystery had been represented, and its expression found. He could see, in the existence of all things, no other explanation and no other excuse.

I do not want to pursue further this digression on Mallarmé's philosophy. I shall end by returning to my beginning. I remarked on the great contrast we perceive between Mallarmé's modest fame when he was alive and his position and importance since his death. This growth in his posthumous power is not due to literary causes only. It is not alone the beauty of his verse, nor the depth of his ideas, nor the formal inventions with their startling elegance that have caused his name to grow, his work to have influence, his figure to impress itself despite the passing years, despite his *obscurity*, his strangeness, despite the absence of attractions that conquer the simple hearts and the minds of the majority.

But this man who was both so profound and so gracious, so simple and so complex, of such modest estate, so worthy, so noble (for nothing was nobler than his attitude, his glance, his welcome, his smile) was the purest and most authentic example of the intellectual virtues. In him there lived and breathed the high dignity of poetry. One could not approach him and hear him speak without feeling, even in his slightest words, that everything in him was ordered toward some secret end, so lofty that it transformed things, appraised, abolished, or transfigured them in the manner of a mystical conviction or illumination. I do not believe anything like it has ever been witnessed in the realm of letters. . . .

I Would Sometimes Say to
Stéphane Mallarmé....

I WOULD sometimes say to Stéphane Mallarmé:

"Some blame you and others ridicule you. You arouse irritation and pity. Any journalist can easily amuse the world at your expense, and your friends shake their heads.

"But do you know, do you feel, that in every French city there is a nameless young man who would let himself be hacked to pieces for your poems and yourself?

"You are his pride, his mystery, his vice. He withdraws from everyone into his undivided love for an intimacy with your work, work so hard to find, to understand, to defend...."

I had in mind a few others besides myself, in whose hearts he was continually present and active and unique; and what I saw flowing from us toward him was the true glory that is not radiant but secret; that is not collective but jealous, personal; and that is based much more, perhaps, on differences and resistances overcome than it is on immediate consent to some common wonderment and delight.

But he, with a masked look, being among those who can expect and enjoy no exaltation save from within, would say nothing.

It is not granted to the deepest minds to admire themselves indirectly through the fervor of others, for they are absolutely certain that no one else can realize either what they demand of themselves or what they hope to obtain from their daemon.

What they give to the public is never anything but what they discard: the rejected fragments, the playthings of their secret hours.

The perfection as well as the consistent strangeness of his rare poems led us to form a picture of the author quite different from one's usual notion of poets, even those of distinction.

Although his unparalleled work amazed us from the beginning, although it immediately enchanted the ear, imposed itself on the voice, and mastered the whole array of speech by creating with the force of art a sort of inevitability in the arrangement of syllables, a moment later it embarrassed and puzzled the mind, sometimes defying it to *comprehend*. Rejecting the instantaneous resolution of words into ideas, it demanded what often proved to be a considerable mental effort on the part of the reader, besides an attentive reexamination of the text: a perilous demand to make and almost always fatal.

Ease of reading has been the rule in literature under the reign of universal haste and of writings that tempt or goad us into still greater haste. Everyone seems inclined to read only what anyone might have written.

Moreover, since it is a question of entertaining the reader or helping him *pass the time*, we must not ask him to make an effort or exert his will; here triumphs the perhaps guileless notion that pleasure and pain are mutually exclusive.

For my part, I confess I derive little or nothing from a book unless it resists me.

To demand that the reader should be intellectually alert; to forbid him the privilege of completely possessing a text except at the cost of a somewhat painful effort; to insist on transforming him from the passive spectator that he would prefer to be into a partial creator—all this was an affront to custom, indolence, and every form of mental inadequacy.

The art of reading at leisure, independently, accurately, and discerningly, which in other days answered the stubborn zeal of the writer with a concentration and a patience of the same quality, is vanishing from our world; it has already vanished. A reader of old who had studied Tacitus or Thucydides, and who had been warned by the obstacles that abound in them not to race from line to line or abandon a sentence or a page as soon as he guessed its meaning, was a partner for whom the author was justified in hesitating over the choice of words and in arranging the elements of a thought in their proper relation. Politics and novels have exterminated that reader. The pursuit of immediate effects and of urgent entertainment have eliminated from writing all that painstaking regard for design, and from reading all that slow intensity of apprehension. The eye now seizes on a crime or a disaster, then flits away. The intellect wanders among a multitude of images, finds them all enchanting, and surrenders to the surprise effects produced by the absence of any law. If dreams (or pictures from memory) are taken as a model, duration and thought give way to the mere moment.

So anyone who did not put aside Mallarmé's involved texts found himself engaged by slow degrees in the task of re-learning how to read. If he tried to give them a meaning that was not unworthy of their admirable form or of the labor those elaborate figures of speech had assuredly demanded of the author, he inevitably came to associate the delights of poetry with a sustained effort of the mind and of its powers of combination. The result was that Syntax, a form of calculation, resumed its rank among the Muses.

Nothing could be less "romantic." Romanticism had decreed that men should no longer be slaves to themselves. One of its essential aims was to abolish the *sequence of ideas*, which is one form of that slavery; hence it encouraged an immense development of descriptive literature. Description absolves us from logical sequence; it admits everything that the eyes admit and allows us to introduce new terms at any moment. The result was that the writer's effort, reduced and concentrated into such moments, was applied to epithets, to contrasts of detail, and to "effects" easy to separate from the body of his work. It was the age of jewelry.

Certainly Mallarmé tried to preserve those beauties of the literary fabric, while at the same time heightening the art of construction. The further he went in his reflections, the more unmistakable in everything he produced was the presence and the firm purpose of abstract thought.

Moreover: the man who offered the world these crystal enigmas, and who dared to introduce such a combination of difficulties and graces into the art of pleasing or touching by way of language, could not but possess a force, a faith, an asceticism, and a contempt for general opinions that had no parallel in Letters; and these qualities cast a slur on all works that were less superb, all intentions that were less rigorously pure—which means on *nearly everything*.

His poems were consciously willed and meditated; as highly elaborated as any poems could be while still fulfilling the absolute requirement that they sing; and their effect on a few was prodigious.

The few are not averse to being few. The many rejoice in being many; they are happy to be of the same indiscriminate opinion, to feel themselves alike, to be reassured by one another. As living bodies huddle together to share one another's warmth, they are confirmed, augmented in their "truth" by the close contact of their equal tepidities.

But the few are persons who differ among themselves. They detest alikeness, which seems to deprive them of their reason for being. *What good is this Self*, they think without putting the thought into words, *if it can be one of an infinite number of copies?*

They want to be like Essences or Ideas, each of which is unique in its species. At the very least they propose to make a world of their own and fill a place in it that no one else could hold.

Mallarmé's work, requiring as it did a personal interpretation by each reader, attracted and attached to itself none but distinct intelligences, won over one at a time, of such as take alarm at the first sign of unanimity.

Everything that pleases the many was expunged from his work. No rhetoric; no stories, no maxims, or only profound ones; no direct resort to common passions; no surrender to familiar devices; none of the "all too human" that degrades so many poems; always an unexpected way of speaking, a diction that never lets itself be carried into the repetitions and vain frenzies of spontaneous lyricism, one that has been purified of all easy-to-find locutions and that consistently obeys the laws of verbal music as well as the poetic conventions that exist to serve as *infallible* obstacles against any lapse into prose—here was a whole collection of negative characteristics, by means of which his poems gradually made us only too aware of the known expedients, the lapses, the

silliness and bombast that unfortunately abound in all poets—
for no venture could be more hazardous or perhaps more
reckless than theirs, and having entered upon it as gods, they
end up as poor mortals.

What is it we seek—if not to produce a powerful sense,
sutained for a fixed period, that there is some sort of harmony
between the sensuous form of a poem and its *exchange value
in terms of ideas*; that the two are conjoined in who knows
what mystical union thanks to which we participate in
quite another world than the one in which words correspond
to deeds? Just as the world of pure sounds, so easily recognized
by our hearing, was selected from the world of noises to
stand against it and constitute the perfected system of Music,
so the poetic spirit would like to do with language. From
that practical and statistical medium it hopes to extract the
rare elements with which it can fashion completely delightful
and distinct works of art.

That is to ask for a miracle. We realize that there is
hardly an instance in which the connection between our
ideas and the groups of sounds that suggest them each in
turn is anything more than arbitrary or fortuitous. But
because we have observed, approved, or obtained a few
admirable isolated effects from time to time, we delude ourselves into thinking that we might some day produce a whole
well-ordered work, without weakness or blemish, compact
of felicities and happy accidents. The fact remains that a
hundred divine moments do not compose a poem, which is a
temporal unit of development and might be called a structure in time, and that naturally poetic element is an exception in the chaos of sounds and images that occur to the
mind. Hence we must devote patience, stubbornness, and
industry to our art if we hope to produce a work which, in

the end, appears to be a series of none but those happy encounters, arranged in the happiest sequence. If we make the further demand that the poem should enchant the senses by the magic of its rhythms, tonalities, and images, while also standing up to and answering the questions raised by the intellect, then we have staked our fortunes on a preposterous game of chance.

Mallarmé was troubled even in late adolescence by an excessively acute awareness of those contradictory requirements and ambitions. He also could not fail to recognize the extreme difficulty of combining his notion of an absolute poetry with a continual grace and rigor of execution. At every step he had against him either his gifts or his principles. He wore himself out trying to strike a balance between time and the moment, a problem that torments all artists who think deeply about their art.

He could therefore produce only a very few works; but those few, once barely tasted, spoiled the savor of any other poetry.

I remember that I was nineteen and had lost most of my enthusiasm for Hugo and Baudelaire when chance made me read some fragments of *Hérodiade*, as well as *Les Fleurs* and *Le Cygne*. At last I had found the uncompromising beauty that I had not known I was seeking. Everything in the poems was based on the magical power of language, and on that alone.

I walked for miles toward the seashore, holding the precious copies that a friend had made for me, and nothing in nature seemed to exist—not the sun in all its power, or blue space, or the dazzlingly white road, or the incense of all the sun-baked herbs—so much had I been moved by those matchless verses, so deeply had they possessed my inmost life.

This poet was the least *primitive* of all poets, yet it came about that by bringing words together in an unfamiliar, strangely melodious, and as it were stupefying chant—by the musical splendor of his verse as well as by its amazing richness—he restored the most powerful impression to be derived from primitive poetry: that of the *magic formula*. An exquisite analysis of his art must have led him toward a doctrine, and something like a synthesis, of incantation.

It was believed for many ages that certain combinations of words had more power than apparent meaning; that they were better understood by things than by men—by rocks, waters, beasts, gods, buried treasures, and by the laws and forces of life better than by the human reason; that they were clearer to spirits than to mind. Death itself would sometimes yield to rhythmic conjurations, and a tomb open to release its shade. Nothing could be more ancient and at the same time more *natural* than this faith in the inherent power of words, based not so much on their *exchange value* as on some vague echo they were thought to arouse in the substance of things.

The efficacy of "charms" lay not so much in a meaning to be derived from the words as in their sonority and in the strangeness of their form. It might be said that *obscurity* was almost essential to them.

Whatever is sung or articulated at the most solemn or critical moments of life; whatever resounds in a liturgy; whatever is murmured or moaned in the extremes of passion; whatever soothes a child or an unfortunate; whatever attests the sincerity of an oath—all these are utterances that cannot be resolved into clear ideas or separated, without becoming vain or absurd, from a certain tone and a certain style. On all such occasions the accent and tempo of the *voice* are more important than the intelligible meaning of what is said, and they are addressed to our lives much more than to our minds.—I mean that the utterances enjoin us to *become* much more than they incite us to understand.

Among the writers of his century, none but this poet had dared to make this sharp division between the power of the word and the ease of comprehension. No one else had so consciously distinguished the two effects of expression by language: transmitting a fact; evoking an emotion. Poetry is a compromise, or a certain proportion of both these functions. . . .

No one else had dared to represent the mystery of all things by the mystery of language.

Why not admit that man is the source and origin of enigmas, when there is no object, or being, or moment that is not impenetrable; when our existence, our movements, our sensations absolutely cannot be explained; and when everything we see becomes indecipherable from the instant our minds come to rest on it and, instead of giving answers, start asking questions?

We may heartily dislike this point of view; we may refuse to recognize any purpose in language save that of transmitting to one person what is clear to another—an attitude that comes down to accepting from another, or from oneself, only what can be understood without effort. But we cannot dispute, first, that the inequality of intelligences leads to great uncertainties in our notions of clarity; next, that if there are obscurities due to the inadequacy of the speaker, there are others inherent in the things of which he speaks— nature has never sworn to present us with no objects except those capable of being defined in simple language; and finally, that neither religions nor emotions refrain from using "irrational" expressions. I might add that the perfect transmission of thoughts is a chimera, and that the total transformation of any discourse into ideas would result in the total annulment of its form. One must choose: either to confine language to the simple transitive function of a system of signals; or else to allow that some may speculate on its sensuous properties, may develop its *virtual* effects, its formal and musical combinations—perhaps to the point of amazing, or perturbing people's minds for a time. Nobody is obliged to read anyone.

These sensuous properties of language also stand in a remarkable relation with memory. Different patterns of syllables, of intensities, and of tempos are quite unequal in their capacities for being retained by the memory, as they are in their ease of emission by the voice. We might say that some have more *affinity* than others with the mysterious power of recollection: each seems to be assigned its own probability of exact restitution, which depends on its phonetic pattern.

An instinct for the mnemonic value of form appears to be very strong and sure in Mallarmé, whose verses are so easy to remember.

I have just been invoking *memory* and *magic*.

That is because poetry most certainly goes back to some human state anterior to writing and criticism. Hence I find a *man of very ancient times* in every true poet. He can still drink from the very springs of language. He invents "verses" almost in the same fashion that the most gifted primitives must have created "words," or the ancestors of words.

It seems to me in consequence that the more or less desirable gift of being a poet bears witness to a sort of *nobility*, one that does not depend on documents attesting to a high descent, but rather on the immediately observable sense of antiquity in the poet's ways of feeling or reacting. Poets worthy of the name in this great sense reincarnate Amphion and Orpheus.

This is mere fancy; and doubtless I should not even have dreamed of this intermittent aristocracy if, in speaking of Stéphane Mallarmé, it had been possible for me to ignore all that was noble and proudly sustained in his attitude and in his art of accepting life. Modest as was his situation in the world of those who eat, earn, and scribble, he somehow suggested those beings, half kings and half priests, half real and half legendary, to whom we owe the belief that we are something more than animals.

Nothing could be more "noble" than the expression, the glance, the greeting, the smile, and the silences of Mallarmé, wholly directed as he was toward a proud and secret purpose. Everything about him had to do with some lofty and well meditated principle. Acts, gestures, remarks, even those made offhand; even his trifling inventions, the infinitely graceful nothings, the little occasional poems (in which he was incapable of not revealing the rarest and most accomplished art), all came from an undefiled source, all seemed in tune with the gravest note of one's being, which is the sense of being unique and of existing once and for all.

So it was inevitable that he should never consent to anything less than perfection.

For thirty and some years he was a witness or martyr to the idea of the perfect. There are no longer many victims of that intellectual passion. An era ended with the renunciation of the lasting. Works that demand time without reckoning, works made to stand for centuries, are scarcely undertaken nowadays. We have entered the era of the provisional. No one has leisure to produce those objects of contemplation that the mind finds inexhaustible and on which it can subsist indefinitely. Time enough for a surprise is our present unit of time.

But it takes a lifelong effort to choose only the best. An obstinate rejection of all the advantages to be gained by facility, of all the effects that are based on the reader's weak-nesses—his haste, his superficiality, his lack of sophistication —may gradually lead to an author's becoming inaccessible. Anyone who makes excessive demands on himself is in extreme danger of demanding too much of the public. If he consumes himself, for example, in the effort to produce a single work that combines the immediately seductive elements essential to poetry with a precious intellectual substance to which the mind can return and on which it can dwell some little time without regret, he decimates his chances of ever being finished with his labors, as well as those of his ever being read.

After the difficulties of the text had been surmounted and its charm had taken effect, the perfection of the workmanship seemed more and more impressive. One could not help attributing it to some incomparable cause. The more one recognized an exquisite intelligence, an inventiveness in the form, and an ingenious depth in Mallarmé's writing, down to his briefest letters, the more one assumed that an inner self, marvelously alone and unparalleled, must be the source of those qualities. It was not that one could not imagine, or refused to admit, that other poets might be more powerful *in action*, but rather that the works and attitude of this poet bore witness to a complete organization of will and intellect that seemed unique.

Few of the great artists inspire us with passionate curiosity about their real and inmost thought. We have a premonition that learning to know their thought as they first knew it themselves would not add much to our love of their works or to our insight. We suspect that they have done hardly more than convey to us the events or situations that moved or dazzled them at some moment, during some moments, just as we ourselves may thereupon be moved or dazzled at second hand. They know hardly more than ourselves about the things they do that are beyond our powers.

But this man as much as commanded us to infer a whole system of thought relating to poetry, a system evolved, tested, and continually renewed *as an essentially infinite work*, of which any realized or realizable works were only fragments, sketches, preparatory studies. Poetry, for him, was doubtless the common limit, impossible to reach, toward which all poems and indeed all forms of art are tending. Having seized upon that notion at an early stage in his career, he had laboriously dominated, modified, and deepened the poet-like-any-other that he was in the beginning. He had sought and recognized the principle of desire that engenders the poetic act; he had defined and isolated its pure element— and he had made himself *the virtuoso of that discipline of purity*, the one who studies and plays faultlessly upon what is rarest in his nature.

I have no aversion for the virtuoso, the man of technical accomplishment. There is a prejudice against him, a *reflex movement*, connected with the vague and seductive ideas awakened in the popular mind by such rather empty words as "creation," "inspiration," or "genius."

This public and proximate judgment of our contemporaries about poetry and any other exciting and astonishing product of the mind can easily be reduced to a principle, as follows. *Everything that is most admirable in a work is owed to the instantaneous mood of its author*, and the mood is as foreign to him as a dream might be to us, or an adventure of the sort that when simply recounted by the most ordinary individual can sometimes move an audience. An author's highest achievement would hence be the one that is farthest from himself or, in other words, least foreseen by himself.

The principle is not completely false; that is why it is dangerous. Where the danger lies is in setting a higher value on special bounties, on extraordinary illuminations and forces, than on the effort to achieve consistency in results or on the acquisition of a permanent capacity by the most sustained and subtle efforts, the soundest observations and revisions, the most precise reasoning. By so doing we exalt the exceptional—more for the surprise it occasions than for any intrinsic quality—and we also surrender to a naïve and idolatrous worship of the marvelous.

But a higher achievement, one that impresses me more than any other, is the man who takes his own measure and refashions himself by his own lights. The finest effort of human beings is to change their disorder into order and their chance into law; that is the true miracle. I like a man to be harsh to his genius. If it cannot be used against itself, "genius" is nothing more to my eyes than an inborn but uneven and inconstant virtuosity. The works that proceed from "genius" alone are curiously fashioned of gold and mud; rich as they often are in brilliant details, time soon dissolves and washes out their clay; nothing remains but a few verses from many a poem. As a result, our very notion of a poem has gradually deteriorated.

The problems, however, that are truly worthy of the most powerful minds—and are also best calculated to arouse them to their full power of transformation—do not appear until a mastery of technical means has been acquired and has become as it were instinctive. The object of all the highest researches is, starting from liberty, to construct some *necessary* edifice or system. The original liberty, however, depends on and develops with one's confident awareness of possessing a full gamut of possibilities. The intuitions that excite the creative impulse show no regard for our faculty of execution: that is their vice and their virtue. But experience, little by little, teaches us the habit of conceiving only what we can execute; it confines us imperceptibly to an exact balance between our ambitions and our deeds. Many are satisfied with this regular and moderate perfection. But there are others with whom the development of technical means is carried so far, and moreover becomes so closely identified with their intelligence, that they succeed in "thinking" and "inventing" in the realm of execution, on the basis of the materials themselves. Music deduced from the properties of sounds; architecture deduced from matter and forces; literature, from the possession of language, from its unique function, and from its modifications—in a word, the real side of the arts giving birth to their imaginary side, the possible act creating its object, what I can do illuminating what I wish, while suggesting projects that are at the same time wholly unexpected and wholly capable of being realized—such are the consequences of an acquired and surmounted virtuosity. The history of modern geometry might also furnish us with excellent examples.

With Mallarmé, the identification of "poetic" meditation with the mastery of language, and the minute study in himself of their reciprocal relations, led to a sort of doctrine of which, unfortunately, we know only the trend.

At times, when considering the new and delightful contrivance of some passage in his poems, I would feel that he had directed his attention to almost every word in our language. The extraordinary book he wrote about English words must have been based on many researches and reflections concerning our own vocabulary.

We must not be misled into thinking that philology covers all the problems raised by language, any more than physics itself, or physiology, prevents or excuses the painter and the musician from having their own ideas about colors and sounds. The problems of creating new works introduce many questions and demand methods of classifying and evaluating that end by constituting a real but individual science for the artist, a form of capital that would be very hard to transfer. Mallarmé had made what was almost a science of *his* words. We cannot doubt that he had examined their patterns, had explored the inner space in which they appeared sometimes as *causes*, sometimes as *effects*, and had estimated what might be called their *poetic charge*; nor again that words—as a result of his tireless effort for precision— were secretly and virtually ordered within the *power* of his mind, according to a mysterious law of his inmost sensibility.

I imagine how he waited, with his mind straining toward *harmonics* and wholly bent on perceiving the emergence of a word in the universe of words, while he forgot himself in the effort to grasp the entire order of connections and resonances evoked by a thought that is struggling to be born. . . .

"I say: A FLOWER. . . ." he wrote.

Most people are blind in that linguistic universe, and deaf to the words they use. Speech for them is only an expedient, and they regard expression as merely *a shortcut*: that minimum defines the purely practical use of language. To be understood, to understand, are the two boundaries within which this practical and therefore abstract language is more and more narrowly confined. Writers themselves seldom linger over terms and forms, except on the occasion of some particular difficulty, some local choice, or an effect to be obtained. Such is the empiricism of the moderns. For a century or more, it has been possible to be a "great writer" while totally neglecting the physics of language, as if it were merely a contemptible agency, a middleman with which the "mind" would like to dispense. Nothing could be further than this opinion from the judgment of all antiquity. Stendhal, therefore, is no pagan. He avoids form, meter, rhythm, figures of speech, and fortifies himself against them by a rigorous study of the Napoleonic Code. If we regard what men do as more indicative of their true nature than what they think and what they say, Stendhal boasts in vain of his sensuality and his claim to be a follower of Condillac, the sensationalist. His language is abstractly intellectual, and he professes the aesthetics of an anchorite.

But Poetry is altogether pagan. The muse imperiously demands that there be no soul without a body, no *meaning*, no *idea*, that is not the *act* of some *remarkable* figure composed of tones, durations, and intensities.

Little by little, in the Poet, Language and Self come to have quite another relation than they have in other men. What the former regards as essential in language is imperceptible or unimportant to the latter. Those others will have no use for the sort of verbal incident that, for us, determines the life or death of a poem. Credulous and abstract, they try to separate *matter* or *substance* from *form*, a dichotomy that has no meaning except in the practical world, where there is an immediate exchange of words for deeds and deeds for words. They do not see that *what they regard as matter is only an impure or, in other words, a confused form.* Our *matter* is composed of incoherent incidents and appearances; sensations, images of all sorts, impulses, isolated words, fragmentary phrases. . . .But before we can transmit that which demands to be transmitted and *wills* to be disengaged from this chaos, all those heterogeneous elements must be represented in a unified system of language and must form a composition. The process of transposing inner events into formulas that consist of symbols belonging to the same type —all *equally conventional*—might well be regarded as the passage from an *impure form* or appearance to one that is *relatively pure.*

But the *given* language we acquired in early childhood, the origin of which is statistical and public, is in general poorly designed to express the states or moments of a process far removed from anything practical. It seldom lends itself to more profound or precise aims than those which determine the acts of daily life: hence the invention of technical languages, including the literary idiom. In every literature one notes the appearance, sooner or later, of a *Mandarin language*, sometimes quite remote from ordinary speech, but derived from that, as a rule, and obtaining from it the words, the figures, and the turns of phrase best suited to the effects desired by the artist in letters. And it happens too that a writer will invent a language of his own.

A poet makes simultaneous use of everyday speech—which meets the one condition of being understood and is therefore purely transitive—and of that other language, which contrasts with it in the same way that a garden carefully planted with selected species contrasts with the wild countryside where every species grows, and from which the gardener carries off a few choice specimens to replant and cherish in the richest loam.

Might it be possible to characterize a poet by the proportion in his work of these two languages, one natural, the other purified and specially cultivated for sumptuary use? A good example would be two poets of the same era, with almost the same background: Verlaine, whose verse boldly mingles colloquial idioms and vulgar terms with the highly artificial poetics of the Parnassian school, and who ended by writing with complete and even cynical impurity—but not without achieving happy effects; and Mallarmé, who created a language almost entirely his own by his refined choice of words as well as by the singular turns of phrase that he invented or developed, while consistently rejecting the immediate solutions suggested by everybody's way of thinking. In effect he was defending himself, even in matters of detail and in the elementary functions of the mental life, *against automatism*.

Mallarmé understood language as if he had invented it. A writer thus obscure had mastered the instrument of comprehension and coordination to such a degree that, forsaking the simple and always personal desires and designs of other writers, he formed the extraordinary ambition of conceiving and dominating the entire system of verbal expression.

In that respect—I said to him one day—he closely approached the attitude of the algebraists who vastly extended the science of forms and the symbolic aspect of their mathematical art. That type of attention has the effect of making the structure of expressions more evident and more interesting than their meanings or values. The properties of transformations offer a higher challenge to our minds than do the objects transformed; and I sometimes wonder whether any thought can exist that is more general than the idea of a "proposition," unless it be our consciousness of thinking anything whatever.

In the linguistic realm, figures of speech, which ordinarily play a subordinate part—which are introduced merely to illustrate or emphasize a meaning, and which therefore seem to be extrinsic, as if they were ornaments that could be stripped from a discourse without affecting its substance— become essential elements in Mallarmé's thought. *Metaphor* in particular, instead of being displayed as a jewel or used as a momentary expedient, seems to have the value here of a symmetrical relation based on the essence of things. With exceptional force and clarity, Mallarmé likewise conceives of art as implying and demanding an equivalence, a perpetual exchange between form and substance, sound and sense, action and subject matter. The modification, and sometimes the *invention*, of action by matter are misunderstood, as a rule, if not ignored by critics of the arts; the fault lies with their *idealism* and with their inexact or inept notion of matter.

Only an extremely rare combination of practice or virtuosity with the highest degree of intelligence could lead to those profound insights, which are also profoundly different from the ideas or idols of literature existing in the popular mind. But it followed that the cult and contemplation of the principles that govern every work of art made it more and more difficult for him to exercise his own art, while giving him fewer and fewer occasions for employing his prodigious resources of execution. In truth we need two lives: one of total preparation, the other of total development.

Is there any sharper torment, any division that strikes deeper into one's being, than this struggle of the Self against the Self, when the soul first identifies with what it desires to achieve, then turns to what it feels able to achieve, and sometimes taking the side of "I can" against "I will," sometimes that of "I will" against "I can," passes back and forth between all and nothing? Each of these "phases" is attended by contradictory or symmetrical ideas and movements, which could doubtless be brought to light by a sufficiently deep analysis of various works in terms of their systematic relations with the author's "can" and "will."

Preciosity, *sterility*, and *obscurity* are the abusive terms applied to Mallarmé by a vulgar type of criticism, which was merely recording as best it could the impression which the results of a sublime inner struggle made upon essentially commonplace and malicious minds. The duty of anyone who undertakes to inform the public about the works of another is to do all he can to understand them, or at least to determine the conditions and restrictions that the author has imposed on himself and that imposed themselves on the author. The critic would then learn that clarity, simplicity, and abundance generally result from the author's employment of familiar ideas and existent forms: the reader can recognize his own thoughts, sometimes embellished. But the opposite qualities often signify intentions of a higher order. Among the great men who were writers, some gratify us precisely by communicating the perfection of what we are. Others strive to allure us toward what we might be, if we had a more complex intelligence or a readier wit or more freedom from habit and everything else that interferes with the broadest combination of our mental powers. I agree that Mallarmé was obscure, sterile, and precious; but if, at the price of those *faults*—and even by means of all those faults, that is, by the efforts they imply on the part of the author and the efforts they exact from the reader—he has made me conceive and value *above all written works* the conscious possession of the function of language and the sense of having a superior liberty of expression, in the light of which any thought is only an incident, a particular event—then this conclusion which I have drawn from reading and meditating on his writings remains for me an incomparable treasure, such that no transparent and facile work has offered its equal.

Mallarmé

OF NECESSITY the most exalted project must also be the most difficult to conceive with precision, to undertake, and above all constantly to pursue.

The most difficult project to conceive, to undertake, and above all constantly to pursue in the arts, and especially poetry, is to *submit the production of a work to the conscious will* without this strict condition, deliberately adopted, being allowed to harm the essential qualities, the charms and the grace, which must be effectively carried by any work of art that aims to lead men's minds to the delights of the mind.

Stéphane Mallarmé was the first artist (and as yet doubtless the only one) who conceived and continued throughout his life to hold to the project of doing *what he wanted* in a domain of the mind wherein, by universal and time-honored consent, the action of the will is almost powerless, success being achieved by the favors of some fatality, or else of fickle gods who are unswayed by prayers and untouched by toil and the sacrifices of time and thought. There was, and there still remains, the mystery of *inspiration*, which is the name given to the spontaneous way speech or ideas are formed in a man and appear to him to be marvels that, of and by himself, he feels incapable of forming. He has, then, been *aided*.

From his twentieth year Mallarmé seems to have felt acutely that the poet's precarious condition was a degradation of the intelligence. He strove moreover to attain the highest purity, which implies accepting only the rarest offering of inspiration. When people speak of *sterility* in Mallarmé (and in some others), they forget that this indigence may be merely the effect of excessive scrupulousness and self-discipline. To obtain a particle of active substance tons of pitchblende have to be treated. At my own risk I shall say that Mallarmé brought the use of the will in art to a supreme degree of application and, going beyond the desire for inspiration which dictates a poetic moment, he came to desire the illumination which reveals the essence of poetry itself.

From 1865 no line he wrote fails to make us feel that its author had thought through language as if, on his own, he were reliving its multifarious invention; and, placing himself from that time on a summit where no one before him had even thought of settling, he remained until the day he died, intimately contemplating a truth whose proof he wished only to communicate by marvelous examples.

This revealed truth was destined, I believe, to initiate an unheard-of insight into poetry that would endow this creation by the human creature, this art of the mind, with a value quite different from the one accepted by naïve tradition and welcomed by the general sloth of the intellect. It was no longer a question of amusement, however sublime. Over and above what is Literature, Metaphysics, Religion, he had perceived the new duty that consisted in exercising and exalting the most spiritual of all the functions of the Word, which neither demonstrates, nor describes, nor represents anything at all; which therefore does not require, nor even allow, any confusion between reality and the verbal power of combining for some supreme end *the ideas that are born of words*.

In the poetry written up to his time he perceived the

fragments of a universal work that had been magnificently adumbrated but not rendered explicit, since none of the great men of the past had been able to conceive its whole or its guiding principle. He saw in the work he felt it to be his duty to write the essential undertaking of mankind, which he stated in familiar terms when he said that "everything would finally be expressed," that "the world had been created so as to end in a beautiful book," that "if there was a mystery of the world it could be contained in a *Figaro* editorial." These assertions proceeded from the substance of his thought, offering mere conversational glimpses of it. The conception was marvelously simple.

I want to picture a most rigorous state of meditation, fraught with anxiety, as though a life-or-death matter, yet inspired by that insignificant object insofar as life is concerned: poetry. To what could this passion of the intellect correspond—tormenting so deeply the man who has it, taking away his ability and, so to say, his right to sleep, making him blind to the most pressing demands of self-interest—if it were not to some Sovereign Good which he perhaps feels existing in himself and which a little more constancy, tension, and keen hope can at any moment allow him to grasp?

His singular consuming mysticism was destined to reach precision in a conception of language—I would almost say, a conception of the Word. In support of this sublimation of language, one may invoke all the uses of speech which do not satisfy needs of a practical nature and have no meaning except in relation to a wholly spiritual universe, deeply similar to the universe of poetry: prayer, invocation, incantation create the beings to whom they speak. Language thus becomes an instrument of "spirituality," that is to say, of the direct transmutation of desires and emotions into presences and powers that become "realities" in themselves, without the intervention of physically adequate means of action.

But neither poetic emotion nor creation is separate from the forms that engender them. Beauty is sovereign appearance. It results from some activity of ours which we bring to bear on a material we find around us. The artist in the material of language is generally happy to develop his talents from one work to the next, according as opportunity or chance gives them a certain subject or theme. Sometimes one fragment comes to his mind as if in sport, inciting him with the temptation or challenge to pursue and equal its perfection by way of his reflective powers. But, as soon as Mallarmé was in possession of his own firm conviction and poetic principle, that is to say, as soon as his *Truth* had *changed into his own true self*, he devoted himself without respite or reservation, without let or halt, to the extraordinary task of grasping in all its generality the nature of his art and, by a Cartesian analysis of the possibilities of language, of distinguishing all its means and classifying all its potential. On one occasion I compared this search to that which led from arithmetic, with its isolated processes, to the invention of algebra.

Language, when once we separate it from its practical uses, can receive certain sumptuary values that we call *philosophy*, or *poetry*, or otherwise. From this point the only question is to stimulate the need for these purposes. This is essential, as these new developments, these sophisticated formations, can be so aberrant that they produce amazement, and resistance on the part of the reader. But the more the need is created, and even aggravated, the more energy the reader finds to solve the problems of the text: from this he will often draw justifiable pride.

Mallarmé's transcendent view of the positive principles of poetry compelled him to undertake a labor of increasing precision which could have no end. Ordinary syntax appeared to him to exploit only a part of the combinations that are compatible with its rules: combinations whose simplicity allows the reader to skim over lines and to know the sense without becoming aware of language itself, just as one is not aware of the quality of a voice that speaks to us of business. Mallarmé sought entirely new arrangements with a daring and ingeniousness that made some exclaim in horror and others in admiration. He demonstrated, by astonishing proofs, that poetry must convey values that are equivalent to the meanings, sounds, the very appearance of words which, when brought unexpectedly together or fused with art, compose lines of poetry possessing a brilliance, fullness and resonance that are unprecedented. Here rhymes and alliteration on one hand, images, tropes, metaphors on the other, are no longer details and rhetorical ornaments that can be eliminated: they are substantial properties of the work. The subject is no longer the *cause* of the form: it is one of its effects. Each line becomes an entity having physical reasons for existence. It is a discovery, a sort of "intrinsic truth" that has been wrenched from the domain of chance. As for the world, all reality has no other excuse for existence except to offer the poet the chance to play a sublime match against it—a match that is lost in advance.

A Kind of Preface

A MANUSCRIPT collection of exercises intended for use in schools, which has recently been discovered and bought by the Bibliothèque Nationale, may serve as the occasion for a few reflections since it is signed by Mallarmé.

In a *totally organized* State—one, that is to say, which decreed, imposed, and from moment to moment maintained economic equality—what would be the chance of survival of a man whose talents and intellectual passion could be applied to nothing but the production of works that are wholly useless to life?

If everything had an exact value, if each man could only exchange public utilities for private ones, the sort of producer I have in mind would die of inanition: the sheer precision of a perfect economy would shut him out. Even if some amateurs were to enjoy his works, they could not buy them, for they would have to pay for them from a portion of their necessities—which, in the State I am imagining, constitute the limits of each man's property. And should it happen that the society itself, agreeing to some imperfection of its mechanism, be willing not to exterminate useless and transcendent industry, how could it single out, and support during his first obscure, silent years, a man who feels it his duty to remain unseen for as long as he needs to mature, and who consumes his days unsparingly in research, correction, and revision? Who can judge the future of an unknown man and his work, when it is still hidden from the man himself?

Then again: a purely useless production, which does not satisfy any of the universal needs of each man's life, escapes any communal estimation that comes from society as a whole and is valid for it as a whole. Neither Law nor the intervention of some administrative body can fix its value: a precise economic machine can only admit commensurable products into the system of its exchanges. It excludes every object that has only the value one chooses: a *stone* for one man, a *diamond* for another.

Finally, as this useless work is arbitrary by its very nature and origin, and as the very essence of it is that *it might not have been*, its accidental character is in turn imposed on the fate of its producer. Since he does not correspond to any real necessity, nor participate in any, he has no place in the cycle of real functions of organized life. He *might* not exist; therefore he *cannot* exist.

From these rather obvious remarks it follows that all the most admirable creations of man were only produced because of the inequality, even the injustice, perhaps the iniquity, of the social systems of different times.

Thus the history of Letters is also the history of the means of subsistence of those who practiced the art of writing through the ages. We find in it all the possible solutions to the problem of making a living that go against man's wits: flattery, praise of the powerful, of the rich or the crowd, beggarliness, fraud, armed theft, house-breaking, burglary, murder, and all the prescriptions of the criminal Code; living off women, extortion of money by threat, the pursuit of nondescript professions from which time is stolen for thinking and writing. Finally there is writing envisaged as a trade, which, from the point of view of literature, is the worst of all these systems. It is useless to speak of the lucky writers since by definition they only owe their good fortune to some inequality in the economic order.

In short, Homer was a beggar; both Vergil and Horace were flatterers; Villon was a thief; Aretino took care to know too much....In the reign of Louis XIV pensions were the goal. Think of all the parasites under Louis XV! Balzac ruined himself with ingenious bankruptcies. Lamartine sent around the hat. Verlaine lived on contrivances and alms. A great many others took bureaucratic posts: dispatch clerks, secretaries, administrative assistants—in the War Office, in the Law Courts, in the Churches, in the Town Hall, everywhere you will find an author. Sometimes he is a celebrity who is the pride of the whole administration: Huysmans gave great luster to the Sûreté.

For his livelihood Mallarmé had chosen to teach English. More than one of his former pupils is still alive but none of them, as far as I know, drew real profit from his classes. The teaching of languages fifty years ago was not what it is today: its method, in one way or another, was rough and ready. The first master I had, in my provincial college, was a good one-eyed man who with his single eye had never seen an Englishman in his life. It showed in his pronunciation. feel certain that since then things have changed considerably.

The relation of Mallarmé to his work was an uneasy one. His profession bored him to death. The lessons he had to give were almost the only thing he was ever known to complain of. He accepted with such loftiness the criticism, the disdain, the mockery his work brought him, that he made of these the natural and necessary homage to his firm faith and hope in his solitary conviction; and he remained marvelously constant in his sovereign will to give his entire life to the finest and most rigorous analysis of the poetic light that he had received one day in his youth.

But this admirable doctor of sublime letters, dispensing around him lessons of spiritual purity, offering us in his low voice a seductively formed doctrine inspired by a kind of applied mythology, suffered less and less silently the obligation to teach anything else, and the wasting of precious hours that had to be sacrificed to his inferior task.

This man who carried to its highest point, into the smallest details of life, the observance of Baudelaire's precept that *one must do to perfection whatever one does*, must have felt cruelly enough the increasing impossibility of giving himself with any love at all to the task that made his living.

Each year, the feeling that his holidays were drawing to a close poisoned the emotion he felt in the supreme moment of summer's funeral rites. He foresaw the new school year and it spoiled the solemn ceremony his beloved Forest was beginning to celebrate around Valvins: the silent all-embracing descent of gold to the earth, the themes and the beauties that were then offered to the mind's eye, were all tainted by the images of a dismal schoolyard and a classroom he knew too well, where for infinite hours he would have to tell heedless children things that have lost all interest and are finally detested and relegated to some servile and miserable region of one's mind.

Nevertheless before Mallarmé lost interest to the point of nausea in his profession, he had made a few attempts to come to terms with teaching. He conceived the idea of composing a few works intended for people who wished to learn English. From these he could envisage a dual advantage: first of all, that of increasing his income somewhat (it was almost wholly limited to his modest salary); secondly, he planned to expound his personal views on the English language and a particular method for acquiring a knowledge of it. I think the only book of this kind he was able to have published and put on sale was *Les Mots anglais*.

It is perhaps pertinent to recall in a few lines the constant preoccupation of his thought which is not absent from his didactic work.

He never stopped meditating in his own way (which was not that of a philologist or a philosopher) on Language, the instrument of his art, which he had made its very substance. The Idea he formed of it came to dominate his whole intellectual life. He had established from an early age that Poetic Reality is preeminently nothing but Language itself, and is inseparable from it, supporting all possible poems, and that each of the distinct elements of which it is composed presupposes a kind of creation. It seems clear that he had conceived and attempted the experiment of writing a poetic literature, the making of which would have been the opposite of the method apparently used by poets. People believe (and poets themselves often believe) that they move from some idea toward form, and from some impression toward the expression that tends to give it back. But that would only be a method of production exactly like the way ordinary discourse is born; if we claim that poetry follows this course and does not involve a completely different manner of using the means of speech, we make it inexplicable. "Common sense" then rightly protests and says: *Why speak in verse?* But whenever poets are truly poets, thought is indivisible from a certain song and the initiative is no longer dependent on thought alone.

I believe I am not betraying Mallarmé here, and substituting my thought for his, when I say that he dreamed of a poetry that would be as it were deduced from the system of properties and characteristics of language. Each work of beauty that had already been created represented for him some page of a supreme Book which would be arrived at by an ever greater consciousness, and purer utilization, of the functions of speech. To the poet's act he attributed a universal meaning and a kind of value that one would be tempted to call "mystical," were this not a forbidden word.

This metaphysics was associated in his case with an extraordinary virtuosity, and he had formulated the most subtle and precise theory of the resources of an art of which he was an unparalleled master. He could doubtless think directly in *poetry*, which is very rare, for poor education, vague terms, magnificently useless notions, scorn for observation, make most of us lose our way in this respect. Many people are quick to agree that they understand nothing about music, that harmony and orchestration appear to them to be mysteries, and they refrain from judging what there is no shame in having failed to study deeply. Yet although poetry is a much more complex and more uncertain art than the art of pure sounds (since it demands that we should at the same time control totally independent parts, that we should establish and maintain a certain indefinable harmony between what is pleasing to the ear and what stimulates the mind), nevertheless very few people, which excludes many who are very cultured, suspect that a particular preparation (which to my knowledge is not provided in schools) is necessary for those who wish to know poetry in any other way than gropingly and according to the style of the moment.

Syntax for this poet was an algebra he cultivated for itself. He loved at times to treat in a generalized way certain turns of phrase that ordinary syntax offers only in exceptional cases, or else to interweave clauses in a sentence and to venture into a kind of literary counterpoint which produced skillfully planned contacts or spacings between terms or ideas. One might say he foresaw what will be discovered one day and which is already evidenced in more ways than one: that forms of speech are patterns of relations and operations which, by allowing us to combine or associate the signs of any given objects and heterogeneous qualities, can help to lead us to the discovery of the structure of our intellectual universe.

One day he came out with a rather significant aphorism: "If there is a mystery of the world," he said, "it could be contained in a *Figaro* editorial."

Sometimes it seemed to me that he had examined, weighed, held up to the light all the words of the language one by one as a lapidary his precious stones: the sound, the brilliance, the color, the limpidity, the meaning of each of them, I would almost say its *orient* luster, became manifestly apparent both in his conversation and his writings, where he brought them together and mounted them with incomparable tactical effectiveness. I have kept the memory of observations he made which bore witness to extreme scrupulousness and refinement. One evening he spoke of the differences he perceived between the possible effects of abstract words according to whether they end with the syllable *té* (as in *verité*), with *tion* (as in *transition*), or with *ment* (as in *entendement*). It did not seem to him a trifling matter to have noticed these nuances....

"Poetry," Voltaire has admirably said, "is made only of beautiful details."

To the study of English Mallarmé tried to apply his infinitely subtle feeling for the musical delicacy of the French language. *Les Mots anglais* may well be the most revealing document we possess concerning his secret research.

Concerning *A Throw of the Dice*

A Letter to the Editor of Les Marges

Dear Sir:

A FRIEND who must bear me a grudge showed me the current issue of *Les Marges*. "There!" he said. I followed his index finger and read, in an article *devoted to poetry*, that "Mallarmé, after choosing a tried and tested artist as executor of his will, has seen—if the dead can still see—that this poet is repeating the exploits of Jean-Baptiste Rousseau."

"Well?" he said.

"Well," I answered, "that definition excludes me. 'A tried and tested artist'—it could not be said that I have suffered many more trials or can be certified as having much more skill than a thousand others. 'Executor of Mallarmé's will'—but that is conclusive: Mallarmé left no will, and I was never appointed in writing or requested by word of mouth to carry out his last wishes. Which leaves J.-B. Rousseau—and what has he to do with me? Long ago I read some poems of his preserved to oblivion in school textbooks. I know nothing about his exploits. I remember vaguely that he was accused of gross slanders and banished on that score. But I am hardly more addicted to slander than most people, and I am not aware of having been convicted by a high court of justice. So, of the three attributes by which you think I was designated, the first is indefinite, the second applies to no one at all, and the third does not apply to me. Be at peace, dear friend. No need to worry on my account. If the author had had something to say to me, it would have been the simplest thing in the world to give my name, besides his own."

But an excited man will not listen to logic. My friend looked at my composure as though it were a fine vase that makes one long to shatter it to bits. He desperately wanted me to write you, my dear editor, and at last he is having his way.

I come to this extremity with a sort of despair, for I have no taste for the fruitless controversies that blossom and wilt away in the back pages of reviews. I have seen too many of them in the last thirty years. There are certain great memories, however, to which I must give way. Perhaps I too have a few words to say about this *Coup de dés* that Mallarmé's new defenders insist on calling *Coup de dé*.

I dare say I was the first man to see that extraordinary work. Almost as soon as he had finished it, Mallarmé asked me to visit him in the Rue de Rome, and took me into the room where, behind an old tapestry, he kept his bundles of notes, all the secret material of his great unfinished work. The notes would stay there until his death, which he had given as the signal for their destruction. On a square table of very dark wood, with twisted legs, he spread out the manuscript of his poem, and he began to read it in a low, even voice, without the least straining for effect, as if to himself.

I like that absence of artifice. The human voice seems to me so lovely in itself, when heard close to its source, that I can seldom bear the professional readers of poetry who claim to *bring out* or *interpret* when actually they are overemphasizing, debauching the author's intentions, corrupting the harmonies of a text, and substituting their own lyricism for the intrinsic melodies of the linked words. What is their trade, their paradoxical proficiency for if not to make the most negligent verses pass for sublime, at least momentarily, while they travesty or annihilate most of the works that exist in their own right? Alas! I have sometimes heard *Hérodiade* declaimed, and even the divine *Cygne*.

After reading his *Coup de dés* as calmly as could be, in simple preparation for a greater surprise, Mallarmé finally showed me how the words were arranged on the page. It seemed to me that I was looking at the form and pattern of a thought, placed for the first time in finite space. Here space itself truly spoke, dreamed, and gave birth to temporal forms. Expectancy, doubt, concentration, all were *visible things*. With my own eye I could see silences that had assumed bodily shapes. Inappreciable instants became clearly visible: the fraction of a second during which an idea flashes into being and dies away; atoms of time that serve as the germs of infinite consequences lasting through psychological centuries—at last these appeared as beings, each surrounded with a palpable emptiness. There amid murmurs, insinuations, visual thunder, a whole spiritual tempest carried page by page to the extremes of thought, to a point of ineffable rupture—there the marvel took place; there on the very paper some indescribable scintillation of final stars trembled infinitely pure in an inter-conscious void; and there in the same void with them, like some new form of matter arranged in systems or masses or trailing lines, coexisted the Word!

I was struck dumb by this unprecedented arrangement. It was as if a new asterism had proffered itself in the heavens; as if a constellation had at last assumed a meaning. Was I not witnessing an event of universal importance, and was it not, in some measure, an ideal enactment of the Creation of Language that was being presented to me on this table at that minute, by this individual, this rash explorer, this mild and simple man who was so unaffectedly noble and charming by nature? I was assailed by the diversity of my impressions, seized by the novelty of what I saw, divided by doubts, and shaken by the thought of developments to come. I looked for some answer in the midst of a thousand questions that I held myself back from asking. Confronted by this intellectual invention, I felt a complex of admiration, resistance, passionate interest, and analogies springing to life.

As for Mallarmé—I think he was considering my astonishment, without astonishment.

On March 30, 1897, when he gave me corrected proofs of the text that would be published in the magazine *Cosmopolis*, he said to me with an admirable smile, betokening the purest pride inspired in a man by his sense of the universe, "Don't you think it is an act of sheer madness?"

A little later at Valvins, on the ledge of a window open to the calm landscape, spreading out the magnificent proofs of the big edition set in type by Lahure (it was never published), he paid me the honor of asking my advice about certain details of the typographical arrangement that was the essence of his undertaking. I searched my mind and offered a few objections, but only in the hope that he would answer them.

My dear editor, I do not question the utter sincerity of the persons who propose to adapt *Un Coup de dés* for the stage and entrust it to the "polyphony" of thirteen executants who will not be executors of a will. If they had known the living Mallarmé, however slightly, and if they had ever had my opportunity of hearing that great man *discuss* (almost in the algebraic sense) the slightest details of the verbal and visual system he had constructed—if they had been privileged to help him as he minutely verified the arrangement of a pattern in which the simultaneity of vision was to be united with the consecutiveness of speech, as though a very delicate equilibrium depended on such fine adjustments—I assure them that they would *never* have dreamed of demolishing by means of interpreters all that profound calculation based on chance.

Late in the evening of the same day, when he was taking me to the train, and the innumerable summer sky enclosed all things in a dazzling array of other worlds, as we were walking—shadowy smokers, in the company of the Serpent, the Swan, the Eagle, and the Lyre—it seemed to me that I was *now* caught up in the very text of the silent universe. A text, I thought, all clarity and enigmas, as tragic or as indifferent as might be; that spoke and did not speak; woven of multiple meanings, assembling order and disorder; proclaiming a God as forcefully as it denied Him; combining all the epochs of the world in its unimaginable totality, each epoch associated with the distance in light years of a celestial body; a text that evoked the most decisive, most evident, and most incontestable form of man's success, the fulfillment of his predictions—carried to the seventh decimal—and at the same time crushed this contemplative animal, this sagacious witness, under the futility of his triumph. . . . We walked on. In the hollow center of such a night, between the remarks we exchanged, I thought of his marvelous undertaking: what a model, what a lesson, there above us! Where Kant, rather innocently, perhaps, had thought to see the Moral Law, Mallarmé doubtless perceived the Imperative of a poetry: a Poetics.

That radiant dispersion; those bushes burning with cold fire; those almost spiritual grains of seed, distinct and simultaneous; the immense questioning suggested by a silence fraught with so much life and so much death—all this, a glory in itself, strange compound of reality and contradictory ideals, was it not bound to suggest to someone the supreme temptation of *reproducing its effect*?

He has undertaken, I thought, *finally to raise a printed page to the power of the midnight sky*.

No more of these memories, and from this point I shall not invoke my own reflections on the poem; I maintain that there is no need to take my word for it. Mallarmé's intention was proclaimed by Mallarmé himself. We have a record in his own hand of what he planned to do: he was trying to "employ thought nakedly" and "fix its pattern." He dreamed of a *mental instrument* designed to express the things of the intellect and the abstract imagination.

His invention, wholly deduced from analyses of language, of books, and of music, carried out over many years, was based on his consideration of the *page* as a visual unity. He had made a very careful study (even on posters and in newspapers) of the effective distribution of blacks and whites, the comparative intensity of typefaces. It was his idea to develop this medium, which till then had been used either as a crude means of attracting attention or else as a natural ornament for the printed word. But a page, in his system—being addressed to the glance that precedes and surrounds the act of reading—should "notify" the movement of the composition. By providing a sort of material intuition and by establishing a harmony among our various modes of perception, or among the *rates of perception* of our different senses, it should make us anticipate what is about to be presented to the intelligence. He introduced a *spatial* reading, which he combined with the *linear* reading; it was equivalent to enriching the literary domain with a second dimension.

It is true that the author (in his preface to the very imperfect *Cosmopolis* edition of the poem) concedes us the liberty of reading it aloud, but that liberty should not be misunderstood; it applies only to a reader already familiar with the text, one who, with his eyes on the splendid array of abstract imagery, can at last use his own voice to animate this ideographic spectacle of an intellectual crisis or adventure.

In a letter written to André Gide, and cited by Gide in a lecture he gave at the Théâtre du Vieux-Colombier, in 1913 (see *La Vie des Lettres*, April 1914), Mallarmé clearly stated his intention:

> The poem is being printed at this moment, in accordance with my conception of the pagination, on which the whole effect depends. One word in heavy type has a whole white page to itself, and I feel sure of the effect. I will send the first clean proofs to you in Florence. You will see that the constellation follows exact laws and, so far as it is possible for a printed text to do so, ineluctably assumes the air of a constellation. When the vessel heels over, it careens from the top of one page to the bottom of the next, etc.: for—and this is the whole point (which I had to omit in a periodical)—the rhythm of a phrase concerning an act, or even an object, has no meaning unless it imitates one or the other, and unless the phrase, when reproduced on paper and read in the original arrangement of words, does render something, after all.

It seems to me that this deposition carries some weight in the case now being argued. But let me say a few words more about the essence of the matter. . . .

I do not think we should regard *Un Coup de dés* as having been composed in two successive operations: one that consisted in writing a poem as it is usually written, that is, without regard to its visual pattern or spatial arrangement, and the other intended to give this definitive text a suitable disposition on the page. Mallarmé's endeavor must necessarily have been of a deeper order. It went back to the moment of conception and was in fact a conceptual method. It involved much more than simply attaching a visual harmony to a preexisting intellectual melody; on the contrary, it demanded an extreme, precise, and subtle form of self-mastery, acquired by a particular course of training, which enabled him to create a complex and momentaneous unity of distinct "parts of the soul," and to conduct that unity from a given origin to a given resolution.

To amplify those statements would require more time and space than I have. I only wanted to show that Mallarmé's last work had all the characteristics of an experiment on which he had reflected patiently and precisely. One may dismiss the poem, laugh at it; or attribute it to a pathological state of mind; all of which is familiar, predictable, I might almost say *correct*. But it is not permissible to present the poem to the public in a version that would utterly misrepresent the intentions and provisions of the author.

When I learned from Jean Royère, as he was telling me about his lecture, that preparations were well under way to present *Un Coup de dés* with a full orchestra, I was stupefied. The notion seemed preposterous. And when Dr. Bonniot brought me the same astonishing news on the following day, I could see at once that he shared my feelings. He had already made up his mind to demand that the undoubted intentions of the author should be respected. I pointed out to him, however, that there was a danger in having reason and even the law on one's side. He was in a delicate situation, for he would be coming into conflict with a zeal that was assuredly disinterested. He seemed to me much less disturbed by the great likelihood of reprisals than he was scrupulously concerned on behalf of Mallarmé's true reputation. But that

fame is not *statistical*. It does not depend on the size of a vague
public. It is composed of isolated individuals who bear little
resemblance one to another. Its possessor acquired it heart
by heart, as he "triumphed over chance, word by word."
One cannot add to that fame, or can one diminish it, by the
usual means. Silence might help it to grow; publicity can
do nothing for such a qualitative penetration. What good
are these appeals to everybody and these invocations of
public opinion. We already heard them when Mallarmé, in
his lifetime, was being put forward as an object of scorn. The
public was told, "See! Read! Judge for yourselves!" and
everyone howled with laughter. This time Bonniot did his
duty. Then came the reactions: with prompt injustice people
wrote the attacks on him that one might have expected.
Among other things, he was treated as a *legatee*; I might even
say that this was the outstanding reproach among the many
addressed to him.

I would rather not mention the pain such a term can
inflict, when it is used against a man who owes his inherit-
ance to the cruelest bereavement. . . . What I must say is that
the sacred legacy of the memory, the manuscripts, and the
fame of Mallarmé is in pious hands. Some day that will be
shown. A prolonged and silent attention will perhaps have
results that could not be achieved by improvised manifestations. Moreover, when people treat the heir with disdain, they do not realize that the principles invoked against
him would also apply to the author himself. The same arguments that would oblige Bonniot—if he accepted them—to
authorize the misrepresentation of *Un Coup de dés* would also
be valid against Mallarmé. Those arguments, in reality, *have
nothing to do with Bonniot's being an heir*; what they demand
is that every writer, dead or alive, must suffer any person

whatever to do whatever he pleases with a published work. Without any obstacle, without possible protest, a poem could be turned into a play, a film, a ballet, a pantomime. The sacredness of art would be invoked against you, the artist! Already those hapless works that are public property have been put to the torture! Shakespeare was no sooner delivered from the music of Ambroise Thomas than he was tossed as a prey into the circus arena. *Athalie* will be filmed. I can picture the *Mystery of Jesus* as the subject of a music-hall sketch. An actor bound to the cross (and we had better not look for him, since he could soon be found) would say in seeming agony to some Pascal-for-the-evening: "This drop of greasepaint has been shed for thee."

The avatar has become a sort of natural law. One is tempted to say that all creations of the mind are subjected, in our time, to an indefinite series of incarnations and reincarnations. The original conceptions do not seem to have profited very much.

Do not think I exaggerate. When Dr. Bonniot was being urged to authorize the performance of *Un Coup de dés* and when he suggested that *L'Après-midi d'un faune* (which was written for the stage) might be presented instead of the other poem (which was not), one of his visitors exclaimed, "How can you think of it, Doctor! Imagine us playing *L'Après-midi d'un faune*...after what Nijinsky has done with it!"

Please allow me to express the highest regard for you, my dear editor, and believe me very truly yours,

PAUL VALÉRY

Literary Reminiscences

MALLARMÉ, whom you have perhaps read, or at least tried to read, is, as you know, a rather difficult author. I shall not talk about his work now; I shall merely say a few words about his personality. He was the most delightful, the most affable, the most courteous man one could imagine. You were received, when you went to visit him, by a man of very modest height with a noble face, a serious and gentle expression, and admirable eyes. His welcome was exquisitely graceful, almost that of another age. He had as it were reconstructed his social being, his visible personality, as he had wholly reconstituted his thought and his language. He offers us a wholly singular example of *self-creation*, of a conscious remolding of the natural personality. Nothing would seem finer than that a man should conceive and carry out this idea of transforming his thought and acts, his work and, in brief, his whole way of life.

Social relations with him were charming. Every Tuesday he grouped together around him, as you know, a few friends and a number of strangers. Anyone who wanted could go to his place, he was equally affable with all. This great accessibility was not without amusing consequences. Every year about the same time you would see a long-haired American who might make you wonder if he had ever opened one of Mallarmé's books or read a line he had written. This unexplained visitor arrived, sat down, said strictly nothing, nodded his approval, then disappeared. He showed moreover the greatest reverence for Mallarmé. One day he wrote to the poet to tell him that, as a souvenir of the enjoy-able evenings spent at his place, around his lamp, he had conceived the idea of baptizing his newly born son *Mallarmé*. So there is at this moment in America a gentleman called Mallarmé who probably does not know the origin of his strange and rare Christian name, nor why he bears it.

I would like to recount a few episodes of my personal rela-tions with Stéphane Mallarmé. One day in the year 1897 he invited me to his home. He wrote that he had something important to communicate to me. I found him in his bed-room; his bedroom and study were one and the same. A modest teacher of English with a very meager income, Mallarmé lived in the Rue de Rome in a flat that was both delightful and utterly simple. He dwelt at the top of the building in minute lodgings that were magnificently decorated with the paintings that had been given to him by his personal friends: Manet, Berthe Morisot, Whistler, Claude Monet, Redon. He received me then in the small room where, not far from his bed, his desk stood, an old square table with corkscrew legs made of very dark wood. A manuscript was in front of him. He took it and began to read a strange text, stranger than any of his I knew at that time. So strange indeed did the manuscript seem to me that I could not take my eyes from the paper Mallarmé was holding. This was how that extraordinary poem *Un Coup de dés* appeared to me for the first time. I do not know if you have ever seen it. It was specially written to give the reader sitting by his fire the impression of an orchestral score. Mallarmé had long reflected on the literary techniques that would enable us, while looking through an album of different typefaces, to rediscover the mood induced in us by orchestral music; and, by an intensely studied and scientific combination of the material means of writing, by a wholly new and profoundly meditated use of spacing, of masses and blanks, of diverse typographical characters, of capital letters, small letters, italics, etc., he had contrived to construct a work whose appearance was truly compelling. It is certain that, as your eye goes over this literary score, as you follow the movement of this visual poem in which certain parts or certain passages correspond to one another—printed as they are in the same characters, adjusting exactly to one another at a distance like musical themes or tones—you imagine, you believe you are hearing, a wholly new type of symphony. You can understand how valuable it would be for poetry to be able to create echoes, harmonies, to pursue one theme across another, and to interweave independent *parts* of a thought. Mallarmé had dared to orchestrate a poetic idea.

Having finished his reading, he asked me if I did not consider him completely insane. I remained silent for a moment, at a loss for words; as excuse I pleaded the extreme newness of the work, the surprise it had given me, and I asked to see the text again at close hand. He handed me the manuscript, and I began to imagine the immense toil the poem must have demanded, to measure the determination, the skill, the depth that it implied in its author.

This man had reflected on every word in the language. His obscurity, which you know of, and which you have perhaps experienced to your cost, is nothing but the result of an infinitely long research that sought to extract from language and poetry everything they could offer the inflexible will to create.

But today I will not insist on considerations of that order. I prefer to remain in the realm of memory, and not to make you follow me in an overarduous analysis. Let us turn again to our memories.

Here is another, the last one, the last dear and painful impression I have of Mallarmé. It dates from the last time I visited him. It was July 14, 1898. He had invited me to spend the day with him in his small property at Valvins. Valvins is a hamlet situated on the very bank of the Seine, facing the edge of the Fontainebleau forest. There Mallarmé used to spend the summer in a modest country house he had arranged with his perfect taste; there he found peace and the labor of meditation during his holiday months; there he had a skiff in which he sometimes took his friends out on the river. And there it was I found him on July 14, 1898. After lunch he led me to his tiny study, which was about two paces wide and six paces long. The proofs of the celebrated *Coup de dés* of which I have just spoken were spread out on the windowsill. Together we looked for a long time at this species of linguistic machine he had so knowingly, patiently, daringly constructed, for nothing could be more daring than this experiment. No one has had more literary courage than this man, who could have been the first poet of his time if he had refused to be wholly himself, and who risked everything to pursue deeply within himself the lifelong quest of an idea.

We considered the proofs for a long time. The perfection of the material execution was essential to his concept, since the visible appearance of the work he dreamt of had capital importance, and every detail had to be specified and carried out with minute care. I remember discussing with him the placing of certain words, the importance of certain blank spaces. And then we went outside. We walked in the warm sunshine. Summer was well advanced and already the wheat in the plain was golden before us. Suddenly he stopped in thought. This man was dreaming of the coming marvels of autumn, autumn that would bring him back to Paris once again and the concerts. . . . I forgot to tell you that he used to go every Sunday to the Lamoureux concerts where you could see him absorbed, not so much listening to the music for itself as trying to force its secrets. You could see him, pencil in hand, noting what he found profitable to poetry in music, trying to extract from it a few types of relationship which could be brought into the realm of language. All summer he would dream of what he had noted in this way during the winter, and would wait impatiently for the time when he could return to Paris and take his place at the concerts, going back, that is, to his source. Considering, then, the golden plains spread before us, this man, obsessed with music, made this final remark. Pointing to the splendor in front of us he said to me: "It's the first cymbal clash of autumn over the earth." That evening he accompanied me to the station. We chatted for a long time beneath an admirable sky. . . . I never saw him again. Three weeks later I received a telegram from his daughter telling me of his death. He had been struck down, literally stifled by an illness for which there is no remedy, in the very arms of the doctor who had come to see him. For me it was a terrible blow.

Let us now say a few words about another writer whom I also loved and admired, although he was very different from Mallarmé.

You know what a strange literary destiny was that of Huysmans. He had begun as a very strict disciple of the Naturalist school, a fervent follower of Zola, one of the writers who collaborated in *Les Soirées de Médan*. His art was extremely sophisticated, refined, nervous—perhaps to excess.

Nevertheless Huysmans acquired a singular influence over three sections of the public by three main works which have kept almost all their savor and power. Each of these books, *À Rebours*, *Là-Bas*, and *En Route*, produced a profound impression on a particular category of readers. *À Rebours* was a revelation for the young men of my time. You know its bizarre plot: the last survivor of an old family shuts himself up in a house that he has built near Paris, and there gives himself over to the extreme cultivation of his sensations. He becomes intoxicated with perfumes that he has curiously and carefully chosen and classified; with liqueurs he composes his own symphonies. Or else he assembles singular objects, extremely rare flowers, which he becomes enamored of and then rejects. But in this same book Huysmans brought to a great number of young men forty years ago the knowledge of writers who were still obscure, painters who were unhailed, artists whom the general public knew least. It was in this book that I learned the names of Verlaine, Mallarmé, Odilon Redon, and a few others, who were then almost unknown.

Huysmans was deputy director of a branch of the Sûreté in the Ministry of the Interior. I was desirous of seeing him and summoned up the courage to ask for an appointment. He wrote to me: "Come to the Sûreté, in the Rue des Saussaies. There, in a dismal but solitary setting, we shall be able to chat." I did not fail to go to this awe-inspiring rendezvous. In the Rue des Saussaies, the office boy led me into a little room that was decorated with files. Huysmans was there enthroned. As I looked around me, trying to put on a countenance, I noticed strange labels on the green files of the deputy director. On one of them the word "cadgers" was written in a firm hand; the other was labeled "bores," and I told myself: "I am not in the left-hand file, but there is a good chance that my letter is in the other." When a man becomes famous, he feels more and more each day the need for files of this kind.

Huysmans' conversation was wildly picturesque. He had the raciest vocabulary imaginable. I truly could not recount to you most of the things he told me. He was rarely considerate and often satirical. He was the most nervously sensitive of men, yet very loyal and helpful. His strange books would bring him bizarre visitors and quite extraordinary letters. Each time I went to see him he had some new story, always surprising.

Now I shall tell you something of the painter Edgar Degas, whom I knew very well and who very naturally takes his place alongside Huysmans and Mallarmé. You know the work of Degas; today it is in the galleries. As a man he was the most uncompromising, the keenest, sometimes the most difficult personality; a wit if ever there was one, and singularly intelligent. At the time I knew him, Degas lived in the Rue Victor-Massé, in a building since demolished, in which he occupied three stories. On the first was his private gallery. He had brought together there, one on top of the other, works of painters he loved. He had some very beautiful paintings by Delacroix, Corot, Ingres, and so forth. Upstairs was his apartment, one of the most cursorily swept and scrubbed apartments I have ever seen. It was all dust and treasures, for his favorite sketches covered the walls. On the third floor was the studio. There you found the bath, the tub and the sponges that were so often used by his models and that appear in such a great number of his paintings. But it is not the painter, nor even the admirable critic I wish to speak of, but a Degas less known, the man of letters and poet.

There was in him a latent writer, and first of all a wit whose pronouncements are so well known that I shall not repeat them here. There was also a Degas who was a poet, and who thus has his place in these literary memories I have been recounting to you today. I will not talk of him as an amateur poet. With his sharp mind he could not bear to stay in the larval state of a beginner. He had an instant and endless curiosity about everything which in the arts constitutes the actual craft—today one would say the "technique." He composed verse, then, feeling it to be a craft of which he was not a master; moreover he composed with the greatest difficulty, which is fitting, since anyone who writes verse easily is not writing verse. When he was in difficulty, when the muse failed the artist or the artist the muse, he took counsel, he would go and lament on the shoulders of men whose art it was. Sometimes he had recourse to Heredia, sometimes to Stéphane Mallarmé. Enlarging on his struggles, his desires, his failures, he would say:

"I've worked for a whole day at this damned sonnet. I have wasted a whole day away from painting writing verse, and I am nowhere near what I want. It's given me a headache."

One day when he was speaking to Mallarmé in this strain he finally said:

"I do not see why I can't finish my little poem; after all I have plenty of ideas."

Mallarmé replied:

"But, Degas, poetry is not written with ideas but with words."

There is an immense lesson in that.

Last Visit to Mallarmé

I FIRST began to see a great deal of Mallarmé at a time when literature was almost the least of my concerns. Reading and writing were a trial to me, and I confess that some of this feeling persists in me to this day. The new preoccupations that seldom left me were self-awareness pursued for its own sake, the clarification of that awareness, and the effort to form a clear picture of my existence. This secret affliction estranges one from literature, even though it originates from there.

Meanwhile, in my inner system of values, Mallarmé was the figure that represented conscious art and the supreme state of the highest literary ambition. For his mind I had formed a deep companionship and hoped that the day would come—in spite of the difference in our ages and the still greater difference in merits—when I should not be afraid to tell him about my difficulties and explain my particular opinions. It was not that he intimidated me, for no one could have been gentler or more delightfully simple; but in those days I felt that there was a sort of contradiction between the practice of literature and the pursuit of a certain rigor and a complete intellectual sincerity. The problem was infinitely delicate; should I bring it to Mallarmé? I loved him and set him above all others, but I had chosen not to worship what he had worshiped all his life, the ideal to which he had sacrificed it, and I could not find in my heart to tell him so.

Yet how could I pay him a more genuine tribute than by confessing what I thought and by explaining how his discoveries, with the delicate and precise analyses that led to them, had transformed the literary problem for me and persuaded me to throw up the game? The fact was that Mallarmé's efforts, opposed as they were to the doctrines and ideals of his contemporaries, tended to rearrange the whole domain of Letters in a logical order based on the general consideration of forms. He had no scientific training, and yet it is most remarkable that a thorough study of his art should have led him to such an abstract conception and one so close to the final speculations of certain sciences. I might add that he never spoke of his ideas except in a figurative way. He was a schoolteacher who loathed his profession, and perhaps that explains his strange aversion for any form of explicit teachings. But in trying to define his tendencies for my own benefit, I allowed myself the inner liberty of giving them names. Ordinary literature seemed to me comparable with arithmetic, that is, with the pursuit of particular results in which it is hard to distinguish the precept from the example; while literature as he conceived it seemed to me analogous with algebra, for it presupposed an intention to emphasize the formal aspects of language, to keep them in evidence through the ideas, and to develop them for their own sake.

"But from the moment that someone has recognized and grasped a principle, he need not waste his time applying it," I said to myself.

The day for which I was waiting never came.

I saw Stéphane Mallarmé for the last time on July 14, 1898, at Valvins. When luncheon was over, he took me to his "workroom," which was four paces long and two paces wide. The window looked out at the Seine and the forest through foliage gashed with sunlight, and the least tremors of the sparkling river were faintly echoed on the walls.

Mallarmé was preoccupied with the final details of the construction of his last poem, *Un Coup de dés*. The inventor was considering and adding pencil touches to the completely novel machine that Lahure's printing establishment had agreed to set up for him.

Nobody had yet undertaken, or dreamed of undertaking, to create a *visual pattern* for his text that would have a meaning and an action comparable to those of the text itself. Just as the daily use of our limbs makes us almost forget their existence and neglect the variety of resources they offer; and just as it sometimes happens that an artist of the human body makes us see all their flexibility, at the cost to himself of a lifetime devoted to exercises and exposed to the perils of his calling—so the customary use of speech, with the practice of cursive reading and the habit of immediate expression, makes us less conscious of those familiar acts and destroys even the idea of their potential power and development,—unless some dedicated person appears who is strangely disdainful of easy ways of thought, but singularly attentive to the possibility of producing something that is free, supple, and completely unforeseen.

I was standing beside such a person. There was nothing to tell me that I should never see him again. No prophetic raven croaked in the gold of that afternoon.

Everything was calm and sure. . . . But while Mallarmé was speaking, with his finger on the page, I remember that my mind became fixed on the dream of *that very moment*. Abstractedly I was giving it a value that seemed to be absolute. At the side of the living man, I was thinking of his destiny as having been fulfilled. Born to be a delight to some, a scandal to others, and a marvel to all—a marvel of folly and absurdity to most men, but a marvel of pride, elegance, and intellectual modesty to those who knew him best—it was enough that he had written a few poems, and they had called the very purpose of literature into question. Difficult as they were to understand, but impossible to overlook, they had divided the lettered community. That he lived in poverty, without public honors, was enough to cheapen all the advantages enjoyed by others, and, though he never asked for it, he could depend on some for an extraordinary devotion. As for himself he gently overwhelmed the universe with the smile of a sage or a lofty victim, and he had never asked anything from the world except the rarest and most precious things it has to offer. These he found in himself.

We went walking in the fields. The "artificial" poet gathered the simplest flowers; we filled our arms with cornflowers and poppies. The air was fire, the splendor absolute, the silence full of eddies and transformations; death seemed impossible or immaterial; everything was formidably beautiful, burning and sleeping; and the soil itself quivered before our eyes.

In the sun, within the immense shape of the pure sky, I dreamed of an incandescent expanse where nothing distinct survived, where nothing lasted and nothing ceased; as if even destruction had destroyed itself before its work was done. I lost the feeling of difference between being and non-being. Music sometimes gives birth to this impression, which is beyond all others. And poetry, I thought . . . might it not also be the supreme play of the transmutation of ideas?

Mallarmé showed me the valley, which the early heat of summer was turning to gold. "*Look!*" he said. "It's the first cymbal clash of autumn over the earth."

When autumn came, he was no longer there.

Stéphane Mallarmé

A TELEGRAM from his daughter, on September 9, 1898, told me of the death of Mallarmé.

The news to me was like one of those thunderbolts that strike to one's depths and even destroy the power of speech. They leave our appearance unchanged and a visible sort of life goes on, but within there is an abyss.

I no longer dared listen to myself, for I felt those intolerable few words waiting for me. From that day there have been certain subjects for reflection that I have truly ceased to consider. I had often thought of discussing them with Mallarmé; they were as if hallowed and forbidden to my mind by his sudden disappearance.

In those days he was very often in my thoughts, but never as mortal. What he signified to me, in the person of a man eminently worthy to be loved for his character and grace, was an utter purity of faith in respect to poetry. I felt that all other writers, by comparison, had failed to recognize the one god and were bowing down to idols.

The guiding motive of his quest was directed toward defining and producing the most exquisite and perfect beauty. From the very first he set out to determine and isolate the most precious elements; then he studied how to combine them without alloy, and at this point he begins to draw apart from other poets, for even the most illustrious of these are sullied with impurities, blemished with inflation, and weakened by lapses. He also drew apart from the majority of readers—that is, from immediate fame and its rewards—by aiming at what was loved and desired by himself alone. He disdained, and was himself disdained. Already he found a recompense in the feeling that what he had composed with so much care was thereby preserved from changing fashions and from the accidents of history. The bodies he gave to his thoughts are glorious bodies, subtle and incorruptible.

In the rich and strange works of Mallarmé there is not one of those casual lapses that flatter so many readers and give them a secret feeling of intimacy with the poet, not one of those displays of humanity that go straight to the hearts of persons who make little or no distinction between what is human and what is common. On the contrary, they embody the boldest and most coherent effort that has ever been made to overcome what might be called *naïve intuition* in literature. This meant a break with the majority of mortals.

Here, perhaps, one should ask whether a poet can legitimately demand any conscious and sustained intellectual effort from his readers. Does the art of writing simply amount to entertaining one's fellows and manipulating their feelings, without arousing their resistance? The answer is simple, there is no difficulty involved: every mind is master in its own home. It can easily reject whatever repels it. You need not hesitate to close our books, let us fall from your hands.

But not everyone is satisfied with that solution, and there are those who become irritable, complain, or do a little more than complain. Although I can think of nothing excellent that has escaped their wrath and not been fortified by their disdain, still I cannot blame them when I try to understand their motives. It is quite a respectable form of impatience that drives people to depreciate and ban and heap with ridicule whatever they do not understand. They are, as best they can, defending their intellectual honor and saving the face of their intelligence. I find it remarkable, and almost admirable, that men cannot bear to impute to themselves a sort of intellectual defeat or to support the weight of it by themselves: they appeal to others of their kind, as though the multiplication of mirrors. . . .

A man who renounces the world puts himself in a position to understand it. The man I am speaking of, who strove toward his supreme felicities by practicing a sort of asceticism, since he had rejected all the facile opportunities of his art and their profitable consequences, fully deserved to understand the depths of it. But those depths depend solely on our own, which in turn depend on our pride.

Love, hate, and envy are all lights for the mind, but pride is the purest light. It has revealed to men all the most difficult and admirable tasks they had to perform. It burns away everything petty and simplifies the personality by detaching it from vanities, for pride is to vanities what faith is to superstitions. The purer one's pride—the stronger and lonelier it is in the soul—the more one's works are lingered over, the oftener they are rejected and put back to be reforged in the fire of a longing that never dies. When attacked by a great soul, the subject matter of art is purified. Little by little the artist divests himself of gross and commonplace illusions, demands immense invisible labors from his inner forces. His years are consumed by implacable choice, and the word *finish* loses its meaning, for nothing is ever finished in the mind.

Meanwhile, stripped of the charms that make it serve the

majority of men, the mysterious action of the idea sheds its ordinary motives and its recognized causes.

Mallarmé justified himself before his thoughts by daring to stake his whole being on the loftiest and most daring of them all. The transition from dream to word occupied his *infinitely simple* life with all the combinations that could be invented by a curiously subtle intelligence. He lived in order to effect admirable transformations within himself. He could see no other conceivable destiny for the universe than to be finally *expressed*. One might say that he placed the Word not at the beginning, but at the very end of all things.

No one else had shown the same precision or constancy or heroic assurance in professing the eminent dignity of Poetry, beyond which he could discern nothing but chance. . . .

FROM THE NOTEBOOKS

Leonardo

O Lionardo

He felt *all* his power and *all* his weakness. And his power came to him when he was faced with obstacles, and his weakness when he was faced with something easy. 1:490

In L. da V. consider his way of universalizing objects of like nature in a scene—all the light objects seen as a group, all the heavy ones, etc. 2:125

Leonardo: painting-pantomime.... 2:670

According to Leonardo (as I interpret him) life in the least animal gives up its dwelling, the body it has made for itself (its work), with great regret—after so much experiment, centuries of precision. He teaches us to value *life*, that miracle of combinations—to admire the organs, the functioning, to sense all the value of an apparatus, a bone. But it is well to reply that life itself teaches us not to esteem too highly any living thing. 3:457

"The Mona Lisa smiling" thinks of nothing. Her smile says: "I am thinking of nothing. Leonardo thinks for me." 4:105

(For L. da V.) Theory of "rough drafts," preparations, inferior goods, things settled prematurely—a sieve. 4:199

Condottieri, Leonardo. And what is Troy to me?...What I judge is not his aim, but his act and his art. Any flag will do, but a victory has to be planned.

This is science, that is art—no matter. Perfection is the essential. 4:439

...Philosophically I am rather with you. But I watch others, and observe carefully.

Because in these matters, no one strangles another, no one makes his way by polemics and cursing—but rather by penetration, illumination, possession of the other, a premonition of the other in himself.

This willed identity, this intelligence—it's much more difficult than war. 4:804

Leonardo clearly saw the problem posed by the fear of death.
4:878

On Leonardo, etc.
...One must be armed with real instruments—drawing and the ability to draw.

Why? Above all, *against* metaphysics, and this is what a few metaphysicians, the subtle and cowardly ones, have been aware of and have tried to replace by *images*.

True philosophy would be nothing but an instrument of thought, not a goal, but reasoned adaptation, a shortcut.

There is no supreme, final knowledge—no divine point of view, no golden balcony.

But maneuver, the trained brain-animal—whose rider is every circumstance, the present, and chance. 5:33

Two men unknown to each other, at different times and in different places, with no contact literary or other, arrive at the same *idea*. So, in Baudelaire's *Mon Cœur mis à nu* I find a very particular thought on love, which is also (to a fraction) found in a manuscript of Leonardo's, and which Baudelaire *could not* have known. 5:750

A man lying in the grass on the bank of a small river and able to follow the destiny of the swirls in the water, to conceive the history of these forms and not disregard them as ephemeral, to grasp the flow of their fluid nets, their narrowing, their spreading out, the whirls they are caught in, to take a notebook of coarse paper and sketch the movement on it; and so reach the banks, sketch the fields, the wet sands, noting the curve of the bed, the opposite bank higher, and noticing that it *must* be so because of the different speed on the two sides of the river. On the near bank, placing the peasant woman as she approaches giving suck to her baby, the weight of her body shifting to the side where the child is not, the right breast vertical to the center of gravity of her body, the right foot hidden by her skirt, the other visible; and the same look and the same hand rising to catch the bird lifted on the waves of the lower air...drifting toward the blue depths, extending analysis into their decreasing transparencies; man all intelligence served by an intrepid hand, by logic and clarity, who for the slightest impression substitutes a complete system—knowing nothing of the vague, the ephemeral, but knowing all the same how to bring them into his art. 6:604

Poe and Leonardo—the character of both. Common characteristics: by analysis and discovered laws, to create fantastic beings or improbable semiviable situations. It must be observed that our metaphysics is of this kind: to define what is not.

The forms of energy, magnetism, etc., considered philosophically—the metaphysics of modern physics. We must not forget that the classical problems in philosophy are all prior to the modern era. Imagine another Aristotle. The ideas of metaphysics are based on images. Outlines of a philosophy of physics in Leonardo.   6:786

It may happen that a rather obscure writer or thinker, one of the third rank, discovered too soon a mode of thought or writing that becomes known several centuries afterwards, and is presented at that time by a man who will be elevated to the first rank.

Leonardo *as* a mode of thought—the kind of man who attempts to be scientific. Cf. Fontenelle—mathematician and writer.   6:882

The hypermuse poet. . . self-muse. Poetics of Aristotle. Put myself on stage. Three steps of pink marble led. . . . The self-styled *seers*, the critics, the engineer—Leonardo. Cerebral machines—Voltaire, Poe. Analysis of literary operations—considerations on poetry. (Cf. *Poe*, 7:205).   7:204

Apropos of Halévy's article on me (May 20):
This portrait, false as it is, makes the model smile and reflect. . . . What I have constantly called Leonardo's method is the control not so much of thought as of its elements. Observation and action understood in this way exclude all mysticism, for there is *no mysticism that can stand up against the whole range of the mind's maneuvers*. Mysticism consists in being maneuvered by some image or some *particular* touch, by way of the impression of inner *extraneity* it gives us. But if we *criticize* this extraneity, if we prove to ourselves that it is

a matter of the too human, if we bring it into the group of ordinary psychic operations. . . .

No *arcana*.   7:489

The debased condition of universities.

Men like Leonardo, Montaigne, Galileo, . . . are not considered in the history of Philosophy. Worse yet, religion is not even mentioned.   7:516

O Lionardo che tanto pensate! Love was the wholly unexpected recompense and punishment for that *quantity* of thought.

8:374

Demon of Socrates

Leonardo would have known how to paint him. But I shall try to describe him. He is simply the fictive being assumed by the *inventive* voice.

That is to say that his conversations are imperative, mysterious, not from obscurity but from being clearer than clarity, and obscuring the clear—obscure in themselves, obscuring the rest, and very brief—broken by long silences. Short phrases—and always in verse rhythms.

What we create is not our own,

Nor really *anyone's*.

What we create is born of circumstances that are present and unable *not to create*, just as electrical charges cannot *not* combine, *with a spark*.

Little by little, or suddenly, the image of what is possible appears.   9:732

For a "Leonardo"

. . . Men pruning a tree: the group of them, with its form and its movement, and the laws of mechanics, and the diversity of points of view. Now colors, now forces and moments, and the works in the fire, and now the value of things and time. The mind dabbles in everything, and passes from one system to another. 9:902

Frontiers of philosophy—Leonardo, Pascal, Montaigne, would figure in ancient philosophy. 10:351

Morphology—Art—Science—Lionardism

Lionardo *rationalized* the natural forms, and *naturalized* the rational forms. First and foremost he understood and *willed* to derive the systematic relations between cause and form, and vice versa. An idea unknown to antiquity was reborn in dynamics ... trajectories ... etc. ... in the eighteenth century. 11:140

But—Reverie

On waking, I thought about knots, about their properties or possibilities—then Leonardo, then the cause of forms. I see the connection with dynamics which became morphology in 17—, by way of the problem of trajectories and that of equilibrium. 11:149

Lionardo

Leonardo, like no other artist, has the sense of *natural forms*. He is the angel of morphology. Cartilage of the larynx, flowers, rocks, draperies are treated by him with the same eye, and that eye always assisted by the will to understand—to be *faithful* and *abstract*—to such a point that his intentions are drawings and must leave him with something he has grasped. It would seem that he perceived the formative forces by drawing them. It is this that gave his fantastic

figures the look of synthetic products, and it was in him
that the characteristics of that power of creating the artificial,
which later triumphed in industry, appeared for the first time
as works of art. Now, on the contrary, we have abandoned
that mode of possession in art.   11:199

Leonardo, a monster of equilibrium.   11:499

Notes on Leonardo

Presentiment of the modern era. Everything is brought
back to precise knowledge, and proved by its results—
inventions, possibilities, etc. Remake the world around man.
"Nature" a particular case; each natural detail a particular
case. The mechanics of phenomena. Even of art. The
reciprocal effect of knowledge on developing action and of
action on conception.

Leonardo, *one of the founders of Europe*.

His means: the role of drawing, of geometry, and of
calculus. The role of images.

Visualization: prelude to the vision of relations in analytical geometry and mechanics. Pattern of the laws, view of the
variations and connections. Develop: symbols, forces.

11:841

Gladiator: modern application

Leonardo—a very simple man, comes down to this, that
he dealt as an *engineer* with human beings and the arts—that
is, with an eye to quantities and precise functions. The
problem of painting, for him, took the form of the imitation
of what is seen, and the composition of a well-defined
subject, very clearly rendered. Hence, his analyses, from
aerial perspective to the psychophysiology of persons.

13:208

Lionardo

Production of the *idea*, and representation by hand of the *thing*, as if from a knowledge of how the thing itself was produced.

And all this is the curious mechanism of imagining inner or creative forces combined with continuous touch and vision—of which the natural and capital product is the *object*, the essential element of our *reality*, its complete *form* and limit.   13:555

A great artist—a Leonardo, a Rembrandt, a Bonaparte—is not a human being. But a synthesis of *pure* angel and pure *beast* who seems a man—although by the power of his senses and his intellect he surpasses the human type and its freedom of action.   14:477

The idea of genius, of something made from nothing, is more an idol in literature than in painting, where *métier*, borrowings, observation, skill, tricks of the trade, are allowed. Cf. Delacroix's *Journal*, Vinci, etc.

But when it comes to language, nothing but moments are needed. It is true that a line of verse, the right word, a page, is more easily detached from a work, than a hand, a *tone*, etc., from a picture.

The memory is totally faithful to a scrap of writing. It is merely uncertain about color and form.   14:479

A complete man is artist *and* poet—that is, clever at making what he is quick and first to conceive. Words and movements chosen by condition and circumstance.

Pro-Leonardo: an artist is a man who takes one of the *senses*, for example the verbal sense, as an external criterion of his self-possession. Whereas the poet *is possessed*.   14:502

Leonardo

The idea or rather the ridiculous and dangerous shadow of an idea of *genius* developed by the "romantics" (sparks, not sustained light) was destructive of *métier*—of what made civilization.

Examples in all the genres—fencing, the dance, painting. Every practice tends either toward improvisation or pure utility. 14:548

For Leonardo

Philosophy is the actual separation of thought from action and invention. Consequences unverifiable—otherwise, science. So it sought justification (though in vain) in logic.

Speculation is the deliberate pursuit of questions in thought, deliberately *separated from all action*—as if, independently of all external consequences, it could reach a terminal state provided with stable properties—("Truth"). To be other than temporary—but definitive.

Philosophy is a speculation limited to a vocabulary and traditional questions.

But if we assign to these inner activities, as an aim, not their objects, not their contents, but the agility, the euphoria, the freedom, the strength, which they give us the sensation of. . . .

Leonardo, or speculation proved by construction. The true value of the work of *art* is perhaps in giving value to speculation, in finding fabrications which are to *speculation* what practical results are to geometry and mechanics. *Here,* there is a possibility of foresight. 14:672

Leonardo was the first to understand that *knowing* and *making* cannot long remain separated without damage. Then metaphysics began to develop, only justifying itself a bit by bringing in an artistic kind of *making*. 15:168

Ego Gladiator

...The excessively little that I knew of Plato, which could have been put into ten or fifteen lines, produced *Eupalinos* for me. Cf. Leonardo also, and Goethe. 18:82

Ego

It appeared to me then (1892) that it was impossible that mental work should be entirely different in different minds or uses of the mind; and the work of the geometer from that of poetry or politics. And I searched naïvely and obstinately for the kind of treatment that would assimilate or differentiate these modes of transformation so different in their effects. (Modes of variation of images.)

The period of my Leonardo. 19:118

Imagination

Has anyone ever so much as dreamed (I did so in the first Leonardo, 1895) of exploring the question of the imagination? of thinking about this possibility and its limits? Is this combinative, which lets itself go in particular cases, capable of researching its whole extent?

And yet we live by it. Our time is occupied entirely by formations that respond to very diverse and very unequal circumstances.

These formations deploy within a domain. 19:301

Bologna, 4 o'clock, April 2, 1937.

Si potrebbe—Leonardo's favorite phrase, part of the substance of his brain, comes back to me here this morning, almost wakes me. This is where Galvani saw the frog dancing.

I don't know how he connected this with amber and the cat skins. Perhaps by Leyden.

I am thinking over the conversations of the past few days with Conti. . . .   19:885

Lionardo

To be what one is, and one's own mathematician, and one's own physicist, and one's own builder—that is, observer, combiner, organizer, and worker.   21:123

Lionardo

Criticism takes over all that a man has done, said, or written, and with that quantity distributed over x decades, and related to a variety of circumstances, of which the great majority is unknowable, makes a monster that not only never was but could not have been.

And so, a *dream*; and all the more as it is more precise, learned, and documented. I have done otherwise—always having more confidence in the *possible* than in the *textual*. Dream for dream, the one that introduces the real presence (and only the *self* can do it) seems to me more instructive than the one that unconsciously mixes things from realms with no communication between them. . . .   21:325

A novel's revelation. I was bathing when the idea of a "novel" came to me, in which the chapters would be: one, a subinvocation of Leonardo; the other, a sub-Rembrandt, etc. (or other names: musicians, mathematicians. . . .) But this for the author only, and with a view to giving a unity to each segment—a "reference."   21:435

In certain artists (Leonardo) drawing is explanatory, *constructive*. In others, *impressionist*. In others (Ingres), it is the search for balance between the *round* and the precise.   21:585

345

One day perhaps we shall have passed the stage of elementary physical eroticism.

These states and maneuvers will be considered with that foreign eye which sees our living organs in transparency on a screen. Leonardo's drawing at Windsor—the "angelic" look. 21:726

On Leonardo: arts of imitation

1) To imitate: deceive the eye (the *primary* idea in painting).

2) To go from imitation of the *living object* as a model to the *fiction* (painted) of an object not given, half-real— Monsters, Angels.

Try to make this compound of the true and the nontrue as possible as possible. So analyze the real to find the elements to be *generalized*, combined, fairly probable. Woman and fish. Youth and eagle. No arms.

3) This brings in anatomy and physiology.

4) Which leads to inventing machines and various laws.

N.B. "Beauty," a *rare* effect—a *rare* product—a Monster? Get it by synthesis, beginning simply by copying beautiful beings, then analyzing these objects. 22:225

For Lionardo

Fame—become the type, the model, the representative of a whole art. 22:303

In my little Leonardo of 1895, I clearly said that the image introduced by Faraday was ... *an image*, and that we must perhaps think about images and their peculiar properties. ... 22:467

Leonardo was not Goethe: the latter does not seem to have looked at *art* (the act of making) *more scientiae*. He saw "nature" in a different way from Leonardo, and consequently *art* (*the making*). There may be *opposition* (in the mind). *This analysis is delicate, but essential.*

Leonardo tried to make syntheses (in the chemical sense) possible in representation: relations between nature and invention.

Leonardo uses language. Importance of his writings. They are not his final aim. In this he is no "philosopher." But a *maker*. Drawing, painting are made like machines.

The functioning hand.

"Nature," model of forms and functions.

But no one can nor wants to copy her.

So—syntheses, combinations.

The person itself seems to have been more loved by Goethe than by Leonardo.   22:507

Implexes: Properties of imagination

"At that time" I saw and tried to exploit the "real" properties of the imagination.

Vinci, Faraday, Maxwell, the vortices of Descartes.

Period of the *Introduction to Leonardo*—'95. So, mental work from '92 to '95.

I thought that to imagine a certain phenomenon was an act of production which *organized* in the *mind's own way* and *completed things in its own way*, and *that this translation into mental life* demonstrated (if one were aware of it) the needs and resources of *our comprehension*—that is, our ability (limited and naïve) to *make* or engender in ourselves a given phenomenon. . . .   22:644

The Complete Man—or Leonardo

"What do you want?"

"I want *ability.* . . ."

His usable thought is made of ideas of his real powers, of his imaginary hands, or rather the *presence* of their forces and opposed forces. If we saw this dynamic-kinetic diagram and a developed drawing....Precision is the quality of an act that produces a certain definite result, as opposed to a multiplicity of unfinished drafts. 22:712

The modern European, from 1400 to....

I should define him in this way: the composite human type (Greco-Romano-Semitic-Nordic) who undertook the adventure of rethinking the "world," of transforming it systematically—tending to identify *knowledge* and "ability" with effective *action-power*.

This type appeared in the 1400s in the form of Leonardo and has never been better represented. Leonardo's aim is not clear. Fame? 22:724

When I fabricated the Leonardo of '95, on an unexpected commission, I constructed-imagined it, and that is very much *me*.

Why I can conceive neither history nor novels. 22:725

I do not see that anyone has tried to represent the fabrication of the "external world," beginning with the incoherence of the senses, the accidental nature of their coming together in succession; and I believe I am the only observer who has noted (in the *Leonardo*, 1895) the instantaneous "sphere" of exteriority that encloses us in its "instant," and whose transformations and invariables—extinctions also, and harmonies and dissonances of presence etc. etc.—play the fundamental role of reference. 22:737

All knowledge (in the sense of "explanation") consists finally in evaluating, or measuring, or reconstituting a given *quid* in the form of acts, things, means of our possession or disposal.

It would be important then to review this fundamental material. An idea that came to me in connection with a piece to be written on Leonardo, which might begin with a notion of the *ordinary man* and his average faculties. *Homo medius...* etc. 22:771

...This dazzling line by Leonardo: "Le soleil jamais n'a vu d'ombre." ("The sun has never seen shade.") Nothing as good as that (the naïveté) in Pascal. 23:175

The philosophers have not been aware or haven't wanted to admit that their occupation lives and moves in language (in this they were mutilating thought) and in the end is merely a matter of form. So they have indulged in all the illusions of language, more manipulated by it than playing with the illusions as the poets do. And in their pride they have not recognized as philosophers such men as Leonardo or Richard Wagner, men I consider prodigiously more universal than the Aristotles and the Platos and the Kants and the Hegels, because they were masters of the means that make it possible to manipulate that in which man can feel, with precision, that he is richer and vaster than necessary for individual life—and what more can philosophy want that is not absurd? 23:642

Eros

Strangeness of the act. Leonardo and the *oprante*. Whence this very strange subject: Adam and Eve have just coupled. *Quis eos edocuit?* All the animals looking on. This was before the Fall, which is consciousness—but of what? It is the creation of the *evil* of the act, and consequently of *nature*. Instinct and gratification, nakedness, etc., condemned. The fruit shared is a magic fruit. It made them sensitive to an instinct and its act, up to that point as simple as the act of eating or drinking (except for the participation of two complementary organs).

However that may be, when the thing is done, the two coupled terms separate, come back to themselves. That moment can become a poem.   24:239

"Hail, Landgrave Hermann!" Hail to you, Richard Wagner, the model of success in the royal way of great Art, who accomplished what only a few have dreamed of, a work produced at the end of a profound analysis, the true POEM in which insight and clear awareness of the problem of art's effect, its technical means, its aesthetic conditions, combine with its natural resources, fed on the energy of passionate life.

Synthesis of the faculty of immediate observation, not secondary but primitive, of the conception of man, of the combinatory and logical capacity—and of the most intense individuality, particularity, sensibility both sensory and felt.

That is a complete being: Poe, Leonardo, Mallarmé also, dreamed of that. Compare *The Philosophy of Composition* and *La Musique et les lettres*.

All these men knew how to give meaning to art. I know of no *painter* except Leonardo who took this way. . . .

24:438

Ego-System

The precise study of the imagination consciously observed—this was my work in '92–'93, and it is indicated in "The Introduction to Leonardo" of '95.

That study seemed to me then to contain, as a particular case or application, the whole explanation of physics—that is, the representation by image of those properties of phenomena which suggested the activity of *hidden bodies*. The atom is a hidden body. Likewise the Ether. Space is a...*Mon Corps d'actes* (My Body as Acts).

Physics has since been obliged to renounce the figurative imagination. The latter requires, among other things, that the order of magnitude of phenomena be correctible by simple similitude. In particular, this makes it legitimate to use the "infinitely small." 24:605

Memoirs of Myself

I was possessed by the daemon of Purity. The idea of separating independent constituents, of making their differences felt in the composition instead of using them mixed. . . . I wanted to apply this in literature, and in *Teste* and *Leonardo* ('95) there are traces of my aim. . . . 25:617

I keep on observing the functions of the mind. I would like to make of this what Leonardo made of the flight of birds.

25:845

The stupidity of men endowed with a mind is very often in failing to perceive the most obvious things.

But often enough, genius is merely in perceiving them. (So, the sun, etc., in Leonardo.) The principle of action and reaction in Newton. 26:445

April 18, 1943

Bestiary

"The spider extracts from herself the subtle and delicate

web which brings her, as a reward, the prey it has captured."
Leonardo.   27:111

Ego

For me, the ideal *thought* is quite the opposite of profound; it is what Leonardo makes with these words: *O sun,
who never see the dark!* That is the sublime.   27:161

Poe

In literature there has been an effort to use the philosophies, but the results are not final, for lack of a sufficiently rigorous psychology. Nevertheless, Poe, Rimbaud, Mallarmé saw the way—and pointed out the possibility.

The technical means are still to be found. The leitmotif is as ineffective as possible in literature.   1:800

Poe—or perhaps some daemon—whispers: the ultimate limit of analysis—is where?   1:809

Poe was lacking in something. Mallarmé in something else. The analysts in something. Others in something.   2:106

What is called consciousness in Poe's sense of the word, that is, the idea that a certain idea is an idea, is merely giving attention to the place of that idea—that is to say, to formal time.   2:120

Poe. Lecture at the Vieux Colombier. Explication of a text by Poe. At about the age of thirty, I spent several years reading nothing but Edgar Poe. Precision. Analytical types: *Arnheim, Morella, Ligeia. The Domain* . . . is of a beauty entirely deductive—Cartesian.

Voltaire: spirit of Shakespeare.

Poe, Diderot—English Romantics.   6:716

Eureka. Man as Poet—dependent on literature but greater than literature, necessarily. The bad in literature is the merely literary. The qualities of the great poet are those of the Head of State, but reduced to governing the dictionary. . . .

Criticism consists in posing new problems. Poe was the first to consider the mental mechanism as the producer of works. No one followed him.

Baudelaire lacked the abstract intelligence that stems from the classics—Voltaire.

Poe, the honor of poetry, being the only one who ever extended it to thought. 6:717

Poe—lecture

Conscious consciousness. Mental hierarchy (opposed to *mystical* hierarchy, life of perpetual union with God).

The principal subjects, then, will be: production of works of the mind, multiplication of possibilities, heuristics (*Eureka*).

But there are two aspects, one pure, the other applied— the latter is an analysis of the patient. 6:767

Exponentiation

Eureka is a symphony and a unique attempt to derive from a simulated identity with the world an explanation of the world, making the latter coincide with Laplace's notion, then integrating again. 6:768

Poe Lecture

One part psychology.
One part combination . . . Leibniz.
One part physicomathematics.
Engineer of the mind.
Literature is application.

Among the many difficulties I shall have in talking to you about Edgar Poe, there is one, and not the least of them, which is to have read him a great deal.

Eureka—to make for oneself what is lacking—that is a metaphysics. Logic. 6:772

(Poe)

Most men have such a vague idea of poetry that, for them, this very vagueness is the definition of poetry.

This definition by vagueness isn't bad. It is worth more than any other except the true—the true and precise.

It takes a lifetime to define the idea of poetry. I agree that the aim is not worth the trouble. 6:775

(Poe)

Credulity, naïveté, are compatible with poetry—whence false naïveté.

Baudelaire: the heresy of the new—inventions.

The place of poetry in a world—the poet knowing what he responds to, what he is a sign of.

It is admirable to see a man as original as Poe insisting on lucidity and turning precision almost against himself, to the point of attacking the idol of originality. He would not, like Baudelaire, have considered the new as having value in itself. That is a failure of discernment. He was aware that the new must not be sought; it appears of itself amongst antiquities. What we call old-fashioned is not so because it is outmoded, dated; the distasteful, on the contrary, comes of our own distaste, which we attribute to things. It is we who seem to us outdated, unable to enjoy, etc.

In general, what we find repugnant is our own superficiality. In the sciences there are no old problems. Weight is an enigma always new, and every reflection on the ancient fact of falling bodies renews it.   6:784

The hyperpoet: Mr. Poe redivivus. The time had come when things *of the mind* had taken on an *entirely* different character.

Man had almost stopped thinking. The era of thought—that is, of groping—was already vanishing.

Thoughts and impressions were as rare as wild beasts. The ancient philosophies were pure curiosities. Asylums for thinkers.

Language was replaced by its functions, precisely regulated and generally mechanized. . . .

Find the solution. The Volapuk era—Graphics, Logistics.

Whence the combinatory problem. Velocity of light.

Pure decoration. Materials. The dark body.   7:205

Consistency

Poe talks about "consistency." I think he meant by it the quality of a thing or a system conceived or existing in such a way that its parts are in symmetrical relation with one another. If A is the cause of B, B is also the cause of A. If A requires B, B requires A, so that every analysis of a particular system is convertible into any other, exactly as an equation may be solved by any one of its letters. . . . In works of art, the *semblance* of consistency must be sought. The study of form may come to this.   7:830

Poe—"New methods in noveling." [Valéry's English.]
                    12:289

Poe was the first to think of giving literary works a theoretical foundation. Mallarmé and myself: I think I was the first to try having no recourse at all to the old notions, but to make a fresh start on purely analytical bases.   12:703

"Modern artists":
> the *Enchanter* type (priest as sorcerer).
> the *Engineer* type (Poe).

Means: meditation on theory.

Creation requires analysis.

"Symbolism" is the use of *magic* in literature. This in a very precise sense, for Symbolism consists in the systematic use of the spoken word, to obtain *limitless, irrational* effects—which literature can manage only by the *contrast* of ideas, combined with unusual sonorities reinforced by the text.   13:9

Male and female form a complete system…like Wegener's continents.

Plato's idea was good.

A case of love might be treated as a complete system from which the two members could be disengaged.

The idea of such a system would be the constant and controlling idea of the work's maker. He would never reveal it explicitly.

A preestablished dependence from which the independence of individuals would be derived.

Notice that this entity is real, although made of subjective bonds in each person.

Nota bene: This at bottom is the idea of *Eureka*—the previous disunion and the present attraction "explained" by the original unity.   13:315

The Occidental ideal 1840–19—

"Scientific" or technical romanticism: Poe, Verne, etc., and a combination of sword-rattling romanticism (Dumas, etc.), one branch of which leads to criminal romanticism, which is a multiple point. . . .   13:412

Guiding themes and types
   Ego
   I no longer know where, nor in which of his works, Poe says that man is far from having realized, in any genre, the perfection he could attain, etc. (Perhaps in *Arnheim*.) But this remark has had the greatest "influence" on me. And this from Baudelaire, speaking of the same Poe: " *That marvelous brain always on the alert.*" This struck me like the sound of a horn, a signal that excited the whole of my intellect, as later on the Siegfried theme.   22:489

If I should write my memoirs, which would be those of a mind with no memory of events, I should have to include the phrase-motifs which greatly excited me when I was nineteen and twenty. Like those of Baudelaire on Poe: "that marvelous brain always on the alert." That is what I envied—and not some "regular" career, a career . . . abroad!
   Or again that phrase from the *Domain of Arnheim* on the highest degree of perfection that man . . . etc. That is what decided my direction.   22:702

Ego
   The inner cults
   The ideal brain—*Leonardo*. Baudelaire's phrase on Poe: "That marvelous brain always on the alert."
   Poe: *The Domain of Arnheim*, perfection.
   Sport—"Gladiator"—*ability*.
   On self-transformation.
   And finally, to consider as movable all that is *movable*—

and substitutable. Possibilities—their urgent possession, and not their accidental presence. Against chance. *Resonance* and Resistance. . . .   23:74

Poe: head-voice under inspiration.   23:123

The *strangeness* mentioned (required) by Poe as an almost indispensable ingredient of poetry, is rather good for creating in someone an interest in poetry, as an initial stimulus. But, on the contrary, once the poetic sensibility has been created, strangeness should rather be rejected—and the poetic, like pure air, breathed without being perceived. . . .
                                                        23:171

Ego
   Arnheim. Poe.
   In this fantasy of Poe's, there is one of those sentences that had so much . . . thematic influence on me at nineteen.
   A sentence on the possibilities of perfection. It said that man is very far from having attained what he could, etc.
   The idea of perfection possessed me. It soon changed into will-to-power, or the possession of power without using it.
                                                        23:188

Marseilles
   Last night I read Stevenson's *Treasure Island*, where I see, like things seen in clear water, the borrowings from Poe and Verne, *The Gold Bug*, *Arthur Gordon Pym*, and the mysterious island (exactly the same subject). Never was piracy more obvious than in this story about pirates.
                                                        24:861

Ego. Memoirs of Myself

Nothing has struck me and "influenced" me more than Poe's sentence about what was possible, and not done, in the realm of perfection (*Arnheim?*).

And Baudelaire's sentence about Poe: "That marvelous brain," etc. These sentences threw my mind into a passion of will-to-consciousness in action.

So one had to change oneself.

And I felt (Mallarmé also taught this, so it seemed to me, by example) the value of "mysticity" in poetry, which, if cultivated, teaches us to set up the whole group of language in opposition to every thought, now become a *local thing* (*of the moment*).   25:625

Poe

Spirituality? Consistency? What meaning can be given to these words? And what meaning can be given: 1) to Mallarmé's attitude? 2) to his aim? (daemon) once it has been deduced (but by hypotheses) from that attitude. That aim can only be *spiritualization*, that is, final substitution.

26:487

The idea of mental *maneuver* long ago *intoxicated* me. . . . Baudelaire's phrase about Poe: "That marvelous brain always on the alert. . .," that sentence, in short, of no *other* importance, was for me a glimpse of the treasure of *A Thousand and One Nights*, or of that simple word *treasure* read with the eyes of a child in the Arabian tale.

For me it was also the call of a horn in the enchanted forest of *Abstract* things. . .etc.   27:234

Ego (1891)

Excited by those few lines of Poe, and overexcited by what seemed to suggest the *experiments* (for, compared to all previous poems, this was the term I had to use) of Mallarmé and Rimbaud, I decided to consider poetry as a general problem—a complex production in which all the constituents of action under conscious or semiconscious or unconscious psychic conditions must figure.   28:252

...The sensation of *force* is of so great an importance and peculiarity that the philosophers make nothing of it, in conformity with Poe's theorem, "Deny what is and explain what is not," which is their Charter.   29:683

Mallarmé

The notable living men I admire *personally* are Messieurs
H. Poincaré, Lord Kelvin, S. Mallarmé, J.-K. Huysmans,
Ed. Degas, and perhaps Mr. Cecil Rhodes. That is six names.

1:116

S. M. Even if he were what you say, he would be, for that
very reason, a thousand times more effective than you. For
you admit his constancy and his stubbornness *in* what he
was doing. You know that no one's reproaches—nor later
on your own, nor those of your clients—ever touched or
shook him.

1:280

On Degas (Letter to S. M.)
  ...but the other's crayon, we know that it would go
where it wanted; every new glance goes beyond the last—
and in the background of a dancer we see an extraordinary
hand, and we are seen by an eye full of authority.

1:424

Mallarme's things engrave themselves in the memory. A
remarkable property. Its root. Relation to interest and
suggestivity?

1:704

On "le coup de dés"
  Current literature—makes gray weather, dull, effortless;
more elevated, it finds itself short of what is indispensable to
the effects and the psychological conduct of the work.
  S. M. inserted blanks.

The problem remains. Lucky music, with its reproducible patterns.   1:798

Thought with its lapses, its evasions, its insinuations, its distinct currents (*uninterrupted by the most irreducible interruptions*) is style—on the condition that it recall (and resist) whatever distance remains absolute between the elements of the one and the other.   1:799

Mallarmé: his perfect knowledge of the language led him to divide his means to the point of displaying the articulations which are for the most part hindrances. Now if we give to each term and its *function* all possible value, what we write necessarily takes on a general character—beyond the complete echoing of the series of meanings in the word, its function in itself is signified (and if the function is tied to the meaning?).   2:129

S.M. His exquisite vocal and verbal invention.   2:141

S.M. attacks the outlines of the voice, that is, enriches the system of notation but by tones of the voice.

To insert in a sentence phrases that are almost entirely irrelevant, and which imitate the *irrational* mixture of the phenomena that follow the *formal*, or time.

This makes an impression. But having observed that this is the *truth* of ordinary discourse, one may imitate this truth by introducing phrases related more or less loosely to the theme of the sentence.   2:191

S.M. A delightful mixture of word-meanings.   2:315

S.M. Inventor. I am writing this book that it may be forgotten and so lead into the beyond ... otherwise it is a failure.

The great new writer will not look for themes or situations, but for what includes them, extends them—the systematically unusual.   2:363

S.M. The logic of a man alone is different from the usual logic—what for him may play the role of a scientific principle cannot do so for the rest of humanity.

Hence the mystics (apparent?) or learned.   2:367

S.M. the astrologer—in disguise.   2:393

The literary man—the greatest—*thinks*, finally, like anyone else, in spite of his skill, his output, his inventions. He differs in this way from the true philosopher, the savant, the saint, from all those who have violated their thought and become a system. ... But there are Mallarmé and a few others who have made the effort to construct themselves.   2:626

It is not the true which matters, it is what can be drawn from the true.

If in a construction one can substitute for the true elements certain invented elements as resistant as the true and as useful, there is no reason not to do so. Cf. metaphors, S.M., etc. Everything that pretends to be true in literature is ridiculous.
2:699

On certain days I celebrate for myself St. Mallarmé's Day, memories, former ambition, admiration and love, sadness, chagrin, greatness. On other days, I celebrate Tiberius, darkly, Archimedes very brightly, or Pascal, or Rome, or London.   2:880

About algebra

Every correct proposition in algebra has a meaning
Why not in language? Cf. S.M.   3:677

A very clear dream: with Mallarmé, I talk to him about
people he must have known—like Nadar, Cazalès—Second
Empire—"Edmond Pourcier," Dr. Roxener, etc., and this
while leafing through some engravings.   4:183

Mallarmé, once, about abstract words in *-tion, -té, -ment.*
The meaning he gave to these endings.   4:208

Mallarmé. His form is certainly the sonnet: *la chevelure
vol*...and his depth is there. The words by themselves
reacting. Somber and rich, hence pure.

  Saved by technique. ... Idealism without value.

  Not to talk philosophically but to act, construct philosophically.   4:262

On Mallarmé

  ...Just as the modern logician in mathematics reconstructs
that very ancient edifice, keeping only those axioms strictly
sufficient to the conduct of his reasoning; so to extract from
the literary tradition only those forms characteristic of
literature, and especially of poetry, to construct a *pure*
system, where nothing is arranged nor enters that is not an
"image," clear sonorities, tempos, appropriate figures, and
the pure and prolonged resonance of the words...; he
managed it *almost* naturally, at the end of an excessively
verbal age.

  ...And whereas each word is clear, all the connections
well defined, the structure almost too clear—the remains or

residues of ordinary language are left in obscurity (concerning this operation)—residues of which it could not rid itself. It is precisely these residues which usually make discourse clear and naïvely intelligible. Since *to understand*, in this sense, is precisely to annul the discourse itself—to see the *thing* as if language did not exist.

Rhyme imitates, in a powerful and naïve manner, the *lucky find*, the threshold crossed, the passage at least probable —in short, the precision that creates the value of a thought, the opposite of common automatic functioning. . . . But as soon as this accuracy itself seems to stem from that functioning, it loses this charm. . . . At times being the least, at other times the most probable, according to the context.

4:440

S. M. What he abstained from, what he had to reject, refuse. What he believed should be done. Abstention as act. Privation as means. 4:450

Stendhal the opposite of Mallarmé

"In a certain sense" their difference is a difference of *distribution*.

The one: all is meaning—that is, he rejects the sign, creates the *real*: *realizing* (as we say *realizing a fortune*). Making of his own literature a definite immediate pleasure— of the same order as real things—the pleasure of seeing clearly, excitement defined by an object.

What to him is "poetic," he puts into song. There is a strange phrase in *Rome, Naples et Florence*—a phrase not so far from Mallarmé.

The other: all is form, defining without naming, indicating by a lacuna. The formation of complex signs, the unimportance of the object, often having no apparent value—the difficulty of such construction—but the construction is what is important. Reconstruct the principal object, evoke the words and attitudes that define it. No isolated object; as itself.

But since in a certain case, a certain name will be "suggested," not uttered; in a certain other case, this name will be pronounced to suggest another. So, it is not the construction of the name which is important *once for all*, but rather the labor itself.   4:481

A poem like *Hérodiade* is made beginning with words and certain conditions imposed by the rhymes, the contrasting words, sonorities, surprises. The ideas are to be looked for in that order.

The marvelous opposite of oratory. The movement of the discourse is elsewhere, in the veins of the rich texture, amid that accumulation.

Artificial, to trace backwards the direction of the ordinary production of words; natural, to look deeply into the laws of their accumulation and construction.   4:652

S.M. Naïve intuition in literature.

Indistinction—confusing the author with things, things with words, objective with subjective words.

Natural confusion.

This grown literary child thinks he has touched the top, grasped an important truth by noting a contrast or a similarity between things dissimilar only in language.

Wise intuition will consist in observing both the language and its effects. . . . So the metaphors, figures, transformations take the leading role. So again, the one who moves from naïve intuition to the highest, crosses a void, a desert. When subjects fail, sterility begins, etc. Crisis—between juvenile habit and the new fashion. . . . 4:680

Mallarmé's art is the limit a literature approaches when research and the division of labor deprive it of its traditional subjects.

Then an art of language in the pure state appears, with a combinative or specious poetics whose end is itself—the aims of the discourse being only to allow it to exist according to tradition, which wants it to have a meaning but hardly more than one. 4:782

"To say all (in verse)"—Victor Hugo.
    And
"To say nothing that is not verse"—Stéphane Mallarmé.
    Two schools, two genres. 4:899

Sterility: the natural condition of the poet (in all genres).

Why?—If it were not so, the *lucky find* would have no *value*. Sterility is in compound proportion to the imposed conditions. "Sterile" means: either a very slight product *or* a very rare one, its rarity being a part of the product's definition. Little or no luck.

Hugo is fertile; Mallarmé is sterile. But if everything that H. wrote had occurred to M., M. would have rejected 85 percent of it. And the rest could not be published alone.

This kind of sterility is not nonproduction, but non-acceptance. It is merely external; since, internally, just as many ideas, images, and words came to Mallarmé as to the other. 4:904

I come back to the idea—half-memory, half-project—of a conversation with my twin, my double; carried as far, one favorable evening, as would ever be possible.

(A few memories of talks almost as profound, with Mallarmé about Poe; and others. . . .)

A mixture of hate and love, a merciless intimacy—with an increasing mutual divination, or closeness, a fury to go faster and deeper into the dear enemy which in itself is like combat, like a race between two only—like coitus.

A close game of chess can serve as a model.

Rules of the game.

Proof of man's existence.

Writing that dialogue would be a project worth all the flabby literatures.   4:908

S. M. Consequences of difficult poetry: when it requires *both* continuous euphony *and* a continuous plenitude of the senses —images, surprises.

Then we instinctively look for a system that allows us a richer vocabulary, to augment the resources needed to cope with more exacting conditions. And the result is a whole personal philosophy.   5:129

In literary matters my ability to admire is strictly limited. Why and by what? If I admire, it is generally a promise.

I see in any literary product nothing more than a make-shift—a mixed advantage.

No writer ever managed to limit himself to the essential and then attain it.

Rare is the writer who has the free use of his means. I find only indirectly in literature any processes of thought, mental operations, realities of form. And that is what, for me, is important. The rest is impurities and excitement of the moment.

Literature does not, like mathematics, introduce *new notions*. The new in literature is always individual, occasional.

If I *adored* Mallarmé, it was precisely my hatred of literature and the sign of that hatred, which was still unconscious.

5:181

The art of Flaubert, and all such, is at the opposite pole from Mallarmé's. The former wanted to make forms and materials out of language; the other to endow the means of language with those movements, those acts that transcend all things, taking them independently of their *remains*, their...*bodies*, which define thought and even language.

And both have this in common: to found art on language, on the function of language, its own resources, and not on the spoken word, which is language considered from the mouth.

5:203

S.M. (Symb. Lit.)

Refers the force of thought, the depth, breadth, extent of what is said, to the act of saying it.

Sets the act to exploring the subject fully (or using the previous inner exploration) however slight the act may be, instead of putting it in the subject itself.

It is better to construct a mouse than a mountain. It is more difficult. An enormous cloud is less than a fly.

For an apparent ability substitute a real one. The greatness is in the connection, the relation, the correspondence, not in the extent.

Show a false object crudely, or represent the true one, which is the mind, subtly—by the slightest means. 5:210

Fame is when someone comes to confess his mind to you.

I don't say his loves, his troubles, his sins. Nor do I mean what is hardest to confess, his ridiculous weaknesses, his fears and phobias and quirks (all of them things that God Himself, of course, doesn't want to know).

I say: *mind.*

One evening in front of the tobacco shops on the Quai d'Orsay, after the concert in the Champs Elysées, I talked for a long time openly to Mallarmé. Either I was laying my mind bare. Or I was fabricating a mind to be laid bare— on that evening in March or a mild November?

To the millionaires you can confess the true sum of your fortune—without shame or fear.   5:634

I take up a highly "finished" poem (as it happens, a sonnet of Mallarmé's) and I decipher it this way:

Find the order in which the elements of the poem were *set down*. Virtual alliterations.

This order is lost when the poem is finished. Up to that point, it existed *as a draft*.   5:693

Rhymes: audition can serve in solving one of the rhymer's most delicate problems—which is, to determine what sound at the *rhyme* must follow another sound. Whether, for example, *oise* is suitable after *cur; il* after *tée*.

Hugo was profoundly ignorant of this detail of the art, and his poetry suffers from it, musically, in the poems with flat rhymes.

Mallarmé was extraordinary in this, as in many other things.   5:869

Villiers was an improviser, a man capable of talking for hours, a café illusionist who could perform all night. His antithesis was Mallarmé, who had the most elegant mind for calculations, a genius for word combinations and words themselves. Vision guided Villier's language, and talking made him drunk. In Mallarmé, the spoken word was the very object of art, the meaning being almost accessory to that function, a consequence rather than the principle.   6:254

Mallarmé's poems, appearing at long intervals and showing each time the peculiar progress of a tendency, a will, a métier, remind us of volcanic summits emerging, the abysses between them being time and inner changes, hidden, impenetrable, with intervening accidents.   6:357

S.M. A very simple psychological device for composing:
1) A first line forming a motif by way of the incomplete, the overhang which it constitutes, the primer—and at the same time the *start*, stirring both the remains and the memory; *instability*, stimulus-need.
2) A mass or group of associations—or even of words in which the simple juxtaposition, if they were mixed and drawn at random in no order, would give the special impression, would require the object which *will be* that of the poem. This is the enigmatic part.
3) The sentence: that is the difficulty.
4) Rhymes, alliteration, etc.   6:425

Mallarmé is an innovator in one way. Rimbaud in another. And the remainder in each is not new, but traditional.

Vision in Rimbaud; in Mallarmé, music—that is to say, the combination of articulations, movement, contrasts, and *the way of cutting off the meaning by the line* (a fraction of elementary meaning for each line) which results in an almost self-created line, self-existent, as suited to the memory as a melody, or a well-known melody's first phrase, heavy with the sequel, out of balance, calling for continuation and further song.

To define this mode, remember the complex relation between the length of a step and the frequency of steps.

Inversions, alliterations, meaningful contrasts combined.

Mallarmé's *obscurity* is the consequence etc., the price that had to be paid for the clarity of structure in his line. To make the line unquestionable, luminous in structure, charged with meaning, and perfectly clear, he is obliged to force the inversion, to play tricks with the syntax, and especially with syntactical habits, reducing to a minimum the heavy apparatus of the propositions, of very short radius, to generalize certain forms. 6:437

(S. M.) "Obscure fist" (*poing obscur*). Obscure refers to the mind of someone showing his fist. This disarrangement is characteristic.

Often, with him, the idea is the group of images evoked by a theme, the logico-syntactic link being the representative of the man himself—the sole real link.

Syntax is employed merely for *lack of something else*, since it implies a causal construction not used here. 6:666

The last poems of Mallarmé are like magnificent rooms uninhabited...or—which comes to the same thing—not otherwise inhabited than by a spirit.

No criticism is more dangerous than the deadly comparison of an ideal with a realized work. 7:9

Mallarmé would sometimes say: "*The world's mystery, if there is one, could be contained in a lead article of the* Figaro."

"Who wouldn't like to write that article?" I said to him. The remark has its depth. Can the words in a dictionary, taken together, be considered as containing among their combinations, one that would be, with respect to the whole knowable group, a valid law, a principle?

This was the whole problem and desire of the Scholastics —Aristotle, Lully, and perhaps Descartes—especially Descartes—for whom the categories were so few that he reduced them to space and time. 7:77

Le Coup de dés

It stares you in the face. The opposite of obscurity—a billboard.

For view *alpha* we have meaning A. For view *beta* we have B. Cf. Poe's *Purloined Letter*.

Also, bringing together is enough, or separating, or waiting, if you would grasp a law of phenomena.

And so, also, music can make us hear and, above all, half-hear the principal idea in the bass, quite slow compared with the excitement in the treble, so this idea may not be clearly perceived but *creates itself* somehow in the air. What is needed, if it is to exist, is that someone should bend his ear a bit more, forgetting the upper register and adding for a moment longer the scattered sounds in the bass.

His idea was the score—the silent-visual orchestra.

Idea of the interval, of pure rapprochement. But such placements correspond to being and nonbeing—since consciousness is or is not, grasps or does not, according to those placements. It sees form or the formless.

So there is an oscillation between Chance and Law. The first *asks*, over and over—the other is response, conclusion, never decisive. . . . 7:273

374

Mallarmé's greatest glory and greatest vice is in being a complete system in himself: in having tried to be an *absolute* system.

An admirable will; he erred in this, that the real elements of his system were borrowed from the common language.

Whence the irresistible impression of perfection, of success, of a closed and self-satisfying world; whence also the impression of the impossibility of nonsystematic developments. 7:471

The most obvious, the most important characteristic of Mallarmé's works is the labor they presuppose.

Literary labor can attain one depth or another: that is, involve this or that depth of language; accept the forms, the locutions, the words, exactly as they are given; or on the contrary, review and revise these elements. We may use as given: syntax, meanings, the usual sonorities—or remake them for our use. The same is true of underlying psychological and logical relations.

For Mallarmé almost nothing was *given*. He tended to redefine words, to reexamine locutions. . . .

This work has no limits. 7:608

Mallarmé found a middle way between the vague and the precise. 7:618

Yesterday at Tisiphone's, the talk was *perversity*! An attentive group. Gide and I. I offered this definition(!): perversity consists in using one's mind where one's body would suffice. Or something of that sort. I said later that this kind of intellectualism, when it goes beyond a certain point, excludes perversity (example: Mallarmé not perverse goes beyond

Baudelaire perverse) since the talent for general forms dominates all possible contents.

All this in a conversational salon manner. The true consists in dissociation of the instincts. Thus: kill the man who does you a favor, or wish to kill him.   7:653

On Mallarmé (Ad inferos)

The polar regions are of no interest to industry, but still they had to be explored; and there had to be a hero to do it, and more than that, a hero with no other thought.   8:648

Literature. Work and its results

Mallarmé simply deduces from work piled on work. Effects of resumption and rumination of a work. Self-criticism endlessly renewed. Perceptible relations. An increase of connections. Obscurity. Contracted habit of no longer accepting from chance the parts of a work not comparable to the perfected parts. Rarefaction.

Link between the scarce, the obscure, and "perfection."

9:118

(Mallarmé) The Withdrawal—*to be defined.* Progress of consciousness.

Bring *before* oneself what is usually in our shadow behind us.   9:148

Mallarmé, first or almost, devoted himself to the production of what could be called synthetic products in literature, by analogy with chemistry—that is, works or more exactly *parts of works* constructed directly out of the literary material which is language, and consequently involving an idea and definitions of language and its parts. An "atomic" idea.

He was brought necessarily to consider combinations—
that is, more or less perfect symmetries, etc., to determine
simple elements, etc.

In that way, he gave a meaning to that whole part of
literature, with all its procedures, which seemed to be merely
difficiles nugae—fixed forms, rhymes, etc. And on the other
hand, he found himself at grips with the opposition that was
bound to arise between the crystalline structures erected in
that way and the systems formed by ordinary practice—
which are said and believed to be immediately *intelligible*.
Cuisine and chemistry.

He was not entirely aware, surely, of what he was doing
in this way. Certain prejudices and a lack of scientific knowledge hindered him. Yet he did profound damage to empirical
literature.   9:206

Mallarmé had in him a sort of taste for flirting with the
Absolute.   9:683

Et cetera. Et cetera.

Mallarmé disliked this word-gesture. He outlawed it. I,
on the other hand, liked it, and was surprised.

The mind has no response more specific. It is the mind
itself that this locution brings into play.

There is no *Et cetera* in nature—enumeration is total. The
part for the whole doesn't exist in nature. The mind will not
tolerate repetition. It seems made for the singular. Once for
all. The moment it perceives law, monotony, it gives up.

10: 105

Mallarmé's attempt to *write* beginning with *words*, whereas
the universal practice is to write *in spite of* words, against

words, and to use them without seeing or hearing them, *to place the attention* (as one *places* the voice) in the object and the result...to such a point that the literary operation would engender the object, rather than be engendered by it, and so would assume capital importance—whereas *the work* would be rigorously impersonal, could have several meanings, would not correspond to the object, and would be not so much the act of a person as of a "mind"—that is to say, *of a system potentially complete.*

This endeavor amounts to finding what is independent of the coordinates *self* and *object*—an *intrinsic* literature. But if the attempt had to be made—and one could hardly admire too highly the premonitions which led Mallarmé to make it —it could not however....   10:154

Mallarmé somehow used *fractions of ideas, irrationals* (especially in his prose). He necessarily used common-sense views to construct expressions.   11:99

Mallarmé's System:

Between him and truth lay the empire of words.

The gigantic problem of *expression* (cf. his brief lines). In a problem of this kind, the details of *the thing expressed* may be capital for *the thing expressing them.*   11:278

Mallarmé's ideas, never revealed:

The extreme novelty of the project—Poe's idea, trimmed down: to make of Literature something more than an amusement, or perhaps to *consecrate* the amusement. In Mallarmé, the *poet* died, became an abstraction, impersonal.

Nevertheless: a complete theory.   11:279

History of French poetry
   (as great music: long lines)
           Corneille — Hugo
      Racine — Baudelaire — Mallarmé
        La Fontaine — Verlaine

                        11:402

Mallarmé: The capital idea for him (clearly marked in the piece on Gautier) was the metaphysical *virtue* of language. Whence the result that poetry is the *final cause*, the supreme object.

And this idea must have come to him from Poe's dialogue: "The Power of Words."   11:515

Certain phrases in Mallarmé's prose are stained glass windows. . . .   13:171

On Mallarmé

The essential point with him, the half-secret idea, fixed, peculiar, venerable, almost morbid, the Idol . . . was expression, the idealized transposition—Literature, Language, Poetry having more value, meaning, and function than can be given by man to any human thing, in the sense of value, meaning, function, the mystical and cosmic value of the word. "Dazzled by his own faith." Where I saw only conventions, he tended to suppose a hidden necessity—an indemonstrable theme and somehow instinctive with him; which can, moreover, be organized rather speciously in developing an idealism* (see below). The extraordinary distance he is accustomed to take, to preserve or forever reconstitute that field.

   *. . . which is a way of accommodating, making it

possible to see all objects as identically *real*, or perhaps identically *apparent*.

Unfortunately he burdened himself with verbal ideas taken from the Philosophers (Hegel). He was also wary of the *teacher's tone*.   14:44

Mallarmé's *sterility* was the result not of impotence with regard to *ordinary* problems—and therefore of inferiority as compared to *ordinary* poets—but of impotence with regard to new problems concerning which no one can say that to pursue them was a chimera—except by counting as a chimera what could not be accomplished.   14:197

The mystics of art and technique: Baucher, Mallarmé, Degas. Flaubert) Evaluations—Deification of excellence.

Ingres, his comic remarks. Sovereign contempt—the small number of connoisseurs. Mysterious language— *irrational*. Sensibility.   14:791

Like Mallarmé, I have refused to use whatever makes use of someone else's weaknesses, exploits his leanings, his non-resistance—in short, the easy.

But also, I have set aside what to me was not precious in depth—merely valid locally and extemporaneously.

It was necessary then that, to be accepted, each element must have not only nonstatistical value but also value in a general system of "myself" (for the advancement of *self in itself*).

This, in short, is a refusal (which can be expressed in the words Pride and Defiance ...) to found that Essential Nothing that one is, or thinks he is, on the *Other*, as on one's own complaisance.   15:44

For the Mallarmé

A remarkable situation: to feel oneself *between* ignorance of the deep self (whose intimacy evades consciousness) and ignorance of the rest (which is, and is not, the whole, and is perhaps part of the Other) and with no faith in a look which, if divine, would unite one with the other, and therefore, being at once the only point of contact and at the same time the consciousness of seeing only what one sees and of giving value and meaning.   15:163

Today we say: Napoleon AND Stendhal. Who would have told Napoleon that one would ever say Napoleon AND Stendhal?

Who would have said to Zola, to Daudet, that this little man so amiable and well spoken, *Stéphane Mallarmé*, by way of his rare little poems, bizarre and obscure, would have a more profound and durable influence than all their books, their observations on life, the "actual experiences" in their novels? A diamond can outlast a city and a civilization. The will to perfection means to make itself independent of time, etc.   15:376

They say (about Mallarmé or me): all this effort and obscurity ...for what? A mite of *thought*. The kernel is hard, its content is a bit of water. The shell is almost inviolable—steel, a triple lock, and inside, a button.

And all this is true. ...   15:799

Just as the Parnassians would first write down their rhymes in a column (there is a page of *Hérodiade* set up in this way, and nothing but rhymes) I would prefer, and with more justification I think, that the page be set up with *rhythms and phrases*, since to get unity of effect one must begin by distinguishing, a priori, *the independent variables.* This unity is precision, which itself is a precise oscillation between expression and idea. *Page* is not the word.

The conditions for the *complete* and the *maximum.* 17:68

Gladiator

I often heard Mallarmé talk about the power of the blank page, a creative power. One sits down before the empty paper. And something writes itself, does itself, etc.

The power of the void—cf. the French *oil* and *ouïe.* Perhaps we understand nothing about sight or hearing so long as we do not understand that these photo- or phono-psychic *cells give and receive simultaneously*—they produce a double effect. 17:178

Poetry

For Mallarmé, the verse line, the kind of *logic* engendered by the existence of regular verse with its form and its studied fullness of sounds (including rhymes) producing the tone and the movement engendered by that structure (cf. decoration-ornament), has led to an effect even on the *syntax* (which existed before in a nascent and timid state: *inversion,* etc.), having already affected the *subject* (which became a *function of the form* and at least *one* of its constituents, not the principal one—things moreover not so much *invented* as observed in the practice of verse; and, for example, felt in the observance of the rhymes and conventional rules)....

The poet's work then tends to keep that relation of exchanges between the constituents, being directed *against* the tendency of the language to *express* in the most direct way—*against* the given, accidental vocabulary.

Certain details of the language then take on enormous importance.... 17:232

London

22 November (1934)

I discover, this morning, on the table that serves as a night table, a volume of poems by a certain Gerard Manley Hopkins—with notes by Robert Bridges. I open it and decipher a bit with a vague grudge and without sensing that I am about to find "twenty minutes" of light. The preface by Charles Williams seems to me ordinary or absurd—at first—then it wakes me, and I grope through the poems and the notes by Bridges. Then I see clearly how all this suits me, *situates* me. An excellent guide that justifies my idea of poetry—which now comes clear to me. I understand also the Englishman's contempt for our poetry, and all the poverty of the French way of teaching language—total negligence of the element of music.

(Incidentally, I notice that Baudelaire, who in places renewed the sense of music, underwent, along with Verlaine and Mallarmé, the English influence.)

The French are not musical, and are disposed to make light of effects of this kind rather than enjoy them. Why? Rhythm and tone hardly exist for them. The weakening of consonants, the muffling of vowels. There ought to be a revolution in this matter, *if today* the thing were worth the trouble.

One note by Bridges is remarkable. He observes that a certain poem by Hopkins, which is "obscure" and strange to the eye (and therefore to be rejected), becomes an entirely different thing if it is read with the ear.   17 : 666

A way of seeing things as equidistant, with an eye to their equivalence in regard to the Self, and a simultaneity necessary to the formation of *expressions*. (This, I believe, would appear in Mallarmé's system of prose.)   17 : 874

Literature

I confess that I appreciate writers only *sub specie utilitatis*. Musset is of no use at all to me. Mallarmé taught me a great deal. "To admire" is to feel that there is a great deal to be learned. Let me add that in many cases a work teaches us a great deal more than the author knew.   18:77

Mallarmé: the attitude of opticoid, pan-psychic *distance*.... (I know what I mean!) This attitude is remarkably implicated in language—the dictionary....   18:116

Poetry

About 1891, it seemed to me that the aim of poetry must be to produce *enchantment*—that is, a state of artificial balance and delight *without reference to the real*.

Nothing was more contrary to reasonable poetry, narrative, the fables of La Fontaine, the oratory of Hugo, and even the sentimental and lyrical "humanity" of Musset, etc., in which I found direct speech. (A selection of those works was enough to make us conceive Pure Poetry.) In Mallarmé, on the other hand, the reciprocal resonances went beyond all meaning (all verse is without meaning or it is not verse).

It was the distancing of man that delighted me. I do not know (no one knows) why we praise an author as being *human*, when all that makes man great is inhuman or superhuman....   18:281

A literary observation

In the 1880s, while all the Huysmanses were using quantities of words of great rarity and introducing unlimited images, the only Mallarmé was inclined to numerous syntactical forms.   18:548

Theta

The soul's withdrawal (as in Mallarmé) tends to put each thing and event in its universal place. This can be seen in his eyes.

It means choosing axes of reference as ... *absolute* as possible. A capital operation, and most important to reveal in anyone to define him.   18:557

Gladiator

Mallarmé or the Artificial.

Repair operation, or Work applied to a part of nature generally left to itself (except at a small number of points)—language.

On the work of man—cf. *Eupalinos*.   18:588

... Another dream the same night. I forget. ... I saw V.H. [Hugo] and S.M. and I said afterwards that I had just shaken hands with these two poets. Then a luncheon where there was Mme de Béhague, and Mallarmé very old arrived late.

19:505

Poetics—Texts

Compare Mallarmé's letters to Aubanel and Cazalis with Rimbaud's letter on "Voyance." These are the most important documents on mystico-poetics, or inner poetics—a glimpse of the *power* to be derived from observing a (banal) dream by way of a "literary" act, the product of which might restore a certain *impression* of the origin. ...

19:658

The "serious" and literature. *Illusionism essential.*

Confusion between thought and mystico-philosophic values (Pascal, Poincaré).

I don't like self-flattery. *Homo* flatters himself with his "thought," etc., and "literature" (Hugo, etc.), whence charlatanism, politics—and autosuggestion (S.M. and P.V.). *Voyances*, *Grandeurs* in drapery—*Poseurs* in three genres (Barrès, Chateaubriand, Nietzsche)....   20:311

Ego: Mallarmé and Me

Beyond the inexhaustible "admiration," wonder, love aroused by his art, to such a point that I could see in his works only the *making*—the impossible *making*, as if in the end one could no longer listen, could hardly hear the sound, so exciting to the mind were the acts of the virtuoso's hands, or those of his phonic apparatus—and later on, more profoundly, the conjectures about the hidden functions, the subtler transformations...the *true Author*—that is, the state of possibility, of which this or that *actual event*, provoked by a certain occasion, is the reflex. In short, the idea of the non-accidental, the "faculty," the *ability*, as *opposed* to its own exercise....

So I felt myself drawn far *away from him*. For he was finally obliged to endow literature, more or less precariously and artificially, *with a value* I could not find in it, being unable to see more than a particular application.

This is the point on which I never had time to question him, for I did not yet dare touch upon that center of his being which my own motives had just located...when he died.

The most important men for me are those with whom I am excessively occupied in imagining their inner operations. They are the only men I value.   20:911

Almost all of Mallarmé's peculiarities are the result of *pure* and precise observations of matters represented in other minds by traditional opinions, impure and imprecise. Now the development of these exact views led him, as always happens, to certain necessarily *paradoxical* practices since they collided with those opinions. 21:529

The level of famous writers 1865–85: the Naturalists very mediocre in intellect—their strength elsewhere. Symbolism. 1870: the difference between young Mallarmé and Z. [Zola] *et al.* must have been extreme—a virtual, implicit difference, but interchangeable opinions. 21:534

Literature and other things:
    Simple consideration of the results of accumulated labor.
    Endless revision. S.M. 21:635

Poetry
    Mallarmé's remarkable idea:
    The verse line considered as a new *word*. Cf. lines made ot proper names, sonorous and bizarre to the ear: *Pasiphaë*, *Oloosone*. Compare these to lines with ordinary words.
                                         21:693

Regrettable words in Mallarmé, words that have always astonished me: *remémore*, *immobilise*, *ignition*, *diffame*. And certain lines that shook me:
    Magnifique mais qui...
    Une nudité de héros tendre diffame (not easy to say).
                                         22:96

Ego
    I dreamed of a man with the greatest gifts—who would do nothing with them, being sure that he had them.

I said this to Mallarmé, one Sunday on the Quai d'Orsay near the Alma bridge, after the concert. He was going to dinner at Berthe Morisot's. We walked back and forth between two bridges, I don't know how many times.

22:600

S.M.

No one understood or guessed (so stupid are the critics) that in Mallarmé the pleasure of devising and that of creating a language of one's own, was bound to win out over any other consideration, and that he could no longer tolerate any *writing* that was not for him at once strange and his own—completely his and perfectly new (all the while believing, perhaps, that he had more generality than what I say of him here concedes).

There was also the model of music.   22:910

Childishness and epic poetry

A great display like *Eviradnus*,★ and many others by Hugo, requires extreme naïveté on the part of the reader, and a will to rootless epic stories in the poet. What energy! What boyishness! Compare this to Mallarmé's "O rêveuse," etc., which is no less "fabricated," as it had to be, but all the nonsense, the flaws, the inflation, are gone from the poetry.

★*Eviradnus* makes me think of the puppet theater in Genoa where there was a whole army of marionettes.

23:131

The conversation with Mallarmé on the Quai d'Orsay after the concert. I said to him that it would be a fine gesture to reject the gift one is sure of having, and to seek...something else!

A childish remark....   23:140

What Mallarmé said to me when he showed me the *Coup de dés*—that he planned to compose *every year*, on this model, a work of a *more intellectual* character than ordinary poetic expression allowed—made me reflect that he was running into a difficulty I knew well, since I had given up poetry some four or five years before, for that reason among others.

There comes a moment when the themes and words possible in French poetry no longer suffice to excite a mind gifted with a certain power of abstraction—and the insoluble problem is put.

I approached it twenty years later, with *La Jeune Parque*.

23:152

Certain poems of Mallarmé, if not all, are admirable *traps*.

23:153

About Mallarmé

What do you expect all those professors to understand about the connection between that completely artificial literature and the profoundest and most... metaphysical sensibility?...

23:155

On Mallarmé

The great role of *refusal* in making those works. 23:159

It was a strange poison that was poured over all other poetry by Mallarmé's—to my mind. It furnished nothing that could have been found by oneself, nothing of immediate and predictable discourse, yet the sonority of the form took effect as strongly and definitively as the surprising difficulty of the meaning, on the contrary, keenly excited the mind's defenses and likewise the whole intelligence.

23:411

S.M.—I am sure that the value Mallarmé certainly attached to the word *abolir* (abolish) played a role in the genesis of the *Coup de dés*.   23:554

To Mallarmé belongs the distinguished merit of having thought out the literary problem in all the generality he could conceive, and this starting from an observation born of practice. His ambition required that he should come *legitimately* to consider every earlier work as a very special case or a very rough, unconscious approximation. And in this, *a will to exhaustion*. . . . He felt that (in order to free his plan of all relativity and make it independent of milieu, etc.) he must give to that view a transcendent value—involve the whole world, etc.   23:884

On Mallarmé

A very important and even essential point with him is the *suppression* of a number of whole elements in ordinary discourse, considered obvious or parasitic or vulgar—or again, useless and harmful to the approach of the effect of absolute discourse, independent of the epoch, etc., and almost of Man.   23:896

Nocturne

I suddenly think of Mallarmé's sonnet of 1880–85: *Le Vierge*. . ., *Le silence déjà*. . .etc., and I believe I see how to interpret the progress of their "obscurity."

I see music as responsible—a question that faced more than one poet in the period 1870–1890. *Wagneris causa*, and in several ways.

Here, it is a matter of the poem's going into action, beginning from the initial *nonbeing of waiting*.

How to make a start?—Of capital importance in poetry. A problem unknown to those who do not distinguish between creating the *state of harmony* and the need of its consequences, which must little by little, and without a break, construct the whole work.... 24:149

On Mallarmé—after reflection on him

...That postponement *to infinity* of the Work willed, accepted, won. And the rest, the actually completed essays—writings to "try his pen."

No doubt he saw the general problem of "harmonic" (and therefore nonrepresentational) literature. In him, this was a transformation by *perspective*, a...*projective* operation which may be taken for a "mystique"...(perfection, pride, the absolute).

This seems to me generalizable. What *is*, what is seen (or is possible)—or what is completely *given*, as the object at once seen and touched—is taken for a degree of purity, or intensity, or *existence*, etc., and corresponding to supposedly increasing values of those variables, an *object* (infinite goodness, power, etc.) or a Being. Whence a transformation of values. 24:371

Memory, matrix of melodies

Mallarmé's profound idea of considering a work as a game played against "chance."

I shall put it slightly otherwise. A "melody" for instance results from a permutation of notes (and the complementary aspects of emission—durations, intensities, frequencies) and the motive force of a *virtual* action more or less signifying affectivity—joy, etc., which distinguishes that permutation from others equally possible, giving it the quality of *unity* and therefore a hold on Memory—that Memory which is the mother and matrix of continuities (*suites*).   24:454

Mallarmé

Generality. First ideal: gymnics. Language: transformations, conjunctions. "Gnostic" and ethical aspect. Unique in literature. Recast oneself—whole. Life also. (Sterility, obscurity: leitmotifs.) Against the rabble: the critics. Triumph of the exception, the *unique*.   24:533

Ego

Nothing made me despair more than Wagner's music. (And I am far from being the only one.) Isn't it the supreme aim of the artist, to bring to *despair*!

So Wagner taught me many things. He made me despair differently from Mallarmé. The latter more directly, since his métier was more intelligible to me. But Wagner brought Mallarmé himself to despair.   24:564

S.M.

Literature has not found its analytical artists and creators of form. Mallarmé is the only case. Even he was hampered by various inadequacies, or by a daemon urging him to take the opposition, to deprive himself of certain means—for no reason.   25:446

Mallarmé?

The first to have a clear insight into the world of literature, at times controlling the springs. But all this was mixed with useless assumptions, residues, marginal interests, etc. The notion of verbal transformations, in the pure state, had developed in him, but confused with a "mystique" half sincere, half political, etc. But useless, otherwise inevitable, considering the date.

The whole of Mallarmé's abstract intuition—and its essential point, that the *content* of forms is more arbitrary than the forms—is naked, as it were, in *Un Coup de dés*.

For me, this says that the infinite number of possible perceptions and ideas corresponds only to a limited number of types of possible verbal acts; and in practice a much smaller number of such acts is used. To which must be added the results of observing sentences or phrases.

Mallarmé introduced numerous asides, and bound the parts together by run-on syntax—often quite cumbersome—encumbered.

It is good that he did so, but at times it has the disadvantage of producing in the reader a sense of contrast between the labor of deciphering and its result. But at times it is a miracle of artistry . . . and psychic truth.

* * *

"In reality," Mallarmé and Rimbaud, simultaneously and independently (or almost—and the notion of influence is here discounted), thinking they were doing something else, "each according to his own nature," introduced into the manner of seeing and making "free" literature (that is, not indebted to . . .) the commanding "point of view," the at least implicit Principate of formal-combinatory action (that is to say, transformations, etc.), action either unconscious or barely conscious, even in the use of poetic language. Whence "new" effects.   25:527–8

In Mallarmé, the consciousness of transformation on an almost purely *formal* base appears—under the disguise of a metaphysics that becomes part of the remarkable precision of an entirely new analysis of language.

Perhaps these foreign ingredients are needed before what is lacking in lures and stimulants can be reduced to the necessary and sufficient.

The fact is, no one has yet managed to dominate and control Language and its Dynamics.   25:529

Mallarmé

It is revolutionary to consider the space of the spoken word—or the universe of language—*prior* to any plan or particular problem; instead of moving toward expression in reaction to an object—that is, to consider *every aim* in the group of possible means, and each *aim* as an application—which leads at once to finding *aims* suggested by their means, aims which the usual way would never have brought to mind. . . .   25:539

On Mallarmé

To *understand* is to *destroy form*. So, that text is *intelligible* which allows its form to be eliminated, and any text that does not, becomes difficult and quickly intelligible.

Now in Mallarmé, form is imposed a priori.
1) The start always excellent for *lyrical instability* or impetus. The initial off-balance of the *Génie de la Bastille*, one foot in the air.
2) End-rhymed and over-rhymed.

All this, and the desire to introduce certain words, or conjunctions . . . and surprises . . . had to be made 1) possible, 2) fairly plausible in "meaning"; and then, here and there, a "fine line" of the ordinary type had to be inserted. Whence the obligation to find a minimum of *meaningful* connection—

which was had by way of allusions, very fragile analogies, and dislocations of order.

The result is that the text has no solution; that is, no equivalent in prose.

It has no *subject* distinct from itself, but a sort of *program* consisting of a collection of words, among which certain *conjunctions as important as nouns* and types of *syntactical moments* (that is, components of forms) and above all, a table of the tonalities of words, etc.   25:557

S.M.

With him, *willed* verbal combinations, and others merely allowed, are ruled by the "more-or-less" in matters of meaning, and a sort of rigor with regard to the psychic and phonic resonance.   25:701

Ego and S.M.

Poetry, for Mallarmé, was the essential and unique object. For me, a particular application of the mind's powers. This was the contrast. Perhaps it should be connected with our respective, easily excited potentialities. . . .   25:706

Ego—Struggle with the Angel—1892

S.M.—Beginning: recognition, reflection, anxiety, when faced with the phenomenon Verse Production. Whence the two themes: *Mystery*, *Chance*, the two aspects of the transformation of (mental) *nothingness* into an *object* (verse). This is the aim. But *nothingness* comes back over the all, and nothing has happened. . . . The words Absolute, Mystery, Chance, here have magic power—rather than meaning.

—But what *rebels* in me against this situation is the wretched status of the art of language in being tied to a locality—to the language of a certain people.

S. M. Treatise on the willed mental deformation in Mallarmé, acquired by means of . . . with the intention of exhausting, at one and the same time, *poetry* in its essence, and himself; with a demonstration of the *constraints* adopted.

The plan of these latter (actual secondary effects imposed on the "natural course") derives originally from *verse*, considered and treated as a language within language.

Verse is *noncertain* language—achieved or not, like the baking of a ceramic.   25:707

This line of Mallarmé's: *Soulève avec l'ennui d'une force défunte* . . . Excellent, that *ennui*. How did this word come into Mallarmé's mind? This is a problem.   25:717

Bâle, August 21, '42
    S. M.
    What is called *sterility* in Mallarmé is of the greatest interest.

It breaks down into two factors:
All he required of himself,
All he rejected.   25:721

S. M. (Gladiator)
    The honor of the mind is in creating its own resistances. *Heroïcity* of style, of rigor. Hence a will to separateness, distinction, to nonimitation and nonimitability, nonequality. . . . "Others" seem to him caricatures of himself. Negative sensibility to reiteration, repetition, as if it were manhood wasted, evolution-time lost.   26:105

Development of self-awareness in one direction.
    Mallarmé came in the end to the idea of the world con-summated by expression.   26:476

S.M.

Poetry: "Creation" plus fabrication alternatively hindered and helped by articulate language.

A remarkable thing: the rules of versification are restraints. *But the body also is a restraint.* All real power is limited —since *the real is a limit.*   26:486

Images of Mallarmé

Mallarmé's daemon

Poe

1) Spirituality? Consistency? What meaning is to be given to these words?

And what meaning is to be given: 1) to Mallarmé's attitude? (daemon), 2) to his aim?—once it has been deduced (but by hypotheses) from his attitude. That aim can only be *spiritualization*—that is, final substitution.   26:487

S.M.

This study might be a chapter of my memoirs.

I was struck by Mallarmé. I admired—from a distance. I loved him. I rethought him. I felt and developed my difference. I sought how it was that what he could do, what he willed (the latter was easier!) differed from what I willed and could do—was in fact its opposite. I also tried to guess not only his thought . . . but his feelings. I saw him creating a new and singular genre. His fame small and profound.

I wept at his death. . . .

Then, that fame grew from decade to decade.

Example of the will to perfection, purity, of some strange zealous curse in the name of the most unshakable certainty man can have, because it depends on no belief.

26:488

... Mallarmé himself acquiesced in a mystagogy....

27:518

Ego

Mallarmé had little effect on my view of things (or my thought), but a great deal on my attitude towards language and Letters. In those days, I sought, I *willed*, I possessed a Secret of thought that was my own discovery. It was "a way of seeing"—a sort of mental projection of everything (also like a *secondary* effect of every ordinary thing that rejected it) on the same plane as every other thing. I said to myself: "*A is a mental phenomenon.*" Hence the idea of looking for relations *among all* things. And if the word "Psychology" can have a meaning, that is precisely *it*.   27:859

Nonsense and poetry

My impressions of 1893 among the "Symbolists," even with Mallarmé. The use of the word *poetry* to designate a state of mind and not something *made*, is responsible jointly with "Romanticism."   29:677

SELECTED LETTERS

Valéry's Letters to his Brother Jules
on the
Introduction to the Method of Leonardo da Vinci

Compiled by his Nephew Jean Valéry

Paul Valéry never dated his letters.

His brother Jules Valéry, however, professor in the Faculty of Law at Montpellier, and eight years his senior, was in the habit of keeping all the correspondence he received and arranging it according to quarterly periods, in large envelopes which he inscribed with the appropriate date and year.

This is how, in the file for October–December 1894, I was able to locate the following letter from Paul Valéry to his brother, the date of which may well be November of that year.

Paris

Weather worse, Foul, humid, rainless.

I'm paying a lot of visits. Madame Gide sent me a book which I took back to her yesterday, without finding her in.

The day before, I had the following letter which I managed to decipher. Here it is verbatim:

18 Boulevard Montmartre

Sir,

Being for the moment overloaded I cannot ask you for an article at once, but my friend Léon Daudet, whose judgment has great weight with me, tells me I might ask you for an article on da Vinci.

Would you care to make a promise of it?

With my compliments,

JULIETTE ADAM

In this way Paul Valéry was called upon to write the Introduction to the Method of Leonardo da Vinci, *dedicated to Marcel Schwob and first published in the* Nouvelle Revue, *which Madame Juliette Adam edited, on August 15, 1895.*

Valéry had been settled in Paris since March 3, 1894. He was barely 23 years old. A few of his poems had appeared in the Revue Blanche.

His friends were Pierre Louÿs, Marcel Schwob, André Gide. He was seeking for his way of life. Perhaps a literary career? Or would he take one of the examinations? J.-K. Huysmans urged him to take a government post. Those who worked in ministerial offices—and Huysmans was well placed to know, being one of them—had leisure hours in which to cultivate the muse or write.

And in fact Valéry sat for an entrance examination to the Ministry of War in June 1895 and passed.

Meanwhile he was working on the Introduction. *In January 1895 he wrote to his brother:*

Vinci glues me to my table and I'm stuffed with him. And at last it begins to take: 30 pages without drawing breath—no narrative trickery!—without the chance of developing a theory (in view of readers, and Reviews, and readers of Reviews)—without stealing from anyone, without descriptions (that sordid filler-up of copy), no details, historical or biographical (delicious stuffing!).

Ah well, it's a long, long business!

If only I'd no ideas on the subject!

How facile and flowing it could be!

But the misery is, having ideas, wanting to discuss only them, and only being able to give the worst—conclusions, notions, vagueness.

In March 1895, in another letter to his brother:

My article now moves into the serious part, which is difficult enough and slow. (The difficulty arising from the nature of the article.) I have to work together the following media: painting, architecture, mathematics, mechanics, physics, and machinery.

I have a good hold on the connecting points which are interesting.

painting { perspective—architecture
{ light, history of light

architecture { partakes of mechanics
{ but also exemplifies
{ molecular structure—crystals

But I don't know at which end to start.

About April Valéry wrote to his brother the essential letter where, at last, he laid out the ideas which he had matured, and which he meant to develop in his article:

My article begins to chew itself over in my head. But I don't know yet whether I'll make it a bargain or a deluxe article, something rich, a high-class novelty, an ornamented shell-comb from London. I am convinced of the newness of the idea and method, but put down on paper, for the *Nouvelle Revue*, which way, what? To carry it through I should need da Vinci's own motto, which appeals to me so much: *Hostinato rigore.* If you feel interested, here's the theme:

I don't give a hang for the erudite-aesthetic side. I rule out the known figure of da Vinci. I want to set up a "model" (in the mechanical sense) of a da Vinci mind, and the problems for me come down to this: "People say he was a *universal* mind." What is the reality, the meaning of such a statement? Is there a method of making oneself universal?

In what way is such a mind conditioned—logically and analogically.

The scientific methods so adroitly put into practice by Faraday, Kelvin, etc.

Which means (what those men of science never brought out clearly) studying the imagination as an instrument of common measurement, and the imaginative faculty as in itself a measurer of the link it *automatically* creates between the most diverse things. Kelvin built models of luminous ether, etc. which fulfill all the analytic conditions of certain molecular movements, etc. Well, from the inductive point of view—inductive-imaginative, say—any human product, and above all a work of art, is the outward sign of a certain number of conditions shaped by the very life of the brain itself. I think I'm the only one to have researched thus far, but not yet far enough in this order of things. It's very difficult.

Let me give a curious example of my conclusions: Imagine all beings classified in accordance with the simplicity or increasing complexity of their structure. From crystal, plants, etc. . . . to man. Number each phase in the symmetry: 1, 2, 3 etc.

Now if one notices in a virgin, natural forest, a row of trees in a straight line, the idea of human intervention arises. One feels a *mind* has been there, the more so insofar as the row continues in length and regularity. Same with a regiment in line etc., a piece of architecture.

Which means that elements, each having the same degree of symmetry, N, form a whole whose degree of symmetry is M, lesser or more than N. The induction works out, and from this position one can draw as from an actual equation the definition of the word: *Mind*; and from the conventional name for the other unknown quantity: *Symmetry*. You follow?

So placing myself at an evolutionary point of vantage I can ask whether this deductive center of things, the mind, has not reached a high degree of complexity simply so as to order things, combine the elements of its perceptions. And I proceed to consider among these elements the elementary laws of matter (to serve as guides). . . .

Two words more in explanation. The mathematical mind par excellence, Laplace for example, studying magnetism would say: Here are two bodies, a certain distance between them, the speed increases as the distance diminishes. I write the equation and that's that. But Faraday's imaginative, *visual* mind, dissatisfied with the measurement which is perfect but too remote from the nature of things, can *see* a field of force, where no one had seen anything but distance, etc., etc.

I've been to the Delisles. All well.

Sent me 1. A sea-biscuit
       2. Police record
       3. Certificate of military service
       4. Life and character.

In a letter to his brother written probably in June 1895, Valéry— who often enjoyed illustrating his letters—drew a man stretched out, smoking a cigarette, and bellied like a pregnant woman.

The legend reads: "The article is in its 8th month. I'm keeping to my chaise longue." *Above the drawing, in a frame like a notice board, he has inscribed:* Madame ADAM, Midwife.

This sense of fun and prankishness reveals a little-known trait in the impulsive and essentially fanciful and artistic nature of Paul Valéry which does not always appear in his writings, though it was one of the charms of his talk and his letters.

II

Letters to and about Mallarmé

[First letter to Mallarmé]

October 1890

Dear Master,

A young man who, though lost in the provinces, has been enabled—thanks to a few rare fragments discovered here and there in reviews—to divine and to love the secret splendor of your works, now takes the liberty of presenting himself.

His conviction is that art can now no longer be other than a city of narrow confines where beauty reigns solitary. He longs, with his private dream, to be among the few lovers of aesthetic purity.

One of these, M. P. Louis, has already mentioned the writer to you, a fact which decided him to send you these lines and these verses.

To make himself known in a few words he ought to say that he prefers poems short, concentrated toward a final impact, in which the rhythms are like the marmoreal steps to the altar, crowning the final line! Not that he can boast of having realized this ideal! It is simply that he is deeply imbued with the cunning doctrines of the great Edgar Allan Poe—perhaps the most subtle artist of this century!

That name alone will suffice to reveal the nature of his Poetics. So let him stop at this point, and yield place to the poems here submitted to you, in the hope of counsels written by that same hand which, in *Hérodiade*, created dazzlement and despair.

Mallarmé's reply to the above was prompt and courteous. "The gift of subtle analysis," *he wrote in his letter of October 24,* "with a music befitting it, this you certainly possess, which is all that matters. . . . As for counsels, only solitude can give you these." *Valéry was to meet the master within the year, but before doing so he wrote him another letter:*

[To Mallarmé]

Montpellier, April 1891

Dear Master,

For the second time I am seeking your advice, in the desire to know whether certain aesthetic meditations which I have stored up this past winter, far away in the provinces, are not altogether wild and illusory.

A poem entitled "Narcisse Parle," which appeared in *La Conque*, throws some light on them, but as often happens, experience has made a mock of theory, and left me perplexed and at a standstill.

Poetry it seems to me is a delicate and beautiful explication of the World, contained within a peculiar and sustained music. Where the art of Metaphysics sees the Universe made up of abstract and absolute ideas, and painting sees it in colors, the art of poetry has to view it clothed in syllables, organized in sentences.

Considered in its naked and magical splendor, the word can be raised to the elemental power of a musical note, a color, or the keystone of an arch. A line of verse takes form like a chord which involves the meeting of two modes, in which the mysterious and sacred epithet, mirror of submerged suggestion, operates like a hushed accompaniment.

A very special devotion to the work of Poe has led me to assign to the poet the kingdom of analogy. He defines the mysterious echo of things, and that secret harmony of theirs which is as real and certain as a mathematical equation to all artist minds, which means to all who are vehement idealists.

Thence arises the ultimate concept of a lofty symphony, uniting the world around us to the world that haunts us, constructed according to a rigorous architectonic order, fixing stylized archetypes upon a ground of or and azure, and liberating the poet from the encumbering aids of banal philosophies, sentimental falsities, and inert descriptions.

The afternoon of the faun, alone in France, achieves this aesthetic ideal; and the dictates of its unprecedented perfection will ensure the disappearance of the pseudo-poets whom it exasperates, and whose mediocrity will overwhelm them as a matter of course.

Here ends this avowal which no doubt you will find ingenuous and childish, alas, but which I had to make in order to justify myself in my own eyes.

I think this, I write that, and where does the truth lie? In our day, the faith of old has lost itself between men of science and men of the arts.

One believes in one's art as in a perpetually crucified one, exalting, denying it, and in hours of pallor and blood one strives to find a word of power, a luminous sign pointing to the future, and that is what I have dared to ask of you, dear Master.

On high in the mystic peace of the plains, calm immensity, clouds widen across the triangle of sky between the mountains, and their flight glides over lakes of oblivion.

A few pale and melancholy figures pasture their vast and pure memories, and bend as they draw down to their faces the tall flowers of tender tints whose naïve chalices are set quivering. . . .

PAUL VALÉRY
3, rue Urbain-V., Montpellier

[First Meeting with Mallarmé]

Saturday, October 10, 1891. Nine o'clock: at Mallarmé's. He opens the door himself. Small. The impression of a quiet, tired bourgeois of forty-nine. Beneath the very dim lamp mother and daughter are *embroidering*. Rosy against the brown tones of a minute dining room. White Monets on the wall. In the corner a tall tile stove. His pipe. He, in a rocking chair. There is quiet at first. (The daughter is classical—charming—a little strange—Greek head—Empire.) Then the conversation gets under way. First the provinces, the Félibres. His eyes half-closed—speech muffled—his voice very low, then suddenly eyes wide open—a loud phrase, with heavy breathing. This man is suddenly learned (I like to see that I have already considered—long ago—all he says)—then epic—then tragic. He talks a great deal about the death of Villiers, who wanted to entitle his work *Devoir français*.

I turn the conversation from subject to subject. From Ghil we come to the color of words. He sees *a* as vermilion, *u* as blue-green (so do I), *o* as black, etc.; then rhythm—it must be inseparable from idea (this is all familiar). The period in poetry.—"I have come to the point," says Mallarmé, "of eliminating punctuation; the verse line is a whole, a new word, never heard before; anyone who uses punctuation needs crutches, his sentence does not move of itself." About free verse. His trouble. The difficulty of writing verse without partitions. *Émaux*, de Régnier.—His *restraint* with the alexandrine, not to let it appear except at high moments. Rhyme—Banville's inspired solution—the Comet. For him, it must be as if the comet did not exist for the poet—but quite alone. Finally—he speaks of the Literary Hero—of his own life, wretchedly depressed by teaching, at the very moment when he was about to produce. To be a hero would mean living with the crowd by crushing it. He would like to work at journalism in his way. Épinal images and, alongside them, refined compositions.

From there, with Louÿs to the *Variétés*, to join Gide.

[To Mallarmé]

Montpellier [January 15, 1894]

If I am late with my greetings, dear Master, it is because my fatigue is proof even against the kindly spark of your card.

Where find a more brilliant—a more lofty—malaise than in sensing a lack of air in some idea by whose means one was on the brink of drawing still closer to oneself—and striking fire thereby?

Yes, I feel a sickening lack of those conditions in which some inspired idea might take charge and set itself in motion. And despite my refusal to attach any value to an idea by itself, to the object one can isolate, I cannot but suffer from this mental minute that stands still.

To take away any overweening import from that word "inspired" that escaped me, and any excess of self-pity from this letter, I will risk giving you a very brief glimpse of the notions—impossible as they are among the thousands I have been trying to work out to some conclusion, and have put off to some better time.

I have simply been trying, dear Master, to include within the same *form* everything which ranks in all respects as the Means—in other words, a theory of the *Instrument*—which would include spade, pen, speech, flute, and even fugues and integral calculus. Man does all he can to exploit them, without giving them any further thought. It is through this ignorance that an object becomes precious in our eyes. And so, in any given undertaking, if one studies what ought not to be mentally worked out, in the delicate equilibrium of the moment where all thought is relative to what one is doing, the result is fatal.

Well, that intellectual *area*, from which one perceives one's world again, would seem to have drawn my mind to the simplicity and purity which belong to it by right.

Forgive my dullness, dear Master, from whom one can seek nothing but detail.

Nearly all my wishes will be going in your direction, if you will accept and pass them on.

P. VALÉRY

[To Jules Valéry] [1898]

I have hardly begun to recover myself, after what has been one of the greatest griefs of my life, and for me an irreparable loss.

Nothing will give me back that friendship with a man unique in his kind, an example of the boldest thought, the most unassuming life, the most incomparable integrity. The feeling he showed for me at times is and will be for me the only external pretext for any self-esteem that I can entertain.

I found his coffin in the garden by the Seine, where his canoe still lay afloat. His daughter fell into my arms as she recalled her father's feelings for me. It is a dreadful blow for her; she had given up all for her father, including the best matches and so on.

People came: quite a few for Valvins, a crowd in fact.

I had a beautiful wreath made at Augustins', and brought it along.

Fortunately, apart from Mendès, there were few literary undertakers.

The church was a long way, then the cemetery, admirably placed, in a position quite like that of his house.

Then Roujon—dressed for the country like everyone (apart from myself who had come from Paris)—nearly all dressed as cyclists or in summer clothes—spoke very simply, and altogether very well—since he said the important thing, that the future of the two women was assured.

Then I was dragged to the graveside and forced to speak.

I babbled a few unconnected and senseless words, for I was choking. Came back to Paris along with Heredia and Régnier.

Le Temps makes me say a couple of things I have no recollection of. ?? However, it doesn't matter to me at all.

Mallarmé died of a strange accident, for that is what it can only be called.

Since Monday he had had a slight throat trouble. The doctor came to see him on Friday, and he felt better and wanted to get up. While he was talking to the doctor, he stiffened, clutched him, and fell dead, asphyxiated by a sudden glottal spasm which had no direct connection with his sickness. It would seem to be a very unusual pathological case.

[To André Gide]

Monday, September 26, 1898

My dear André, here are some details. It will be some relief to write, for I have not slept for three nights, and I weep and choke like a child. In fact I have lost the man I loved best in the world, and nothing will in any way replace him, in my feelings or in my way of thinking. I had grown into the habit, on his initiative, of feeling as close to him as a son. And then he could understand every kind of thought, and my most peculiar vagaries would find in him a "precedent," and if need be a support—all opinions excepted. All this is irrecoverable. Six or seven weeks ago, I spent the day there. He seemed to me tired, very white, and he told me he had given up his canoe—which was still floating there on its rope, yesterday. We went to talk in his room. He showed me a few roughs of *Hérodiade* in progress, etc., changed his underwear while I was there, gave me water for my hands, and then some of his own perfume. That evening with his daughter he saw me back to the station at Vulaines—never-to-be-forgotten conditions of darkness, calm, and talk for three voices.

Friday evening I came back late, about eleven. I found Geneviève's telegram: Father is dead. . . .

I won't go into that night, one of the most frightful I have ever known, along with last. In the morning I telegraphed Paris friends, wrote to you, and so on.

P.L. [Pierre Louÿs] at the last minute did not want to go down there. I set off with Régnier and Heredia. I let them go off to lunch and went to the house.

I don't know if you know it? Here's a little plan:

[Here there is a plan of Mallarmé's house at Valvins.]

The coffin was in A, some people arranging it with flowers. I put a wreath of roses at the head.

That's Mallarmé's room.

The moment I entered the garden, his daughter threw herself weeping into my arms, saying "Ah, monsieur V. Papa was so fond of you!"

Then I saw his wife too, but in what a state; but that poor girl who gave up all for her father, and who made with him such a pure and delicate bond—an "antique" morality.

This is how he died. It was an accident, and quite without precedent. Since Monday he had had tonsillitis—not at all severe—but being delicate in that respect he went to bed. On Friday the doctor came to see him. He felt better and naturally wanted to get up. While he was talking to the doctor, a spasm of the glottis killed him outright, by asphyxiation; he stiffened, threw himself on his knees, clinging to the doctor, and fell back dead. It seems such cases are extremely rare. This fatal spasm had very little to do with his actual throat trouble. Perhaps he could have been saved if this remote contingency had been thought of, and all had been ready for an immediate tracheotomy.

He died at 11 in the morning. His daughter insists that at the one critical minute, he understood, and that he looked in her direction. I can see that look ever since she told me.

Gradually, people came along. Catulle, Roujon, Dierx, etc.... the Natansons—quite enough to fill the garden in fact and, myself apart, I believe everyone was in country clothes, in all colors, cycling costume, and so on.

We went to the church at Samoreau, in fearful heat, and then to the cemetery which is beautifully placed. He would have the same view there as from his window.

Roujon spoke with great emotion, and he gave the necessary assurances about the future of the two women.

Then Quillard forced me to come up to the grave, and say farewell in the name of the Young! And I was absolutely incapable of saying anything but confused babblings, I was suffocating, and no one else understood any better than I the three or four sounds I made. You'll see some traces of this in today's papers.

The last rending, public farewells of his daughter followed, then they took her away from the grave and we left.

All this came back to me in the night, and being unable to breathe I got up, made fumigations, then a tremendous storm broke, and I slept for an hour.

Please keep this letter which is an exact account of yesterday. I'll ask you for a copy later, because I have neither the wish nor the courage to write it all out for myself just now.

Your VALÉRY

[To Émile Verhaeren]

Wednesday, 28 [1898]

Sir,

The Mallarmé ladies have recently been talking to me about the publication of the poetical works of Stéphane Mallarmé by the firm of Deman.

The latter, it seems, bought the rights—at a contemptible price, as befitted him. The agreement, made in the poet's lifetime by himself, resulted in no written document.

We are afraid the publisher will give his fancy full rein regarding these precious texts, and at the moment we are trying to find means of limiting his powers as much as possible in this respect.

It occurred to me—forgive me—to consult you, and/or alternatively to put you in contact with these two ladies for the present purpose.

The recollection of my having sometimes met you, and my awareness of Mallarmé's feelings toward you, decided me to overcome my hesitation in intruding on your hard-working leisure.

So if you do not object to the inconvenience, let me ask for a meeting (in the evening, because of my working hours) or else, which would be preferable, I will put you into direct contact with Madame and Mlle Mallarmé.

Let me renew my apologies, and assure you of my admiration and respect.

PAUL VALÉRY
12, rue Gay-Lussac

P.S.—Gide has perhaps already talked to you about all this.

[To Émile Verhaeren]

Tuesday [1898]

Sir, thank you for the reply you were good enough to send. I imagine you are back from Belgium, and I take the liberty of troubling you once more.

Unfortunately I cannot just now suggest our meeting, because I am both unwell and overloaded with the duties of my post. The simplest, then, and the most practical thing would be for you to see the Mallarmé ladies, who are longing to discuss with you the matter of this Deman edition.

The problem of this business, which worries them very much, is the fact that they do not know the real extent of M. Deman's rights in the poems of Mallarmé.

They are convinced they will not receive a penny for this publication, but to what degree are they debarred from bringing out an edition themselves of these poems, in France?

Then there is the *integrity* of this Deman edition. I have seen and partly corrected the proofs: I was surprised at the order adopted in arranging the poems. And finally, there are certainly some gaps.

Such is the position in which your advice would be so invaluable—whatever it be.

Please accept my thanks and apologies, together, sir, with the assurance of my respectful admiration.

P. VALÉRY
12, rue Gay-Lussac

[To Albert Thibaudet]

Sunday [1912]
40, rue de Villejust

Dear Sir,

Sunday, with a little more time to myself, different sounds in the street from ordinary days, I must seize the chance, and try to write to you. If only I could thank you "by word of mouth!" I'm bored with the pen, good only for spoiling the pleasure of being born and dying with each instant.

But already I've been talking for days about your book, to anyone I can.

To begin with my surprise. The fact that you have made the most living likeness of Mallarmé, baffling those who knew him, is astonishing enough. And then that really nothing escapes your eye in the technique of his verse, so much so as to make one wonder if you don't on the quiet practice the art yourself. Am I wrong?

As for the expositions, I leave you in the clutches of M. de Gourmont, whose *Petit Carême* devoted to you I have just been reading. His is a very distinguished mind, but one feels too clearly that he is confined within his article and goes not an inch farther. I don't always care for this elegant form of limitation, which doesn't really work with me. I cannot care for the idea of making such a point of stopping at the first decimal.

So, with regard to these expositions, my view is: that I find them as precise—barring some overtones—as their object will allow. Above all I feel that they were something *that had to be done.* As an enterprise, they should offer an important precedent—the first to my knowledge of a serious form of literary criticism within definite limits.

Some other comments—without order or example (I feel vague to a dominical degree!).

A touch of Bergsonism made me shy imperceptibly at certain points.

I am as ignorant of this philosophy as might be. I can see you are fond of it, but I like you better when you display here and there a sort of Mallarmism which replaces or dismisses all philosophy.

Besides, it seems to me, allowing for my ignorance, that Bergson can throw no light on any other activity than his own. He (perhaps) creates a world, but not the explanation of a world. Etc.

With regard to *Un Coup de dés*, it is not the case that Mallarmé drew the idea from reading some of Nietzsche. I am sure he knew nothing of him.

Moreover there is a manuscript work of 1868–1869, "Le Prince Igitur," known to Villiers and Mendès. A remarkably strange piece. One chapter is entitled "Un Coup de dés"; but the whole work deals with Chance, with chance as defined by M.

The strange hero of this work utters the word "madness," with the same impetuous emphasis as in the poem of 1897.

I have seen rather than read this early text twice over a period of years, and each time only for a few minutes. There is no doubting that this was the germ. I was not able to point this out at a useful time, having only seen the manuscript again a few days since.

One great praise I must not forget to offer you concerns your capacity to make your reader think—or keep him strictly to the literary problem.

Literature, *ad libitum*, is all, all or nothing. Consequently it is nothing, or nearly.

How that nothing can take over a whole life, become its reality or function, or strive to do so—perhaps this will be seen in your case, regarding Mallarmé. *That would be all-important.*

For my own part, between the all and the nothing of it, I have oscillated. I knew Mallarmé, *after* having undergone his influence to the limit, and at the very moment when in my own mind I wanted to guillotine all literature.

I worshiped that extraordinary man at the very time when I saw in him the one—invaluable—head to cut off in order to decapitate all Rome. You can easily guess the passion a young man of twenty-two can feel, crazed with contradictory desires, incapable of distracting them, intellectually jealous of every idea that seems to him to combine power with precision: a lover not of *souls*, but of minds the most various, as others are of bodies. . . .

Intolerable, in short—and above all to himself. Yet this secret wrestling, only with *angels*, amounts to a disease like alcohol—but a highly significant one. . . .

In other words, with a total, instinctive force I put the whole *question* on a different level: I reduced everything—poetry, analysis, languages, exploitation of the real and of the possible—to the single brute notion of mental power. Half-knowingly I was committing the error of replacing *being* by *doing*, as though one should have been able to construct oneself—by what means? The question was, not to be a poet, but to be able to be one.

This is what corrupts my vision. And it is why that formless sketch, "M. Teste" (made up of fragments, for a particular occasion) has so little to do with Mallarmé.

But between that concept of what one *must* be and the concept of Mallarmé there is a very curious relationship.

Like those smoke rings of the scientists which pass in succession one into another—each in turn attracting and growing larger than what it attracts—or again, one might think of those Arab magicians who take on monstrous forms to outdo each other. In this case, a struggle between forms and contents. . . . To go further is to return.

Forgive my straying so far from the object of this letter. I have many other things to say to you, but my quarter of a Sunday is nearly used up, and no leisure tomorrow.

I must cut short, with the wish that I may see you some time at one place of encounter or another. . . . I read some of your recent articles in the *Revue Française* with an overall pleasure sharpened, as it ought to be, by certain problems. I cannot yet make out the system of your mental world; I won't say your system. For me you still remain in a state of plurality. I can feel the link between the closely neighboring personalities on the page, but cannot identify it as I should like to. I cannot see what connects you with such and such a particular taste. Perhaps in you it is a case of "historical" sentiment—which in me is nonexistent or wiped out.

Be assured of my very high esteem, for your book and you—and of my thanks for your too kind references to me.

(Yet there is an element of paradox in immolating what I understand to be the gigantic work of Mauclair before the pinch of dust which is all I represent.)   P. Valéry

[To Albert Thibaudet]

[1912]

As for my letter, if the fragments of it can be of use, do as you choose: I should be hard to please if I did not want to appear in such a book as yours will be. If in fact the letter repeats neither the order nor the form of my views on the subject, our agreement as to an essential part is enough to assure me that we could not differ very widely as to the rest.

Only this: the ideas must not appear as coming authentically and expressly from Mallarmé. I have no peculiar right to testify as to his real thinking. I am not one to come and declare what an author neither wished, nor knew how, nor thought good to say for himself. He told me nothing in confidence which was not pure Mallarmé, and no less marvelous than his writings.

I must be placed on your level, not on his.

I was brought to feel his power most by a reading of Poe. I read in him what I wanted and caught that fever of lucidity which he communicates.

Consequence: I gave up writing verse. That art, which became impossible for me from 1892, was already simply an exercise, or an application of researches that were more important. Why not develop within oneself that which alone, in the genesis of a poem, is of interest to oneself? (All this is sheer history, not a thesis or an argument.)

My last poems—very inferior Mallarmé—were a part of this mental gymnastics.

In this state of mind, I enjoyed Mallarmé's friendship, greedily. Time passed.

One evening, a conversation on Poe, growing more and more concentrated, transformed the admirable host into a supreme, fatherly friend. What an evening for me, as centrally important as the stretto of a fugue—when the gropings of a dialogue growing more and more condensed arrive at a sense of pure unanimity—what a scholastic might call a dream—at the very source of individuation. As though, in the strange movements of two involved opponents who foresee less and less their own actions, a threshold had been crossed, almost that very one which speech itself forbids to talkers-in-general.

"M. Teste" has for me no willed connection with Mallarmé. It is, like everything else of mine, an occasional work. With the aid of notes quickly thrown together, I made up that pseudo portrait of nobody, a caricature if you like of someone who might have been invented by—Poe, once more.

As to Mallarmé's influence, my view briefly is that it was almost nonexistent. Certain results of that labor of precision were "taken up without delay into the industry," and this shows in all of us.

Nothing could be more curious than the varieties of its effect on the personal styles of a number of writers. The graph of imitation rises abruptly, and after a level of a few years, sinks again. . . . And it was a sort of fever. Many were happily restored to their normal temperatures, which is no cause for surprise.

It was really not in the order of things for Mallarmé to have influence: a proposition which can be demonstrated.

Influence signifies imitation or continuation. To imitate someone so singular was to shout imitation from the rooftops. To imitate an art so perfect is a disastrous business: it costs more than the risks of being "original."

And someone of much purer mind, if he were to take on the task of prolonging as though giving a second life to the originator, *exactly as he was*, supposing he dared to think of starting out from what was already a spiritual extreme, such a monster would have to accept sacrifices so great, admit such defeats, that there cannot be two men of that kind; and I do not know even that *one* who perhaps does exist.

No, my task is not to follow Mallarmé, either if my

purpose is to do my very best work, *or* if the goal is to win whatever profit depends upon other people. By this process of elimination, you can see how few the possibilities of influence were.

But the real effects lay in the moral order. This was felt even by those who could not understand him. He served, and still serves as a conscience to some: in some cases a *good* conscience, in others a bad one.

Here is a painful fact, which you ought to be made aware of.

Towards the last quarter of his life, he knew something of an exquisite kind of fame. The performers were few, but the tone and intensity without compare. No orchestral fanfares à la Hugo in this case: simply a quartet of passionate connoisseurs.

But an hour struck. Certain ones seemed to wake up with a start. What, am I 35, 40 years of age, and neither rich nor famous! If I stand still I perish. And always that sense of domination, of inferiority. Something instinctive made them plunge—into journalism, the theater, academic life, ministries, publishing, public life: all the latrines of the herd. . . .

This was natural, right, unavoidable; irreproachable animal instinct—whatever the elements of calculation.

Only, someone was left wounded. After so many struggles, the joy of that veneration, the living response to what he had so admirably done, and then, before his death, this desertion.

Never a word said. No hints, even of the slightest. As though he had noticed nothing. I was so astonished by this, and I felt the change of atmosphere so keenly on his behalf that I could not but mention it—in terms rather strong—one day when we were alone.

And I could see, from the sheer absence of surprise lighting up all his silence with a smile, what he really suffered.

Believe me, I do feel, in the very penetrating study you have made, a tribute to the memory of Mallarmé that shows a devotion which others have refused. Which proves that if they sometimes understood the letter, the spirit escaped them.

That consideration—and more personal ones having to do, no doubt, with some of my inmost feelings—of something that I most love (though I know that it bores or puzzles almost everyone else) has made me write too long a letter.

You have only yourself to blame, and be assured that you tempted me.

P. VALÉRY

[*Death of Mme Geneviève Bonniot-Mallarmé*]

Mme Geneviève Bonniot, daughter of Stéphane Mallarmé, died on May 26. All the great poet's friends can remember the young girl who received them with such grace, in the little apartment on the Rue de Rome; who alongside her father offered such a refined and transparent emblem of the tenderest and most anxious daughterly love, and who would then retire under cover of the smoke we made, toward the moment when the talk was about to fix or fuse into that incomparable soliloquy which those who never heard cannot imagine how wonderful it was.

And now she has retired forever; leaving us that adorable *Fan* which her father made for her from the tenderest words, the most subtle images, from the most precious of thought substances: a poem so rare in its perfection, music, charm as to be Mallarmé's masterpiece, if there were one.

To that father she had given all the zealous devotion a poet could wish. With the aid of her husband Dr. Bonniot, whose zeal for Mallarmé's fame was equal to her own, she brought out the volume of the *Poems* and the *Coup de dés*. Other works, which will appear after her death, took up her time until her very last days.

Geneviève Bonniot will lie beside her parents in the little cemetery at Samoreau where we left Mallarmé one day in September 1898, on one of the most blazing and implacable of Afternoons.

PAUL VALÉRY

[To Albert Mockel]

Thursday, April 1921

Dear and Excellent Friend,

. . . .

What a capital question, this one of Mallarmé! The fact of Mallarmé, the individual; at first elaborated within a diamantine consciousness, which then proceeded to impress itself on all the purest minds of our generation; and which has remained inarguable, impossible to deny, neglect, or accept!

Each one of us has striven as well as he might against this miracle, and in one way or another against this same god who came to inhabit all of us.

There is nothing more extraordinary in all literary annals. . . .

. . . .

I would have given so much to render to Mallarmé some tribute really worthy of him!

. . . .

PAUL VALÉRY

[To Henri Mondor]

16 February 1941

Dear Friend,

For two nights now your devil of a book has kept me down to two hours' sleep. I was foolish enough to take it up in the evening, and it stirred up so much in my mind, memories on one hand and problems on the other, that to read, this time, was to relive—and to relive is not to sleep. You cannot imagine, for instance, how the period when Mallarmé becomes the creation of Poe and arrives at a final judgment on Baudelaire put me back into my years of 1891–1892, when I too was obsessed with Poe. (Though it is remarkable that in my case this influence worked perhaps more against the purpose of poetry than for it.)

You have discovered and revealed a Mallarmé at his beginnings, of which I had only the vaguest idea. The essential problem is thus elucidated, thanks to your researches. For me, it amounts to this: how and whence was born that strange and unshakable *certainty* on which Mallarmé was able to found his whole life, his renunciations, his unparalleled daring, his so triumphantly successful undertaking to recreate himself, to make himself in fact the man of a work he did not accomplish and which he knew could not be accomplished. All this, thanks to your impressive harvesting of texts and your commentary, can now be situated and circumscribed with much greater accuracy than one could once have hoped. But in another way, this book gives me to think something quite different. Surgeon as you are, you have laid the poetry open, and exposed all that was hidden beneath the final states of the poems. I was extremely struck, even more than surprised, to see in several cases how excellence, perfection, was founded only on the

426

ruins, until now unknown, of various successive texts, at times mediocre enough. But I know from experience to what degree endless rewritings are the condition of the final sureness and purity. And nothing to my mind is more agreeable than to work on a rough draft which without doubt forces us to react against the imperfections we can feel, and delivers us from having to fill that "empty sheet" where the vertigo of beginnings hovers.

I greatly like that Lefébure whose name only I knew. There was a real friend. He makes me think of Pierre Louÿs, who was the soul of zeal on my behalf, as he was for that monster Debussy who repaid him so shabbily.

You have drawn a portrait of a Marie Gerhard [Mme Stéphane Mallarmé] who seems a charming figure, and pathetic indeed. I knew her well, since it was she, with Vève as her accomplice, who had the idea of getting me married, and did all the necessary in order to carry out this plan. But I knew her only at an age and in conditions that were sad enough. . . . Sad is the word. I realize now what it really is, this terrible becoming. I can no longer recognize the old man I meet in a corner mirror, or the old brain that talks to itself without managing to be interested in what it says. You see, I fall to grumbling instead of telling you what I wanted to say. First, I meant to thank you for the book and its dedication; next to assure you that you have written a *very important* work. You have even overcome the difficulty of how to draw the likeness of a man you never met, for some who did know him and who, all in all, have found nothing to "shock" in this posthumous portrait. It was quite a big risk. But the book will mark an era in the career after death of the great, the one and only Mallarmé.

Altogether yours,   PAUL VALÉRY

[To Henri Mondor]

March '42

Dear Friend,

Really I must throw in the sponge. I am definitely incapable of replying to this book, which affects me in a thousand ways, as I really ought. God knows how many memories, or patches of life consumed, or sparks of yesteryear it revives in me. It is strange to rediscover in oneself, as though by force of influence, or the approach of an electrified body, a certain young man of 24... half a century later!

The fact of Mallarmé exerted an influence on what was to be my life, both extraordinary and complex in the extreme, which will not be simplified into some form of intellectual change. On the contrary, I might almost say!—if that were not all too simple. I do now know what I would have been if M. had not existed, or if I had not known of his existence, and I can only make a few necessarily vain hypotheses. What is certain is that for about ten years the way of thought which I judged to be his intrigued, preoccupied, charmed, and sometimes shocked me, always provoking me to re-imagine and resist it—rather as one resists a passion. Until that fatal summer of '98, I had hoped that our increasing intimacy would one day enable me to talk to him as I argued with him in my own mind. And note this, that in my then state of mind, a conversation of that sort at the level I imagined,—in some indefinable "absolute"—would have had more importance than any conceivable piece of writing!

All this, as you can imagine, was very much stirred up in my ancient substance by this second volume, which I cannot approach as an ordinary reader—a fact which authorizes me to pay you a particular compliment. I mean you have resolved the principal or rather the essential problem of the task you took on. There was everything to be feared of a portrait painted after death, by a painter who never knew the sitter, while there are still men who saw and studied him in life.

Well, I have found almost nothing in your work that is inconsistent with the idea of the real past—I am speaking of the *tone*, the most elusive value of an era, for as far as documents are concerned, you have assembled the fullest possible body of material. But the *tone*, the atmosphere of the time as it was breathed at the Rue de Rome, that you could only recreate for yourself; and yet the synthesis works triumphantly. I feel that that was something not to be hoped for—an extraordinary thing, in fact, and the true consequence of your devotion to a noble theme.

How many things, in the course of reading, brought me to a stop, demanding a station—like the stations of the cross! I confess I almost regretted that you did not say in passing what I cannot disclose myself... the—panatolian—reasons for my resounding silence in the Académie—my justification resulting from what you give to understand concerning the "Parnasse" affair.

. . . .

I could go on forever. This volume demands one from me. Along with the first, from now on it will stand as a fundamental monument to the glory of Mallarmé, which is in itself the paradoxical fact par excellence of the history of the Mind. It works out just as though the Great Work he dreamed of, and which was by its very nature not to be realized, had in fact been realized, thanks to one or two people, and recognized as such.

And it came about in a dark and squalid epoch like this one.

Thanks, dear friend. I am altogether yours

PAUL VALÉRY

NOTES

NOTES

vii. PREFACE: From Valéry's introduction to *Autour de Paul Valéry*, by René Fernandat (Grenoble: Arthaud, 1933); revised, 1944. See *Œuvres II*, Pléiade (1960), p. 1536. Translated by Malcolm Cowley.

3. INTRODUCTION TO THE METHOD OF LEONARDO DA VINCI: First published as "Introduction à la méthode de Léonard de Vinci" in *La Nouvelle Revue*, August 15, 1895. Dated 1894 and reprinted with "Note et digressions" (in the plural) (Gallimard: Paris, 1919); in *Variété I* (Paris, 1924). Published with "Note et digression" and "Léonard et les philosophes," "commentés et annotés" by the author, in *Les Divers Essais sur Léonard de Vinci* (Paris: Éditions du Sagittaire, 1931); and in *Œuvres I: Les Divers Essais sur Léonard de Vinci* (Paris: N.R.F., 1938); reprinted alone but with Valéry's marginal notes in *Tout l'œuvre peint de Léonard de Vinci* (Paris: N.R.F. [Galérie de la Pléiade], 1950). See *Œuvres I*, Pléiade (1960), p. 1153. Translated by Malcolm Cowley.

Marcel Schwob (1867–1905): A prolific writer of tales, novels, and essays, but best remembered for his brilliant researches into the literature, life, and language of France in the fifteenth century, particularly with reference to Villon.

17n. *Poincaré*: Henri Poincaré (1854–1912) lectured from 1881 at the Sorbonne on almost all branches of pure and applied mathematics. In 1892 he published his *Méthode nouvelles de la mécanique céleste*; in 1906, a paper on the dynamics of the electron in which he obtained many of the results (independently of Einstein) of the special theory of relativity. Like Valéry, Poincaré had a particular interest in the psychology of mental discovery, deduction, and creation. He believed that certain mathematical ideas precede logic. In a famous essay he made an original analysis of the psychology of mathematical discovery and invention.

31. *Langevin*: Paul Langevin (1872–1946), a French physicist whose work covered research into ions, magnetism, relativity, and supersonics. (See also *Collected Works*, Vol. 13, p. 26n.)

39. *Diderot*: Denis Diderot (1713–1784). Valéry admired and at times enjoyed a sense of identification with the *philosophes* of eighteenth-century France. Perhaps the most versatile of them was Diderot—Encyclopedist, playwright, critic of acting, painting, and music, and a speculator in the scientific field. His *Le Neveu de Rameau*, translated into German by Goethe before the French text was published, has some qualities in common with Valéry's own dialogue, *L'Idée fixe*. (See *Collected Works*, Vol. 5.)

57. *Lagrange*: Joseph-Louis Lagrange (1736–1813). French mathematician born and educated at Turin. At the age of nineteen he evolved a method of dealing with the isoperimetrical problem out of which grew a new calculus of variations. This calculus led to the work of Hamilton and Maxwell and was continued in the work of Einstein and others. Lagrange lived for twenty years at the court of Frederick the Great, where he wrote his *Mécanique Analytique* (Paris, 1788). At the death of Frederick he was invited to Paris by Louis XVI, was treated with respect during the Revolution, and in 1797 became a professor in the newly founded École Polytechnique. He is buried in the Panthéon.

D'Alembert: Jean Le Rond d'Alembert (1717–1783). A founding Encyclopedist and secretary of the French Academy. His mathematical work was chiefly devoted to differential equations and mechanics. His *Traité de Dynamique* appeared in 1743.

Laplace: Pierre-Simon, Marquis de Laplace (1749–1827), mathematician, physicist, and astronomer. Apart from his work on the solar system, comets, and tides, and the cosmology that bears his name, he also established the basic laws of electromagnetism.

Ampère: André Ampère (1775–1836). A contributor to the sciences of mathematics and chemistry, as well as a philosopher; he became the discoverer of electrodynamics by deducing the similarity between electric currents and magnetic fields of force.

Maxwell: James Clerk Maxwell (1831–1879), author of the electromagnetic theory of light.

Faraday: Michael Faraday (1791–1867), the great physicist and chemist who discovered the laws of electrolysis, the theory of electrostatics, and, among much else, electromagnetic induction.

59. *Lord Kelvin*: William Thomson (1824–1907) discovered the Second Law of Thermodynamics. Otherwise, he is best known for his work on electricity with respect to submarine telegraphy. In the context of Leonardo and Valéry, perhaps his most sympathetic trait is that having undertaken in 1879 to write a series of articles on the mariner's compass, he found so many questions rising in his mind that the second article appeared only after five years' exhaustive work on the subject.

Boscovich: Ruggiero Giuseppe Boscovich (1711–1781), Serbian Jesuit, who became professor of mathematics and

physics at Rome, and later Directeur de l'Optique de la
Marine at Paris; he wrote numerous studies on mathematics,
physics, and astronomy.

64. NOTE AND DIGRESSION: Written as "Note et digressions," dated 1919, and published as the preface to *Introduction
à la Méthode de Léonard de Vinci* (Paris: N.R.F., 1919);
reprinted in *Variété I*; in *Divers Essais sur Léonard de Vinci*;
and in *Œuvres I: Les Divers Essais sur Léonard de Vinci*. See
Œuvres I, Pléiade (1960), p. 1199. Translated by Malcolm
Cowley.

66. *Juliette Adam* (1836–1936): Her long literary career
began as early as 1858, and by 1873 she had published a
dozen books, stories, sketches, travel impressions and
polemics on love, woman, and marriage. She founded *La
Nouvelle Revue* in 1879, with a manifesto declaring its
political, social, and philosophical aims. Her salon was
famous and influential at the turn of the century.

Léon Daudet (1868–1942): son of Alphonse Daudet. He
wrote novels and memoirs, and was an early collaborator on
Le Figaro, Le Gaulois, etc. He is best known as a journalist,
political figure, and the founder in 1907 (with Charles
Maurras) of *L'Action française*, the daily newspaper of the
extreme right, whose program was to combat liberal and
democratic ideas in the interest of "nationalisme intégral."
It continued publication until 1944.

78. ... *the crudely defined opposition between the spirit of
finesse* ...: Valéry is referring here to Pascal's *Pensées*
Pléiade edn., Art. 21, p. 826).

79. ... *at a time when he might have honored France* ...: A
few years after Pascal's death in 1662, the infinitesimal calculus was developed independently by Newton and Leibniz.

No abyss opening on his right: "Abîme de Pascal"—the abyss Pascal is said to have seen always beside him. The legend is founded on a letter written long after Pascal's death, by Abbé Boileau, to console a young lady subject to imaginary terrors: "I am reminded," he wrote, "of Pascal.... That great mind believed that he always saw an abyss at his left side, and he had a chair placed there to reassure him. I know the story at first hand." (*Lettres de l'Abbé Boileau*, 1737 edn.) Voltaire perpetuated the story, but since Pascal's contemporaries—even his enemies—say nothing whatever about it, its authenticity is doubtful.

88. *Durus est hic sermo*: "This is a hard saying."

93f. *As the consciousness emerges...*: The whole of this passage, and the entire evocation of what Valéry calls the "perfected consciousness," is of added interest when considered in the context of *La Jeune Parque*. As a gloss of that poem, it is perhaps more illuminating than anything else written about it.

100. *... jeu de l'amour et du hasard*: The title of Marivaux's best-known comedy has passed into the language as a proverb.

103. *... tot capita, tottempora*: "as many times as there are persons."

104. *...intus et extra*: "inwardly and outwardly."

109. *Ader and the Wrights*: Clément Ader (1841–1925); Wilbur Wright (1867–1912); Orville Wright (1871–1948): French and American pioneers in aviation.

Fresnel's optical theories: Augustin-Jean Fresnel (1788–1827), French physicist, who studied crystals and the double refraction of light; collaborated with Arago on the study of polarized light; invented the double convex optical lens.

M. Duhem: Pierre Duhem (1861–1916), physicist,

mathematician, historian of science, and author of a theory of energetics. He wrote his *Études sur Léonard de Vinci* in 1906, and before his death he had published seven volumes of his projected *Le Système du Monde: Histoire des doctrines cosmologiques*.

110. LEONARDO AND THE PHILOSOPHERS: "Léonard et les philosophes, Lettre à Leo Ferrero," first published in *Commerce XVIII* (Paris, Winter 1928), with this note: "Préface à l'ouvrage de M. Leo Ferrero qui doit paraître sous le titre: *Leonardo o del arte*." Reprinted in Leo Ferrero, *Léonard de Vinci ou l'œuvre d'art, précédé d'une étude "Léonard et les philosophes" de Paul Valéry* (Paris: Simon Kra, 1929); with marginal notes written in 1929-1930, *Les Divers Essais sur Léonard de Vinci*, "commentés et annotés" by the author (Paris: Éditions du Sagittaire, 1931); *Œuvres I: Les Divers Essais sur Léonard de Vinci*, with a note on the death of Leo Ferrero (Paris: N.R.F., 1938); *Variété III* (Paris: Gallimard, 1936 and 1946). See *Œuvres I*, Pléiade (1960), p. 1234. Translated by Malcolm Cowley.

Leo Ferrero: (1903-1932), the son of Guglielmo Ferrero (1871-1942), Italian sociologist and historian. An opponent of the Mussolini regime, Leo took up residence in Paris in 1928. See Valéry's note, p. 157.

113. ...*ultra vires*: beyond the power or authority of the person or body in question.

125. *Pascal tells us*...: Pascal counted himself an "esprit fin" as well as a mathematician, but he was quite impervious to the values of the visual or other arts. Having denounced the vanity of painting, he goes on to animadvert against the folly of putting an inestimable value on a picture of a basket of fruit or flowers when the actual objects of the painting would be worth only a few cents.

135. *All the rest is literature*: "Tout le reste est littérature". The final line of Verlaine's *Art Poétique*. Because it could be so variously and ambiguously applied, it became and remains a standard expression in the French language.

149. . . . *res inter alios actas*: "transactions among people."

161. ON POE'S "EUREKA": "Au sujet d'*Eureka*," written as the Introduction to the new edition of Baudelaire's translation of Poe's *Eureka*, Éditions d'art Édouard Pelletan (Paris: Helleu et Sergent, 1923); appeared in *La Revue Européenne*, May 1, 1923; in *Variété I* (Paris, 1924); reprinted in *Œuvres choisies* (Lausanne, 1947); see *Œuvres I*, Pléiade (1960), p. 854. Translated by Malcolm Cowley.

Lucien Fabre: (1889–1952), scientist, novelist, and poet; a friend for whom Valéry wrote two prefaces. (See *Collected Works*, Vol. 7, pp. 39 and 231.) Valéry once described him as "a man of the Renaissance displaced in our time."

169. *Boltzmann's theories*: Ludwig Boltzmann (1844–1906), Austrian physicist who worked chiefly on the kinetic theory of gases, and the electromagnetic theory of light.

Carnot's principle: Nicolas-Léonard-Sadi-Carnot (1796–1832), physicist, studied the laws of heat, the comparative expansion of gases and the application of steam to mechanics. "Carnot's principle" is found in his *Réflexions sur la puissance motrice du feu et les machines propres à développer cette puissance* (1824); it is a formulation of one of the two fundamental laws of thermodynamics.

170. . . . *the late Svante Arrhenius*: (1859–1927), Swedish physicist, Nobel prize-winner in 1903, chiefly remembered as author of the theory of ions. In his later career as an astronomer, he tried to evaluate the effects of the pressure of light on the movement of stars.

177. SOME FRAGMENTS FROM POE'S "MARGINALIA": "Quelques Fragments des Marginalia, traduits et annotés par Paul Valéry," published in *Commerce*, XIV (Paris, Winter 1927), where Poe's text in Valéry's translation is on the righthand pages with the gloss on the left. Valéry gave his own subtitles, "De l'Expression" and "Fatale Supériorité" to his translations from the *Marginalia*. Valéry's gloss translated by James R. Lawler.

193. THE PLACE OF BAUDELAIRE: "Situation de Baudelaire," given as a lecture at Monaco, February 19, 1924; published as a plaquette at the Imprimerie de Monaco, 1924; in *La Revue de France*, September 15, 1924; again as a plaquette by Lesage, Paris, 1924; as an Introduction to Baudelaire's *Fleurs du mal* (Paris: Payot, 1926); reprinted in *Maîtres et amis* (Paris: Marcel Lacou et Émile Lainé, 1927); *Poësie* (Paris: Collection Bertrand Guegan, 1928); *Variété II* (Paris: N.R.F., 1929); *Œuvres, Vol. G: Variété* (Paris: Gallimard, 1937). See *Œuvres I*, Pléiade (1960), p. 598. Translated by James R. Lawler.

207. *Luxe, forme et volupté*: Valéry is adapting the famous line *Luxe, calme et volupté* from Baudelaire's "L'Invitation au voyage."

215. THE EXISTENCE OF SYMBOLISM: "Existence du Symbolisme," an address given at Liège on May 28, 1936, to celebrate the fiftieth anniversary of Symbolism and of *La Wallonie*, one of the first Symbolist reviews, founded at Liège in 1886 by Albert Mockel; the address was reprinted in the brochure-program, *Le Symbolisme 1886–1936*, Brussels, Institut National Belge de Radiodiffusion, for their broadcasts on Symbolism, June 15, 1936; revised and enlarged,

published by Stols, Maastricht, 1939; reprinted in *Écrits divers sur Mallarmé* (Paris: N.R.F., 1950). See *Œuvres I*, Pléiade (1960), p. 686. Translated by Malcolm Cowley.

216. *Arago*: François Arago (1786–1853), the great astronomer and physicist; an antimonarchist and member of the 1848 emergency government which followed the deposition of Louis-Philippe.

220. Valéry is here citing the leaders of the conventional criticism of the day. Francisque Sarcey (1828–1899) was drama critic of *Le Temps* for over thirty years. Jacques Fouquier founded the daily *Le Petit Parisien*, and wrote theater criticism for *Le Figaro*. Ferdinand Brunetière (1849–1906) and Jules Lemaître (1853–1914) presided over the academic literary criticism of the day. Anatole France (1844–1924), the novelist and essayist, shared many of the conventional views of his time. As a member of the editorial board of the third anthology of *Le Parnasse contemporain*, he rejected all the contributions of Mallarmé, Verlaine, and Charles Cros. (See *Collected Works*, Vol. 11.)

231. *The Cirque d'Été*: "the Summer Circus," established in 1841 as a counterpart to the Cirque d'Hiver, famous since its founding in 1785. Pulled down in 1902. It was used for the concerts of the French conductor Jules Pasdeloup (1819–1887), who created his famous series of popular concerts of classical music in 1861.

240. LETTER ABOUT MALLARMÉ: First appeared in *La Revue de Paris*, April 1, 1927; in *Mallarmé, précédé d'une lettre sur Mallarmé de Paul Valéry*, by Jean Royère (Paris: Simon Kra, 1927); as a plaquette in Éditions de la Nouvelle Revue française (Paris, 1928); in *Poésie: Essais sur la poëtique et le poète* (Paris: Bertrand Guégan, 1928); in *Variété II* (Paris,

1929); in *Œuvres choisies* (Lausanne, 1947); in *Écrits divers sur Mallarmé, op. cit.* See *Œuvres I*, Pléiade (1960), p. 633. Translated by Malcolm Cowley.

244. *Corneille's elder Horace*: The elder Horace is speaking of his son and namesake:

> Julie: *Que vouliez qu'il fît contre trois?*
> Le Vieil Horace: *Qu'il mourût,*
>   *Ou qu'un beau désespoir alors le secourût.*
>   What could he do against three?
>   He could have died,
>   Or else some fine despair could have come to his aid.
>   *Horace,* III, 6.

246. *You would not read me...*: Valéry is parodying a famous *pensée* of Pascal's (Pléiade edn., Art. 736, p. 1062): *Tu ne me chercherais pas si tu ne m' avais pas trouvé*: "You would not seek me if you had not found me".

251. *...Caligula*: A reference to the Emperor's famous wish that the Roman people had only one head so that it could be dispatched at one blow.

254. STÉPHANE MALLARMÉ: Originally given as a lecture at the Université des Annales, "Conférence de M. Paul Valéry avec l'éminent concours de Mme Marguerite Moréno," January 17, 1933. Published that year in *Conférencia*, Paris, April 15, reprinted in *Écrits divers sur Mallarmé, op. cit.* See *Œuvres I*, Pléiade (1960), p. 660. The texts of the Mallarmé poems read by Mme Moreno have not been reproduced here. Translated by James R. Lawler.

Marguerite Moreno was an eminent actress, a contemporary and friend of Colette. From her early days she had been an admirer of Mallarmé, and as a young actress had wanted to give a première performance of the never-to-be-completed *Hérodiade*.

268. *Aubanel*: Théodore Aubanel (1829–1886), a Provençal poet; his best-known work is *La Grenade entr'ouverte*.

... *the Félibrige group*: There are various theories about the meaning of *Félibre*, the name chosen for themselves by the seven Provençal poets who in 1854 founded the literary school which they called *Le Félibrige*. Mistral had discovered the word in a medieval poem in which the Virgin tells how one day she found her son in the temple "parmi sept félibres de la loi" ("among seven *félibres* of the law"). The word is probably derived from Low Latin *fellebris* ("nursling" of the Muses), from *fellare*, "to suck."

The best known of the founders of *Le Félibrige* are Roumanille, Mistral, and Aubanel; its aim was to restore to the Provençal language its poetic and literary use, and to preserve the original character of the literature, art, and costumes of southern France.

... *light my lantern*: An allusion to the fable by Florian, of the monkey who wanted to display a magic lantern, but overlooked one detail: to light it.

269. ... *on which I used to hang myself*: Presumably an allusion to the final lines of an early poem by Mallarmé, "Le Guignon": "Ces héros... Vont ridiculement se pendre au réverbère." ("These heroes [the poets]... Ridiculously go and hang themselves to a lamppost.")

272. I WOULD SOMETIMES SAY TO STÉPHANE MALLARMÉ...: "Je disais quelquefois à Stéphane Mallarmé...," written as a preface to an edition of Mallarmé's poems, published by La Société des Cent-Une, Paris, 1931; reprinted as a plaquette by the same, 1931; in *La Nouvelle Revue Française*,

May 1, 1932; *Variété III* (Paris: N.R.F., 1936); *Écrits divers sur Mallarmé*, *op. cit.* See *Œuvres I*, Pléiade (1960), p. 644. Translated by Malcolm Cowley.

288. *Condillac, the sensationalist*: Étienne Bonnot de Condillac (1715–1780), philosopher, leader of the "École sensualiste"; his two most important works are *L'Essai sur l'origine des connaissances humaines* (1746), and *Le Traité des sensations* (1954), both influenced by John Locke.

294. MALLARMÉ: First published in *Le Point*, Lanzac par Souillac (Lot), February–April, 1944; reprinted in *Vues* (Paris: La Table Ronde, 1948); and in *Écrits divers sur Stéphane Mallarmé*, *op. cit.* See *Œuvres I*, Pléiade (1960), p. 706. Translated by James R. Lawler.

299. A KIND OF PREFACE: "Sorte de Préface" first appeared in *Le Figaro*, December 5, 1936, under the title "Quand Mallarmé était professeur d'anglais." It was written as the preface to Mallarmé's *Thèmes anglais pour toutes les grammaires: Les mille proverbes, dictons et phrases typiques de l'anglais groupés d'après les règles de la grammaire* (Paris: Gallimard, 1937); reprinted in *Écrits divers sur Mallarmé*, *op. cit.* See *Œuvres I*, Pléiade (1960), p. 680. Translated by James R. Lawler.

301. *Aretino took care...*: Pietro Aretino (1492–1556), contemporary and friend of Titian, who painted a famous portrait of him. A satirist and one of the most licentious writers of all time, he made a fortune from the bribes of eminent contemporaries who wished to be spared his tongue, and his pen—the wages of silence.

307. CONCERNING "A THROW OF THE DICE": "Le Coup de dés: Lettre au Directeur des *Marges*," written as a letter and

published February 15, 1920, under the heading "Controverse sur un poème de Mallarmé"; reprinted in a slightly abridged and definitive form in *Fragments sur Mallarmé* (Paris: Ronald Davis, 1924); in *Poësie, op. cit.*; in *Variété II*; in *Écrits divers sur Mallarmé*. See *Œuvres I*, Pléiade (1960), p. 622. Translated by Malcolm Cowley.

Jean-Baptiste Rousseau: Poet and dramatist (1671–1741). In 1712, convicted of grossly slandering other poets, he was exiled from France for life.

310. *...set in type by Lahure*: Auguste-Charles Lahure (1809–1887) was a pioneer printer in France. His press, one of the largest and best equipped of his time, had been in existence for fifty years, inherited from his father and grandfather. His press printed the Hachette universal dictionaries, and produced the first French periodical illustrated in color.

314. *Dr. Bonniot*: Dr. Edmond Bonniot, having married Mallarmé's daughter Geneviève in 1901, became at his wife's death in 1919 the guardian and trustee of the poet's works and of the rights attached to them. (See p. 424.)

316. *Nijinsky*: Vaslav Nijinsky (1890–1950), the famous Russian dancer, first appeared in Paris with the Diaghilev Ballet in 1909. He had already scored perhaps his greatest success in *Le Spectre de la Rose*, based on a poem of Théophile Gautier. In 1912 he created his own choreography for *L'Après-midi d'un Faune*, a ballet based on Mallarmé's poem and set to the prelude which Debussy had composed for that work as early as 1890.

317. LITERARY REMINISCENCES: An extract from "Souvenirs littéraires," a lecture given (with Hélène Vacaresco) at the Université des Annales, November 18, 1927; published in *Conférencia*, March 20, 1928; reprinted in *Œuvres*, Vol. K:

Conférences (Paris: Gallimard, 1939). See *Œuvres I*, Pléiade (1960), p. 777. Translated by James R. Lawler.

321. *Lamoureux Concerts*: Charles Lamoureux (1834–1899), born at Bordeaux; conductor and violinist, founder of the Concerts Lamoureux, a series famous in his day and since, and which still bears his name. (See *Collected Works*, Vol. 11, p. 196.)

325. LAST VISIT TO MALLARMÉ: "Dernière Visite à Mallarmé" was first published in *Le Gaulois*, Paris, October 17, 1923. It appears in *Variété II*, in *Écrits divers sur Mallarmé*, and other collections. See *Œuvres I*, Pléiade (1960), p. 630. Translated by Malcolm Cowley.

329. STÉPHANE MALLARMÉ: First published in *Le Gaulois*, October 17, 1923; reprinted in *Fragments sur Mallarmé*, in *Poësie, Variété II, Écrits divers sur Mallarmé*. See *Œuvres I*, Pléiade (1960), p. 619. Translated by Malcolm Cowley.

333. FROM THE NOTEBOOKS: Valéry's *Cahiers* were published in facsimile, in twenty-nine volumes, by the Centre National de la Recherche Scientifique, Paris, 1957–1961. The excerpts were selected and translated by Jackson Mathews.

399. SELECTED LETTERS: translated by David Paul.

401. *Jean Valéry*: son of Paul Valéry's brother Jules. He lived all his life in his father's house, 1 rue Fournarié, Montpellier, and was director of a journal for winegrowers, *Le Midi vinicole*.

406. *First letter to Mallarmé*: sent by Valéry with his poems "Le Jeune Prêtre" and "La Suave Agonie" in October 1891. (See Collected Works, Vol. 1, pp. 338 and 348.)

Published by Henri Mondor, to whom the two poems had been given by Mallarmé's daughter, Mme E. Bonniot, in his *Vie de Mallarmé* (Paris: Gallimard, 1941); and more completely in Mondor, *La Heureuse Rencontre de Valéry et Mallarmé* (Paris-Lausanne: Éditions de la Clairfontaine, 1947). Reprinted in Valéry, *Lettres à Quelques-uns* (Paris: Gallimard, 1952). See *Œuvres I*, Pléiade (1960), p. 1581.

407. *Second letter to Mallarmé*: published by Henri Mondor in his *Vie de Mallarmé*; reprinted in Valéry, *Lettres à quelques-uns*. See *Œuvres I*, Pléiade (1960), p. 1740.

"Narcisse parle": See Collected Works, Vol. 1, p. 28.

409. *First Meeting with Mallarmé*: a "resumé drawn from a note written at the time," published by Julien P. Monod in *Regard sur Paul Valéry* (Lausanne: Editions des Terreaux, 1947). This translation by James R. Lawler is based on the original manuscript, now in the *Valeryanum* of the Doucet Library, Paris, which differs in some details from that published by Monod, and reprinted in *Œuvres I*, Pléiade (1960), p. 1741.

Valéry had completed his second year of law studies at the University of Montpellier. He went to Paris with his mother on September 19, 1891, where he stayed for five weeks at the Hotel Henri IV in the Rue Gay-Lussac. On September 25 he met Huysmans; a fortnight later Pierre Louÿs arranged a meeting for him with Mallarmé, to whom Valéry had written for the first time a year earlier. (See p. 406.)

...*the Félibres*: See p. 268n. Mallarmé became acquainted with the Félibres during his stay in Avignon. Valéry was also in touch with Félibre circles; in June 1891, *La Cigale d'or* had published his sonnet, "La Belle au bois dormant," with a translation into Provençal by Joseph Loubet, one of the

Félibre poets. (See "Au bois dormant," Collected Works, Vol. 1, p. 18.)

...*his voice very low*: Deeply impressed by Mallarmé's voice, Valéry wrote a poem in free verse in 1912 or 1913 to evoke his memories of it. This early version which he set down in his Notebooks (*Cahier* 4:684) has the initials S.M. written alongside it. He later published the poem in *Tel Quel*, without mention of Mallarmé, under the title "Psaume sur une voix." (See *Collected Works*, Vol. 2, p. 185.)

...*Devoir français*: The homely term for a French school-boy's homework.

René Ghil: Pseudonym of René Guilbert (1862–1925), the founder of the "École instrumentiste" and creator of a so-called "poésie scientifique." Mallarmé wrote a famous foreword to Ghil's *Traité du Verbe* (1886).

Emaux: A reference to Théophile Gautier's collection of poems, *Émaux et Camées*, which appeared in 1852. Mallarmé acknowledged his admiration of Gautier in a prose poem, "Symphonie littéraire," and in the long threnody "Toast funèbre," which transforms Gautier into the symbol of the Poet par excellence.

De Régnier: Henri de Régnier (1864–1936), poet, novelist, and critic, was deeply influenced by Mallarmé, who admired Régnier in turn and, in a celebrated interview with Jules Huret in 1891, praised him as the most accomplished of the younger poets.

...*Banville's inspired solution*: Théodore de Banville (1823–1891), a disciple of Gautier, published several collections of verse and a widely read treatise on versification (1872) in which he says, "La rime est tout le vers. ... C'est pourquoi l'*imagination de la rime* est, entre toutes, la qualité qui constitue le poète. ..." ("The rhyme is everything. ...

That is why imagination in rhyming is, above all, the quality that makes the poet.") This perhaps is the "inspired solution" that Mallarmé referred to.

...*the Comet*: One of the fundamental tenets of Mallarmé's aesthetic was the compelling need to achieve "la disparition élocutoire du poète," thus making the poem an impersonal expression of beauty. Here he uses a characteristic image which likens the poem to a comet illuminating the sky with its sudden grace, freed from the bonds of an author's personality.

410. *Epinal images*: episodes of a historical or legendary nature represented in the manner of the popular colored sheets produced in the Vosges town of Epinal.

Letter to Mallarmé: in *Lettres à quelques-uns*. See *Œuvres I*, Pléiade (1960), p. 1741.

Letter to Jules Valéry: written in 1898 to his brother on the occasion of Mallarmé's death. First published in a special number of *Les Lettres*, under the title *Stéphane Mallarmé 1842–1898* (Paris, 1948); reprinted in *Écrits divers sur Stéphane Mallarmé*. See *Œuvres I*, Pléiade (1960), p. 1742.

Jules Valéry: see herein, p. 401.

412. *Letter to André Gide*: published in *L'Arche*, No. 10, October 1945; in André Gide, *Paul Valéry* (Domat-Montchrestien, 1947); in *Écrits divers sur Stéphane Mallarmé*, and in *Correspondance: André Gide–Paul Valéry* (Paris, Gallimard, 1955). See *Œuvres I*, Pléiade (1960), p. 1743.

415. *Letters to Verhaeren*: published in *Écrits divers sur Mallarmé*. See *Œuvres I*, Pléiade (1960), pp. 1745f.

417. *Letters to Albert Thibaudet*: about his book, *La Poésie de Stéphane Mallarmé* (Paris, N.R.F., 1912), which the author had sent to Valéry in proofs. These letters, "made available by Mme Paul Valéry, François Valéry, and Julien P.

Monod," were first published in the review *Fontaine*, No. 44, 1945; reprinted in *Écrits divers sur Stéphane Mallarmé*, and *Lettres à quelques-uns*. See *Œuvres I*, Pléiade (1960), pp. 1746–1751.

424. *Death of Mme Geneviève Bonniot-Mallarmé*: first published in *Le Mercure de France*, No. 504, June 16, 1919; reprinted under the title "Geneviève Bonniot-Mallarmé" in *Petit Recueil de Paroles de Circonstance* (Paris: Collection Plaisir de Bibliophile, 1926). See *Œuvres I*, Pléiade (1960), p. 1751.

425. *Letter to Albert Mockel*: published in *Écrits divers sur Stéphane Mallarmé*. See *Œuvres I*, Pléiade (1960), p. 1752.

Albert Mockel: see p. 215n.

426ff. *Letters to Henri Mondor*: written to Dr. Henri Mondor concerning Volumes I and II of his *Vie de Mallarmé*, published respectively in 1941 and 1942 (Paris: Gallimard). The letters were published in *Lettres à quelques-uns*. See *Œuvres I*, Pléiade (1960), p. 1753ff.

428. ...*electrified body*: assuming that *électricité* in the original is a mistake or misprint for *électrisé*. [Tr.]

429. ...*panatolian—reasons*: This can only be a reference to Anatole France's well-known hostility to the work of Mallarmé, who was almost his exact contemporary. As coeditor of the third "Parnasse" anthology, France had thrown out all Mallarmé's contributions. Valéry was elected to the French Academy to fill the chair left vacant by Anatole France's death. In his duty speech in praise of his predecessor, he never spoke France's name nor did he refer to the "Parnasse"affair. (See *Collected Works*, Vol. 11, pp. 3ff.)

INDEX

INDEX

This colophon was chosen from a number of drawings by Paul Valéry of his favorite device.